D1488021

PUERTO RICO

1st Edition

**Where to Stay and Eat
for All Budgets**

**Must-See Sights
and Local Secrets**

Ratings You Can Trust

Excerpted from *Fodor's Puerto Rico*

Fodor's Travel Publications New York, Toronto, London, Sydney, Auckland

www.fodors.com

FODOR'S IN FOCUS PUERTO RICO

Series Editor: Douglas Stallings

Editor: Molly Moker

Editorial Production: Evangelos Vasilakis

Editorial Contributors: Mark Sullivan

Maps & Illustrations: David Lindroth, cartographer; Bob Blake and Rebecca Baer, *map editors*

Design: Fabrizio LaRocca, *creative director*; Guido Caroti, Siobhan O'Hare, *art directors*; Ann McBride, *designer*

Photography: Melanie Marin, *senior picture editor*

Cover Photo (Vieques): Francesco Lagnese Photography/Jupiter Images

Production/Manufacturing: Matthew Struble

COPYRIGHT

1st Edition

ISBN 978-1-4000-1891-8

ISSN 1939-9871

SPECIAL SALES

This book is available for special discounts for bulk purchases for sales promotions or premiums. Special editions, including personalized covers, excerpts of existing books, and corporate imprints, can be created in large quantities for special needs. For more information, write to Special Markets/Premium Sales, 1745 Broadway, MD 6-2, New York, New York, NY 10019, or e-mail specialmarkets@randomhouse.com.

AN IMPORTANT TIP & AN INVITATION

Although all prices, opening times, and other details in this book are based on information supplied to us at press time, changes occur all the time in the travel world, and Fodor's cannot accept responsibility for facts that become outdated or for inadvertent errors or omissions. **So always confirm information when it matters,** especially if you're making a detour to visit a specific place. Your experiences—positive and negative—matter to us. If we have missed or misstated something, **please write to us.** We follow up on all suggestions. Contact the Puerto Rico editor at editors@fodors.com or c/o Fodor's at 1745 Broadway, New York, NY 10019.

PRINTED IN THE UNITED STATES OF AMERICA

10 9 8 7 6 5 4 3 2 1

Be a Fodor's Correspondent

Your opinion matters. It matters to us. It matters to your fellow Fodor's travelers, too. And we'd like to hear it. In fact, we *need* to hear it. When you share your experiences and opinions, you become an active member of the Fodor's community. Here's how you can help improve Fodor's for all of us.

Tell us when we're right. We rely on local writers to give you an insider's perspective. But our writers and staff editors also depend on you. Your positive feedback is a vote to renew our recommendations for the next edition.

Tell us when we're wrong. We update most of our guides every year. But things change. If any of our descriptions are inaccurate or inadequate, we'll incorporate your changes in the next edition and will correct factual errors at fodors.com *immediately*.

Tell us what to include. You probably have had fantastic travel experiences that aren't yet in Fodor's. Why not share them with a community of like-minded travelers? Share your discoveries and experiences with everyone directly at fodors.com. Your input may lead us to add a new listing or a higher recommendation.

Give us your opinion instantly at our feedback center at www.fodors.com/feedback. You may also e-mail editors@fodors.com with the subject line "Puerto Rico Editor." Or send your nominations, comments, and complaints by mail to Puerto Rico Editor, Fodor's, 1745 Broadway, New York, NY 10019.

Happy Traveling!

Tim Jarrell, Publisher

CONTENTS

ABOUT THIS BOOK

Our Ratings

We wouldn't recommend a place that wasn't worth your time, but sometimes a place is so experiential that superlatives don't do it justice: you just have to be there to know. These sights, properties, and experiences get our highest rating, Fodor's Choice, indicated by orange stars throughout this book. Black stars highlight sights and properties we deem Highly Recommended places that our writers, editors, and readers praise again and again.

Credit Cards

Want to pay with plastic? **AE, D, DC, MC, V** following restaurant and hotel listings indicate whether American Express, Discover, Diners Club, MasterCard, and Visa are accepted.

Restaurants

Unless we state otherwise, restaurants are open for lunch and dinner daily. We mention dress only when there's a specific requirement and reservations only when they're essential or not accepted— it's always best to book ahead.

Hotels

Unless we tell you otherwise, you can assume that the hotels have private bath, phone, TV, and air-conditioning. We always list facilities but not whether you'll be charged an extra fee to use them, so when pricing accommodations, find out what's included.

Many Listings
- ★ Fodor's Choice
- ★ Highly recommended
- ⊠ Physical address
- ✛ Directions
- ⌂ Mailing address
- ☎ Telephone
- 🖷 Fax
- ⊕ On the Web
- ✉ E-mail
- 🎟 Admission fee
- ☉ Open/closed times
- Ⓜ Metro stations
- ▱ Credit cards

Hotels & Restaurants
- 🏨 Hotel
- ⇆ Number of rooms
- ♨ Facilities
- ⵝⵔ Meal plans
- ✕ Restaurant
- ⌒ Reservations
- ↘ Smoking
- 🆈 BYOB
- ✕🏨 Hotel with restaurant that warrants a visit

Outdoors
- ⅄ Golf
- ⚐ Camping

Other
- ♺ Family-friendly
- ⇨ See also
- ⊠ Branch address
- ☞ Take note

Puerto Rico

KEY
- - - - Ferry lines
🌴 Rainforest

Isabela

Hatillo

Puerto
Tortugu

Pta.
Agujereada

Pta.
Borinquén

Bahía de
Aguadilla

**Playa
Crashboat**

Quebradillas

Camuy

Arecibo

Aguadilla

Bosque
Estatal
Guajataca

Manati

129

10

22

22

Pta.
Gorda

Aguada

Rincón

San
Sebastián

111

Utuado

Jayuya

149

115

Bahía de Añasco

Mayagüez

105

Maricao

Adjuntas

Bosque
Estatal
Toro Negro

102

Bosque Estatal
Maricao

Joyuda

Cabo
Rojo

San
Germán

10

Juana Díaz

102

52

**Balneario
Boquerón**

101

116

Guayanilla

Ponce

Boquerón

La
Parguera

Guánica

El Combate

Bahía
Salinas

Bahía
Sucia

Bahía
Fosforescente

**Playa
Santa**

Ensenada
Las Pardas

**Playa
Ballena**

Pta.
Jagüey

Caja de
Muertos

Caribbean Sea

0   20 miles
0   30 km

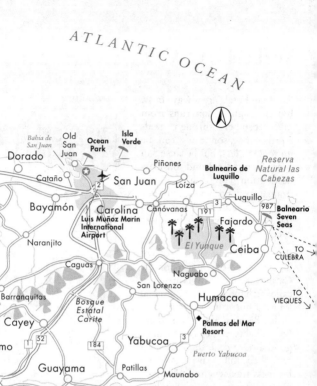

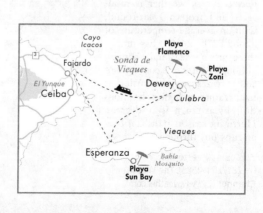

WHEN TO GO

San Juan hotels are always busy, but the high season runs from mid-December through mid-April; off-season rates can be up to 25% less, but because San Juan is a year-round business destination you don't see the dramatic savings you see in some other destinations. Elsewhere on the island, prices will be lower except at deluxe resorts.

Puerto Rico can be an excellent hurricane-season option for the Caribbean, especially when you can watch the weather report and know a hurricane isn't about to strike. Because of the large number of flights, you can often find a good airfare deal, though flights are often full year-round with business travelers and with people transferring through San Juan for other Caribbean destinations.

Climate

Puerto Rico's weather is moderate and tropical year-round, with an average temperature of about 82°F (26°C). Essentially, there are no seasonal changes, although winter sees cooling (not cold) breezes from the north, and temperatures in higher elevations drop by as much as 20 degrees. Hurricane season in the Caribbean runs July through November.

Forecasts **Puerto Rico Weather** (☎787/253–4586). **The Weather Channel** (⊕www.weather.com).

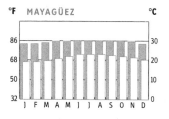

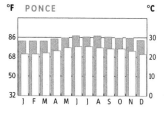

San Juan

WORD OF MOUTH

"There is so much to do in Old San Juan. Especially if you like to eat and shop. There is so much history there and it is such a great place. It is a beautiful city. I am sure you will have a fantastic time."
—MIM04

SAN JUAN IS PARADISE'S BABY in an urban comforter. Puerto Rico's sprawling capital is bordered to the north by the Atlantic and to the east and west by bays and lagoons. More than a third of the island's 4 million citizens are proud to call themselves *Sanjuaneros*. They go about their business surrounded by the antique and the modern, the commercial and the residential, the man-made and the natural.

By 1508 the explorer Juan Ponce de León had established a colony in an area now known as Caparra, southeast of present-day San Juan. He later moved the settlement north to a more hospitable peninsular location. In 1521, after he became the first colonial governor, Ponce de León switched the name of the island—which was called San Juan Bautista in honor of St. John the Baptist—with that of the settlement of Puerto Rico (Rich Port). The capital of paradise was born.

Defended by the imposing Fuerte San Felipe del Morro (El Morro), Puerto Rico's administrative and population center helped to keep the island firmly in Spain's hands until 1898, when it came under U.S. control after the Spanish-American War. Centuries of Spanish rule left an indelible imprint on the city, particularly in the walled area now known as Old San Juan. The area, with its cobblestone streets lined with brightly painted, colonial-era structures, has been designated a UNESCO World Heritage Site.

Old San Juan is a monument to the past, but the rest of the city is firmly in the here and now. It draws migrants from elsewhere on the island to jobs in its businesses and industries. It captivates both residents and visitors with its vibrant lifestyle as well as its balmy beaches, pulsing nightclubs, and mesmerizing museums. Wrap yourself up in even one small patch of the urban comforter, and you may never want to leave this baby.

EXPLORING SAN JUAN

San Juan's metro area stretches for 12 mi along Puerto Rico's north coast, and defining the city is rather like assembling a puzzle. Neighborhoods are irregular and sometimes overlapping—not easily pieced together—and the areas most visited by tourists run along the coast.

SAN JUAN TOP 5

■ Getting lost among the cobblestone streets of Old San Juan, a UNESCO World Heritage Site.

■ Climbing the battlements of Fuerte San Felipe del Morro, the 16th-century fort that dominates the waterfront.

■ Window shopping along Condado's Avenida Ashford, where you can find most of the city's designer boutiques.

■ Catching a few rays at Balneario de Carolina, the award-winning beach at the eastern tip of Isla Verde.

■ Dining at one of the other stellar restaurants along the southern end of Calle La Fortaleza, a strip so trendy that locals call it "SoFo."

Farthest west is Old San Juan, the showplace of the island's rich history. On this peninsula you will find the city's finest museums and shops, as well as excellent dining and lodging options. To the east is Puerta de Tierra, a narrow strip of land sandwiched between the ocean and the bay. There are a couple of famous hotels and two noteworthy parks, the Parque de Tercer Milenio and the Parque Muñoz Rivera. Beyond Puerta de Tierra is Condado, a strip of shoreline crowded by resort hotels and apartment buildings. Here you can find designer fashions in the boutiques and on the people strolling down the main drag of Avenida Ashford. Ocean Park, to the east, is a mostly residential neighborhood; the handful of inns and restaurants here are among the city's best. Beyond Ocean Park is Isla Verde, which looks a lot like Condado.

WHEN TO TOUR SAN JUAN

The high season is roughly mid-December through mid-April. Winter hotel rates are a bit higher than in the off-season, and hotels tend to be packed, though rarely entirely full. A less expensive time to visit San Juan is during the "shoulder" seasons of fall and spring, when the weather is still fantastic and the tourist crush is less intense.

OLD SAN JUAN

Old San Juan is compelling. Its 16th-century cobblestone streets, ornate Spanish town houses with wrought-iron balconies, busy plazas, and museums are all repositories of the island's history. Founded in 1521 by the Spanish explorer Juan Ponce de León, Old San Juan sits on a peninsula separated from the "new" parts of the city by a couple of miles and a couple of centuries. Ironically, it's youthful and vibrant. It has a culture unto itself, reflecting the sensibilities of the stylish professionals, the bohemian art crowd, and the skateboarding teenagers who populate its streets. You'll find more streetfront cafés and restaurants, more contemporary art galleries, more musicians playing in plazas, than anywhere else in San Juan.

At the northwest end of Old San Juan, Calle Norzagaray leads to El Morro, the old city's defense bastion. On the north side of Calle Norzagaray you'll note a small neighborhood at the foot of an embankment, bordering the ocean—this is La Perla, a rough neighborhood that you would do best to avoid. The west end of the old city faces San Juan Bay, and it's here that the sandstone walls of the original city are most in evidence. On Old San Juan's south side you can find the commercial and cruise-ship piers that jut into San Juan Harbor.

Old San Juan is a small neighborhood, approximately seven city blocks square. In strictly geographical terms, it's easily traversed in a day. But to truly appreciate the numerous museums, galleries, and cafés requires two or three days. If you're limited to a day, you'll need to pick and choose sights according to your interests. It can be done—it's just not quite so rewarding.

Free trolleys swing through Old San Juan all day, every day—they depart from the main bus terminal area across from Pier 4 and travel through the Old City. Taxis can be found in several spots: in front of Pier 2, on the Plaza de Armas, or on Calle O'Donnell near the Plaza de Colón.

Numbers in the text correspond to numbers in the margin and on the Old San Juan map.

WHAT TO SEE

⓮ **Alcaldía.** San Juan's city hall was built between 1604 and 1789. In 1841, extensive alterations were made so that it would resemble the city hall in Madrid, with arcades, towers, balconies, and an inner courtyard. Renovations have refreshed the facade of the building and some interior rooms, but the architecture remains true to its colonial style. A municipal tourist information center and an art gallery with rotating exhibits are on the first floor ⊠ *153 Calle San Francisco, Plaza de Armas, Old San Juan* ☎ *787/724–7171* ⊠ *Free* ⊙ *Weekdays 8–4.*

🔟 **Capilla del Cristo.** According to legend, in 1753 a young horseman named Baltazar Montañez, carried away during festivities in honor of San Juan Bautista (St. John the Baptist), raced down Calle Cristo and plunged over its steep precipice. A witness to the tragedy promised to build a chapel if the young man's life could be saved. Historical records maintain the man died, but legend contends that he lived. (Another version of the story has it that the horse miraculously stopped before plunging over the cliff.) Regardless, this chapel was built, and inside is a small silver altar dedicated to the Christ of Miracles. You can visit any time, but the gates are only swung open on Tuesday. ⊠ *End of Calle Cristo, Old San Juan* ☎ *No phone* ⊠ *Free* ⊙ *Tues. 10–3.*

🔟 **Casa Blanca.** The original structure on this site was a wooden house built in 1521 as a home for Ponce de León; he died in Cuba without ever having lived here. His descendants occupied its sturdier replacement, a lovely colonial mansion with tile floors and beam ceilings, for the next 250 years. From the end of the Spanish-American War in 1898 to 1966 it was the home of the U.S. Army commander in Puerto Rico. Several rooms decorated with colonial-era furnishings are open to the public. A guide will show you around, and then you can explore on your own. Don't miss the stairway leading down from one of the bedrooms; alas, despite local lore it leads to a small room and not to a tunnel to nearby El Morro. The lush garden, recently reopened to the public, is a quiet place to unwind. ⊠ *1 Calle San Sebastián, Old San Juan* ☎ *787/725–1454* ⊕ *www.icp.gobierno.pr* ⊠ *$3* ⊙ *Tues.–Sat. 9–noon and 1–4.*

9️⃣ **Casa del Libro.** On a pleasant side street, this 18th-century house contains a museum dedicated to the artistry of the printed word. The 6,000-piece collection includes some 200 rare volumes dating back more than 500 years, as well as what appears to be legal writing on a fragment of clay from 2,000 years ago. Also on hand are several antique printing presses, one constructed in 1812 in France and later brought to Puerto Rico. There are interesting tem-

El Campo
Del Morro

Calle del Morro

City Wall

San Juan

San Se

Sol

Luna

Las Monjas

Bahia de
San Juan

San Jose

Cristo

Fortalez

Tetuár

Paseo de la Princesa

0   200 yards
0   200 meters

Exploring
Old San Juan

ATLANTIC OCEAN

San Miguel
Bajada Matadero
zagaray
Tanca
Sol
Luna
O'Donnell
San Francisco
San Justo
Recinto Sur
Comercio
Paseo Gilberto Concepción

City Wall

23

Muñoz Rivera
24
Ponce de Léon
25
Paseo de Covadonga

Gen. Harding
Gen. Pershing

◆ Frank Santaella
Parking Lot

◆ Terminal de Guaguas
(bus terminal)

de Gracia

1
La Casita
Tourist
Information
Center

Pier
1

Pier
2

Pier
3

Cruise Ship Piers

Pier 4

*Bahía de
San Juan*

TO CATAÑO

KEY

⚓ *Cruise ship terminal*

⛴ *Ferry*

IF YOU LIKE

ARCHITECTURE

San Juan has been under construction for nearly 500 years. The Old City's colonial Spanish row houses—brick with plaster fronts painted in pastel blues, oranges, and yellows—line narrow streets and alleys paved with *adoquines* (blue-gray stones originally used as ballast in Spanish ships). Several churches, including the Catedral de San Juan Bautista, were built in the ornate Spanish Gothic style of the 16th century.

BEACHES

Just because you're staying in the city doesn't mean you'll have to forgo time on the playa (beach). San Juan's beaches are among the island's best, and Condado, Isla Verde, and Ocean Park—to name just a few sandy stretches—are always abuzz. The government maintains 13 balnearios (public beaches), including two in the San Juan metro area.

MUSIC

Music is a source of Puerto Rican pride, and it seems that, increasingly, everyone wants to live that *vida loca* (crazy life) espoused by Puerto Rico's own Ricky Martín. The brash Latin sound is best characterized by the music–dance form salsa, which shares not only its name with the word "sauce," but also its zesty, hot flavor. Dancing to it is a chance to let go of inhibitions.

porary exhibits as well. ⊠*255 Calle Cristo, Old San Juan* ☎*787/723–0354* ⊕*www.lacasadellibro.org* ⊒*$2 donation suggested* ☉*Tues.–Sat. 11–4:30.*

🄬 **Casa de Ramón Power y Giralt.** The restored home of 18th-century naval hero Don Ramón Power y Giralt is now the headquarters of the Conservation Trust of Puerto Rico. On-site are several displays highlighting the physical, cultural, and historical importance of land and properties on the island under the trust's aegis. You can find a display of musical instruments that you can play, a bird diorama with recorded bird songs, an active beehive, and a seven-minute movie discussing the trust's efforts. Displays are in Spanish; the movie is in English or Spanish. A gift shop sells toys and Puerto Rican candies. ⊠*155 Calle Tetuán, Old San Juan* ☎*787/722–5834* ⊒*Free* ☉*Tues.–Sat. 10–4.*

❶ **La Casita.** With a name that means "Little House," La Casita was built in the 1930s to handle traffic at the nearby port.

Today the beautiful building, with yellow stucco walls and a barrel-tile roof, serves as an information center run by the Puerto Rico Tourism Company. The friendly staff will give you all the maps and brochures you can carry. ⊠*Plaza de la Dársena, Old San Juan* ☎*787/722–1709* ⊕*www. gotopuertorico.com* ⊙*Sat.–Wed. 8:30–8, Thurs. and Fri. 8:30–5:30.*

❺ Catedral de San Juan Bautista. The Catholic shrine of Puerto Rico had humble beginnings in the early 1520s as a thatch-roof, wooden structure. Hurricane winds tore off the thatch and destroyed the church. It was reconstructed in 1540, when it was given a graceful circular staircase and vaulted Gothic ceilings. Most of the work on the present cathedral, however, was done in the 19th century. The remains of Ponce de León are in a marble tomb near the transept. The trompe-l'oeil work on the inside of the dome is breathtaking. Unfortunately, many of the other frescoes suffer from water damage. ⊠*151 Calle Cristo, Old San Juan* ☎*787/722–0861* ⊕*www.catedralsanjuan.com* ⊠*$1 donation suggested* ⊙*Mon.–Sat. 8–5, Sun. 8–2:30.*

❽ Centro Nacional de Artes Populares y Artesanías. Run by the Institute of Puerto Rican Culture, the Popular Arts & Crafts Center is in a colonial building next to the Casa del Libro and is a superb repository of island crafts, some of which are for sale. ⊠*253 Calle Cristo, Old San Juan* ☎*787/722–0621* ⊠*Free* ⊙*Mon.–Sat. 9–5.*

❿ Convento de los Dominicos. Built by Dominican friars in 1523, this convent often served as a shelter during Carib Indian attacks and, more recently, as headquarters for the Antilles command of the U.S. Army. Now the beautifully restored building is home to some offices of the Institute of Puerto Rican Culture containing religious manuscripts, artifacts, and art. The institute also maintains a crafts store and bookstore here. Classical concerts are occasionally held here. ⊠*98 Calle Norzagaray, Old San Juan* ☎*787/721–6866* ⊠*Free* ⊙*Mon.–Sat. 9–5.*

❼ La Fortaleza. Sitting on a hill overlooking the harbor, La Fortaleza was built as a fortress in 1533. Not a very good fortress, mind you. It was attacked numerous times and taken twice, by the British in 1598 and by the Dutch in 1625. When the city's other fortifications were finished, La Fortaleza was transformed into a palace. Numerous changes to the original primitive structure over the past four centuries have resulted in the present collection of marble and mahogany, medieval towers, and stained-glass galleries. The Western Hemisphere's oldest executive mansion in continuous use, it's still the official residence of the island's governor. Guided tours are conducted in English and Spanish; both include a short video presentation. Call ahead, as tours are often canceled because of official functions. The tours begin near the main gate in a yellow building called the Real Audiencia. ⊠*Calle Recinto Oeste, Old San Juan* ☎*787/721–7000 Ext. 2211* ⊕*www.fortaleza. gobierno.pr* ⊠*Free* ⊙*Weekdays 9–3:30.*

㉓ Fuerte San Cristóbal. This stone fortress, built between
⟳ 1634 and 1785, guarded the city from land attacks. Even larger than El Morro, San Cristóbal was known in the 17th and 18th centuries as the Gibraltar of the West Indies. Five freestanding structures are connected by tunnels, and restored units include an 18th-century barracks. You're free to explore the gun turrets, officers' quarters, and passageways. Along with El Morro, San Cristóbal is a National Historic Site administered by the U.S. Park Service; it's a UN World Heritage Site as well. Rangers conduct tours in Spanish and English. ⊠*Calle Norzagaray, Old San Juan* ☎*787/729–6960* ⊕*www.nps.gov/saju* ⊠*$3; $5 includes admission to El Morro* ⊙*June–Nov., daily 9–5; Dec.–May, daily 9–6.*

★ Fodor'sChoice **Fuerte San Felipe del Morro.** On a rocky prom-
㉒ ontory at the northwestern tip of the Old City is El Morro
⟳ (which translates as "promontory"), a fortress built by the Spaniards between 1540 and 1783. Rising 140 feet above the sea, the massive six-level fortress covers enough territory to accommodate a nine-hole golf course. It's a labyrinth of dungeons, ramps, barracks, turrets, towers, and tunnels. Built to protect the port, El Morro has a commanding view of the harbor. You're free to wander throughout. The cannon emplacement walls are thick as a child's arm is long, and the dank secret passageways are a wonder of engineering. The history of the fortress can be traced in its museum. Tours and a video show are available in English. ⊠*Calle Norzagaray, Old San Juan* ☎*787/729–6960* ⊕*www.nps. gov/saju* ⊠*$3; $5 includes admission to Fuerte San Cristóbal* ⊙*June–Nov., daily 9–5; Dec.–May, daily 9–6.*

⑯ Iglesia de San José. With its vaulted ceilings, this church is a splendid example of 16th-century Spanish Gothic architecture. It was built under the supervision of Dominican friars in 1532, making it one of the oldest churches in the Western Hemisphere. The body of Ponce de León, the Spanish explorer who came to the New World seeking the Fountain of Youth, was buried here for almost three centuries before being moved to the Catedral de San Juan Bautista in 1913. At this writing, much-needed renovations were underway; the church was expected to reopen in 2007 at this writing. ⊠*Calle San Sebastián, Plaza de San José, Old San Juan* ☎*787/725–7501.*

⑮ Museo de Arte y Historia de San Juan. A bustling marketplace in 1855, this handsome building is now the modern San Juan Museum of Art and History. You can find exhibits of Puerto Rican art and audiovisual shows that present the island's history. Concerts and other cultural events take place in the huge interior courtyard. ⊠*150 Calle Norzagaray, at Calle MacArthur, Old San Juan* ☎*787/724–1875* ⊯*Free* ⊙*Tues.–Sun. 10–4.*

㉑ Museo de las Américas. One of the finest collections of its type in Puerto Rico, the Museum of the Americas is on the second floor of the imposing former military barracks, Cuartel de Ballajá. Most exhibits rotate, but the focus is on the popular and folk art of Latin America. The permanent exhibit, "Las Artes Populares en las Américas," has religious figures, musical instruments, basketwork, costumes, farming implements, and other artifacts of the Americas. ⊠*Calle Norzagaray and Calle del Morro, Old San Juan* ☎*787/724–5052* ⊕*www.museolasamericas.org* ⊯*Free* ⊙*Tues.–Fri. 10–4, weekends 11–5.*

⑥ Museo del Niño. This three-floor, hands-on "museum" is pure fun for kids. There are games to play, clothes for dress-up, a mock plaza with market, and even a barbershop where children can play (no real scissors here). One of the newer exhibits is an immense food-groups pyramid, where children can climb to place magnets representing different foods. Older children will appreciate the top-floor garden where bugs and plants are on display. For toddlers, there's a playground. Note that when it reaches capacity, the museum stops selling tickets. ⊠*150 Calle Cristo, Old San Juan* ☎*787/722–3791* ⊕*www.museodelninopr.org* ⊯*$5, $7 for children* ⊙*Tues.–Thurs. 9–3:30, Fri. 9–5, weekends 12:30–5.*

⑱ Museo de Nuestra Raíz Africana. The Institute of Puerto Rican Culture created this museum to help Puerto Ricans understand African influences in island culture. On display over two floors are African musical instruments, documents relating to the slave trade, and a list of African words that have made it into popular Puerto Rican culture. ⊠*101 Calle San Sebastián, Plaza de San José, Old San Juan* ☏*787/724–4294* ⊕*www.icp.gobierno.pr* ⊡*$2* ⊙*Tues.–Sat. 8:30–4:20.*

⑰ Museo Pablo Casals. The small, two-story museum contains memorabilia of the famed cellist, who made his home in Puerto Rico from 1956 until his death in 1973. Manuscripts, photographs, and his favorite cellos are on display, in addition to recordings and videotapes (shown on request) of Casals Festival concerts, which he instituted in 1957. The festival is held annually in June. ⊠*101 Calle San Sebastián, Plaza de San José, Old San Juan* ☏*787/723–9185* ⊡*$1* ⊙*Tues.–Sat. 9:30–5:30.*

⑪ Parque de las Palomas. Never have birds had it so good. The small, shaded park bordering Old San Juan's Capilla del Cristo has a large stone wall with pigeonholes cut into it. Hundreds of *palomas* (pigeons) roost here, and the park is full of cooing local children chasing the well-fed birds. There's a small kiosk where you can buy refreshments and bags of seed to feed the birds. Stop to enjoy the wide views over the bay.

❷ Paseo de la Princesa. This street down at the port is spruced up with flowers, trees, benches, street lamps, and a striking fountain depicting the various ethnic groups of Puerto Rico. Take a seat and watch the boats zip across the water. At the west end of the paseo, beyond the fountain, is the beginning of a shoreline path that hugs Old San Juan's walls and leads to the city gate at Calle San Juan.

⑬ Plaza de Armas. The old city's original main square was once used as military drilling grounds. Bordered by calles San Francisco, Rafael Codero, San José, and Cruz, it has a fountain with 19th-century statues representing the four seasons, as well as a bandstand and a small café. This is one of the most popular meeting places in Old San Juan, so you're likely to encounter everything from local bands to artists sketching caricatures to street preachers imploring the wicked to repent.

㉔ Plaza de Colón. A statue of Christopher Columbus stands atop a high pedestal in this bustling Old San Juan square. Originally called St. James Square, it was renamed in honor of Columbus on the 400th anniversary of his arrival in Puerto Rico. Bronze plaques on the statue's base relate various episodes in the life of the great explorer. On the north side of the plaza is a terminal for buses to and from San Juan.

❹ **Plazuela de la Rogativa.** According to legend, the British, while laying siege to the city in 1797, mistook the flaming torches of a *rogativa*—religious procession—for Spanish reinforcements, and beat a hasty retreat. In this little plaza statues of a bishop and three women commemorate the legend. The monument was created in 1971 by the artist Lindsay Daen to mark the Old City's 450th anniversary. ⊠*Caleta de las Monjas, Old San Juan.*

❸ **Puerta de San Juan.** Dating back to 1520, this was one of the five original entrances to the city. The massive gate, painted a brilliant shade of red, gave access from the port. It resembles a tunnel because it passes through La Muralla, the 20-foot-thick city walls. ⊠*Paseo de la Princesa, Old San Juan.*

❷❺ **Teatro Tapia.** Named after the Puerto Rican playwright Alejandro Tapia y Rivera, this municipal theater was built in 1832 and remodeled in 1949 and again in 1987. It showcases ballets, plays, and operettas. Stop by the box office to find out what's showing. ⊠*Plaza de Colón, Old San Juan* ☎*787/721–0169.*

GREATER SAN JUAN

Modern San Juan is a study in congested highways and cement-block housing complexes, as well as the resorts of Condado and Isla Verde. Sightseeing in the modern city requires more effort than it does in Old San Juan—the sights are scattered in the suburbs, accessible by taxi, bus, or a rental car, but not on foot.

Avenidas Muñoz Rivera, Ponce de León, and Fernández Juncos are the main thoroughfares that cross Puerta de Tierra, just east of Old San Juan, to the neighborhoods of Condado, Ocean Park, and Isla Verde. South of Condado and Ocean Park is Santurce, a mostly commercial district where you'll find the Museo de Arte de Puerto Rico and the Museo de Arte Contemporaneo.

Numbers in the text correspond to numbers in the margin and on the Greater San Juan map.

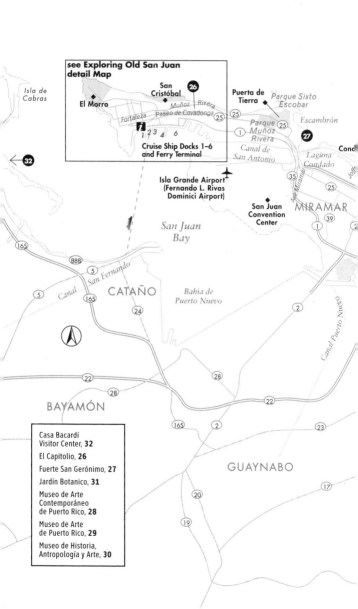

see **Exploring Old San Juan** detail Map

Isla de Cabras

El Morro

San Cristóbal

26

Puerta de Tierra

Parque Sixto Escobar

Fortaleza

Muñoz Rivera

Paseo de Covadonga

25

25

25

Escambrón

Parque Muñoz Rivera

1

Cruise Ship Docks 1–6 and Ferry Terminal

1 2 3 4 6

Canal de San Antonio

1

27

Cond

32

←

Isla Grande Airport (Fernando L. Rivas Dominici Airport)

San Juan Convention Center

35

Laguna Condado

25

Joff

MIRAMAR

1

39

2

San Juan Bay

165

888

5

San Fernando

5

Canal

165

CATAÑO

24

Bahía de Puerto Nuevo

Bahia de Puerto Nuevo

Canal Puerto Nuevo

2

165

22

28

BAYAMÓN

28

165

2

22

23

GUAYNABO

17

20

19

Casa Bacardí
Visitor Center, **32**

El Capitolio, **26**

Fuerte San Gerónimo, **27**

Jardín Botanico, **31**

Museo de Arte
Contemporáneo
de Puerto Rico, **28**

Museo de Arte
de Puerto Rico, **29**

Museo de Historia,
Antropología y Arte, **30**

Exploring
Greater San Juan

ATLANTIC OCEAN

na Ashford
Luchetti
Wilson
C Mc Leary
Taft
Loiza
Park Blvd
C Cacique
Guerrero
Noble
Punta
las Maias
Isla Verde
Gardenia
Amapola
Rosa
Violeta
29
26
37
Parque
Barbosa
Loiza
37
26
37
SANTURCE
35
25
Sagrado Corazón
de Jesús
Avenida Eduardo Conde
Laguna
Los
Corozos
26
187
Calle Tapia
36
RÍO PIEDRAS
27
Avenida Rexach
Constitucion
Luis Muñoz Marín
International Airport
Martín Peña
1
25
Teodoro
Moscoso Br.
CAROLINA
23
17
8
41
25
27
17
17
181
30
31
47
1

KEY	
🚢	Ferry
🛈	Tourist Information

WHAT TO SEE

㉜ Casa Bacardí Visitor Center. Exiled from Cuba, the Bacardí family built a small distillery here in the 1950s. Today it's one of the world's largest, with the capacity to produce 100,000 gallons of spirits a day and 221 million cases a year. You can hop on a little tram to take a 45-minute tour of the bottling plant, distillery, and museum. Yes, you'll be given a free sample. If you don't want to drive, you can reach the factory by taking the ferry from Pier 2 for 50¢ each way and then a *público* (shared van) from the ferry pier to the factory for about $2 or $3 per person. ⊠*Rte. 165, Km 6.2, Cataño* ☎*787/788–1500* ⊕*www.casabacardi.org* ☎*Free* ⊙*Mon.–Sat. 8:30–5:30, Sun. 10–5. Tours every 15–30 min.*

㉖ El Capitolio. The white-marble Capitol, a fine example of Italian Renaissance–style, dates from 1929. The grand rotunda, which can be seen from all over San Juan, was completed in the late 1990s. Fronted by eight Corinthian columns, it's a very dignified home for the commonwealth's constitution. You can watch the legislature in action—note that the action is in Spanish—when it's in session, most often Monday and Tuesday. Guided tours, which take 45 minutes and include visits to the rotunda and other parts of the building, are by appointment only. ⊠*Av. Ponce de León, Puerta de Tierra* ☎*787/724–2030* ☎*Free* ⊙*Weekdays 9–5, Sat. 9–2.*

㉗ Fuerte San Gerónimo. At the eastern tip of Puerta de Tierra, this tiny fort is perched on a hilltop like an afterthought. Added to San Juan's fortifications in the 18th century, it barely survived the British attack of 1797. Restored in 1983 by the Institute of Puerto Rican Culture, it's now open to the public. To find it, go to the entrance of the Caribe Hilton. ⊠*Calle Rosales, Puerta de Tierra* ☎*787/724–5477.*

㉛ The Universidad de Puerto Rico's main attraction is the **Jardín Botánico** *(Botanical Garden)*, a 75-acre forest of more than 200 species of tropical and subtropical vegetation. Gravel footpaths lead to a graceful lotus lagoon, a bamboo promenade, an orchid garden with some 30,000 plants, and a palm garden. Signs are in Spanish and English. Trail maps are available at the entrance gate, and groups of 10 or more can arrange guided tours ($25). ⊠*Intersection of Rtes. 1 and 847 at entrance to Barrio Venezuela, Río Piedras* ☎*787/767–1710* ☎*Free* ⊙*Daily 9–4:30.*

★ **Fodor'sChoice Museo de Arte Contemporáneo de Puerto Rico.** This
❷❽ Georgian-style structure, once a public school, displays a
dynamic range of works by both established and up-and-
coming Puerto Rican artists. Many of the works on display
have strong political messages, including pointed commen-
taries on the island's status as a commonwealth. Only a small
part of the permanent collection is on display at any time,
but it might be anything from an exhibit of ceramics to a
screening of videos. ✉*Av. Ponce de León at Av. R. H. Todd,
Santurce* ☎787/977–4030 ⊕*www.museocontemporaneopr.
org* ✍*Free* ☉*Tues.–Sat. 10–4, Sun. noon –4.*

★ **Fodor'sChoice Museo de Arte de Puerto Rico.** One of the big-
❷❾ gest museums in the Caribbean, this 130,000-square-foot
building was once known as San Juan Municipal Hospital.
The beautiful neoclassical building, dating from the 1920s,
proved to be too small to house the museum's permanent
collection of Puerto Rican art dating from the 17th century
to the present. The solution was to build a new east wing,
which is dominated by a five-story-tall stained-glass window, the work of local artist Eric Tabales. The collection
starts with works from the colonial era, most of them commissioned for churches. Here you can find works by José
Campeche, the island's first great painter. His *Immaculate
Conception*, finished in 1794, is a masterpiece. Also well
represented is Francisco Oller y Cestero, who was the first
to move beyond religious subjects to paint local scenes. His
influence is still felt today. A gallery on the top floor is filled
with works by artists inspired by Oller. ✉*299 Av. José de
Diego, Santurce* ☎787/977–6277 ⊕*www.mapr.org* ✍*$6*
☉*Tues. and Thurs.–Sat. 10–5, Wed. 10–8, Sun. 11–6.*

❸⓿ The Universidad de Puerto Rico's **Museo de Historia, Antropología y Arte** *(Museum of History, Anthropology and
Art)* has archaeological and historical exhibits that deal
with the Native American influence on the island and
the Caribbean, the colonial era, and the history of slav-
ery. Art displays are occasionally mounted; the museum's
prize exhibit is the painting *El Velorio (The Wake)*, by the
19th-century artist Francisco Oller. ✉*Av. Ponce de León,
Río Piedras* ☎787/764–0000 Ext. 5852 ⊕*www.uprrp.edu*
✍*Free* ☉*Weekdays 9–4:30, Thurs. 9–9, weekends 9–3.*

Saints on Parade

Each of Puerto Rico's 78 municipalities has a patron saint, and each one celebrates an annual festival near the saint's birthday, sometimes lasting a week or more. These festivals are a great opportunity to hear live music and buy local arts and crafts. San Juan celebrates its patron-saint feast in the *noche de San Juan* on June 23, when locals take to the beach. The event culminates at midnight, when crowds plunge into the Atlantic to flip over backwards three times, a cleansing ritual expected to bring good fortune. The "San Juan" for whom the city is named was St. John the Baptist, and it is his feast day that is celebrated on June 24; the feast coincides with the summer solstice.

WHERE TO EAT

In cosmopolitan San Juan, European, Asian, and Middle Eastern eateries vie for your attention with family-owned restaurants specializing in seafood or *comida criolla* (creole cooking). U.S. chains such as McDonald's and Subway compete with chains like Pollo Tropical, which specialize in local cuisine. Although each of the city's large hotels has two or more fine restaurants, the best dining is often in stand-alone establishments—don't be shy about venturing to such places.

WHAT IT COSTS IN U.S. DOLLARS				
AT DINNER				
$$$$	$$$	$$	$	¢
over $30	$20–$30	$12–$20	$8–$12	under $8

Prices are per person for a main course at dinner.

OLD SAN JUAN

ASIAN

$$–$$$ ✕**Dragonfly.** It's not hard to find this little restaurant—look for the crowds milling about on the sidewalk. If you can stand the wait—as you undoubtedly will since reservations aren't accepted—then you can get to sample chef Roberto

Trevino's Latin-Asian cuisine. (For the best chance of avoiding a line, come at 6 PM, which is opening time.) The *platos* (plates) are meant to be shared, so order several for your table. Favorites include pork-and-plantain dumplings with an orange dipping sauce, smoked salmon pizza with wasabi salsa, and lamb spareribs with a tamarind glaze. The dining room, all done up in Chinese red, resembles a bordello. There's no children's menu, but you probably won't want to bring the kids anyway. ⊠*364 Calle La Fortaleza, Old San Juan* ☎787/977–3886 ⌂*Reservations not accepted* ⊟*AE, MC, V* ⊗*Closed Sun. No lunch.*

$$–$$$ ✕**Tantra.** Sitting square in the middle of Old San Juan's up-and-coming restaurant district, known as SoFo (short for South Fortaleza Street), this little gem serves a combination of Indian, Asian, and Caribbean flavors, with traditional dishes like tandoori chicken and inventive surprises like beef tenderloin in a cassava purée. The jewel-tone interior invites you to linger, and many patrons do so for an after-dinner puff on an Asian water pipe. ⊠*356 Calle Fortaleza, Old San Juan* ☎787/977–8141 ⊟*AE, MC, V.*

CARIBBEAN

$$–$$$ ✕**La Ostra Cosa.** With brilliant purple bougainvillea tum-
★ bling down the walls and moonlight streaming through the trees, this restaurant's courtyard is one of the city's prettiest alfresco dining spots. If that doesn't inspire romance, the succulent prawns, grilled and served with garlic butter are supposed to be aphrodisiacs. Well, everything on the menu is rated for its love-inducing qualities. (Look out for those labeled "Ay, ay, ay!") The gregarious owner, Alberto Nazario, brother of pop star Ednita Nazario, genuinely enjoys seeing his guests satisfied. He'll sometimes take out a guitar and sing old folk songs. ⊠*154 Calle Cristo, Old San Juan* ☎787/722–2672 ⊟*AE, MC, V.*

$$–$$$ ✕**Parrot Club.** Loud and lively, this place is intent on making sure everyone is having a good time. You're likely to strike up a conversation with the bartender as you enjoy a passion-fruit cocktail or with the couple at the next table on the covered courtyard. Something about the atmosphere—ear-splitting salsa music and murals of swaying palm trees—makes it easy. (If you want to avoid the nighttime noise, come for a quiet lunch.) The menu has contemporary variations of Caribbean classics. You might start with mouthwatering crab cakes or tamarind-barbecued ribs, followed by blackened tuna in a dark rum sauce or seared

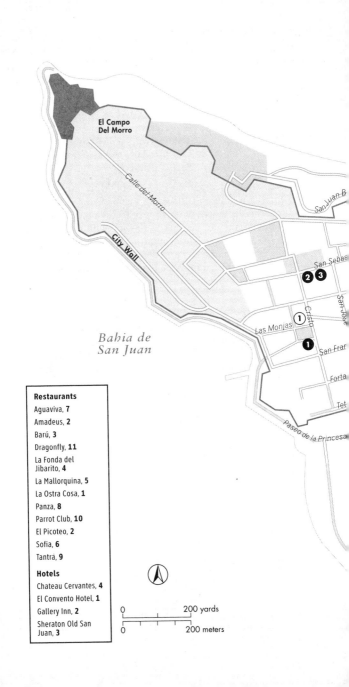

El Campo Del Morro

Calle del Morro

City Wall

Bahia de San Juan

San Juan B

San Sebas

2 3

San Jose

Cristo

Las Monjas 1

1 San Frar

Forta

Tet

Paseo de la Princesa

Restaurants
Aguaviva, **7**
Amadeus, **2**
Barú, **3**
Dragonfly, **11**
La Fonda del Jibarito, **4**
La Mallorquina, **5**
La Ostra Cosa, **1**
Panza, **8**
Parrot Club, **10**
El Picoteo, **2**
Sofia, **6**
Tantra, **9**

Hotels
Chateau Cervantes, **4**
El Convento Hotel, **1**
Gallery Inn, **2**
Sheraton Old San Juan, **3**

0 — 200 yards
0 — 200 meters

Where to Stay & Eat in Old San Juan

ATLANTIC OCEAN

City Wall

San Miguel

Norzagaray

Tanca

Sol

O'Donnell

4

Luna

6

San Francisco

Muñoz Rivera

9 **10** **11** **7**

Ponce de Léon

Paseo de Covadonga

5 Fortaleza

8 **(4)**

San Justa

Tetuán

Recinto Sur

Gen. Pershing

Gen. Harding

◆ Frank Santaella
Parking Lot

🚌 Terminal de Guaguas
(bus terminal)

Comercio

de Gracia

Tanca

Paseo Gilberto Concepción

(3)

Bahía de
San Juan

Pier
3

🛈 La Casita
Tourist
Information
Center

Pier
2

⚓ Cruise Ship Piers

Pier 4

Pier
1

🚢

↓ TO CATAÑO

KEY	
1	Restaurants
(1)	Hotels
⚓	Cruise Ship Terminal
🚌	Ferry
🛈	Tourist Information

sea bass with lobster, leek, and scallop confit. ⊠*363 Calle Fortaleza, Old San Juan* ☎*787/725–7370* ⚐*Reservations not accepted* ⊟*AE, DC, MC, V.*

$–$$ ✕**La Fonda del Jibarito.** Sanjuaneros have favored this casual, family-run restaurant for years. Specialties on the menu of *comida criolla* include conch ceviche and chicken fricassee. The back porch is filled with plants, and the dining room is illustrated with fanciful depictions of life on the street outside. Pedro J. Ruiz, the ever-present owner, is filled with the desire to ensure that everyone is happy. ⊠*280 Calle Sol, Old San Juan* ☎*787/725–8375* ⚐*Reservations not accepted* ⊟*AE, MC, V.*

ECLECTIC

$$$–$$$$ ✕**Panza.** Tucked discreetly behind gauzy curtains, this restaurant doesn't have to shout to be heard. But chef Roberto Pagan's creative cooking speaks loud and clear. Although it's rather too quaintly divided into sections called Preface, Essays, and Contents, the menu is a wonderful mix of different-size dishes, so you can have your own or share a few with friends. Don't miss the bacon-wrapped dates with blue cheese aioli and the tiny tacos stuffed with slow-cooked duck. If you can't decide, there are two tasting menus: five courses for $70 or seven courses for $95. The half-moon banquette in the front window is the perfect place to try any of the 550 wines from the extensive cellars. ⊠*329 Calle Recinto Sur, Old San Juan* ☎*787/724–7722* ⚐*Reservations essential* ⊟*AE, D, DC, MC, V* ⊘*Closed Sun.*

$$–$$$ ✕**Amadeus.** Facing Plaza San José, this bright and airy restaurant often throws open the doors and lets its tables spill into the square. If you want a little more privacy, there's also an interior courtyard and an intimate dining room with whitewashed walls, linen tablecloths, and lazily turning ceiling fans. Try nouvelle Caribbean appetizers such as dumplings with guava-rum sauce or plantain mousse with shrimp and entrées such as ravioli with a goat-cheese and pork with an apple-molasses sauce. ⊠*106 Calle San Sebastián, Old San Juan* ☎*787/722–8635* ⊟*AE, MC, V* ⊘*Closed Sun. No lunch Mon.*

$$–$$$ ✕**Barú.** The well-traveled menu has earned Barú a solid reputation among Sanjuaneros, so it's often crowded. The dishes, all served in medium-size portions so you can order several and share, range from Middle Eastern to Asian to Caribbean. Favorites include oysters in a soy-citrus sauce, risotto with green asparagus, and carpaccio made from beef, tuna, or salmon. More substantial fare includes filet mignon with horseradish mashed potatoes and pork ribs with a ginger-tamarind glaze. The dining room, set in a beautifully renovated colonial house, is dark and mysterious. ⊠*150 Calle San Sebastián, Old San Juan* ☎*787/977–7107* ⊟*AE, MC, V* ⊗*Closed Mon. No lunch.*

ITALIAN

$$–$$$ ✕**Sofia.** Ignore the tongue-in-cheek recordings of "That's Amore." Everything else in this red-walled trattoria is the real deal, from the gleaming vegetables on the antipasto table to the interesting vintages on the small but well-chosen wine list. Start with the squid stuffed with sweet sausage; then move on to the linguine with clams and pancetta or the cannelloni filled with roasted duck and topped with mascarpone cheese. The plates of pasta are huge, so you might want to consider a half order (which is more the size of a three-quarter order). Save room for—what else?—a tasty tiramisu. ⊠*355 Calle San Francisco, Old San Juan* ☎*787/721–0396* ⊟*AE, MC, V.*

LATIN

$$–$$$ ✕**La Mallorquina.** Dating from 1848, La Mallorquina is thought to be the island's oldest restaurant. The menu is heavy on such basic Puerto Rican and Spanish fare as *asopao* (a stew with rice and seafood) and paella, but the atmosphere is what really recommends the place. Friendly, nattily attired staffers zip between tables agains peach-color walls and beneath the whir of ceiling fans. ⊠*207 Calle San Justo, Old San Juan* ☎*787/722–3261* ⊟*AE, MC, V* ⊗*Closed Sun.*

SEAFOOD

$$–$$$$ ✕**Aguaviva.** The name means "jellyfish," which explains why this ultracool, ultramodern place has lighting fixtures shaped like that sea creature. Elegantly groomed oysters and clams float on cracked ice along the raw bar. The extensive menu is alive with inventive ceviches, some with tomato or roasted red peppers and olives, and fresh takes on classics like paella. For something more filling, try dorado served with a shrimp salsa or tuna accompanied with seafood enchiladas. You could also empty out your wallet for one of the *torres del mar,* or towers of the sea, a gravity-defying dish that comes hot or cold and includes oysters, mussels, shrimp—you name it. Oh, and don't pass up the lobster mashed potatoes; those alone are worth the

trip. ⊠*364 Calle La Fortaleza, Old San Juan* ☎787/722–0665 ⌕*Reservations not accepted* ☰*AE, D, MC, V.*

SPANISH

$$$ ✕**El Picoteo.** You could make a meal of the small dishes that dominate the menu at this tapas bar. You won't go wrong with the sweet sausage in brandy or the turnovers stuffed with lobster. Small plates are best shared. If you're not into sharing, there are five different kinds of paella that arrive on huge plates. There's a long, lively bar inside; one dining area overlooks a pleasant courtyard, while the other takes in the action along Calle Cristo. ⊠*El Convento Hotel, 100 Calle Cristo, Old San Juan* ☎787/723–9621 ☰*AE, D, DC, MC, V.*

CONDADO

CARIBBEAN

$$–$$$$ ✕**Ajili-Mójili.** In a plantation-style house, this elegant dining ★ room sits on the edge of Condado Bay. Traditional Puerto Rican food is prepared with a flourish, with flourishing prices to match. Sample the fried cheese and *bolitas de yautía y queso* (cheese and yam dumplings); then move on to the *gallinita rellena* (stuffed cornish hen). The plantain-crusted shrimp in a white-wine herb sauce is delicious, as is the paella overflowing with shrimp, octopus, mussels, chicken, and spicy sausage. ⊠*1006 Av. Ashford, Condado* ☎787/725–9195 ☰*AE, DC, MC, V.*

$$–$$$ ✕**Yerba Buena.** Tables on the terrace are hard to come by at this restaurant, one of the most popular in Condado. That's fine, because the glassed-in dining room is even more comfortable and has exactly the same view. Cuban classics such as *ropa vieja* (meat cooked so slowly that it becomes tender shreds) seamlessly blend local dishes with imaginative presentation. The shrimp has a coconut-and-ginger sauce, the halibut fillet one of mango and orange liqueur. The restaurant claims to use the "original" recipe for its *mojito*, Cuba's tasty rum, lime, and mint drink. Live Latin jazz is played many nights. ⊠*1350 Av. Ashford, Condado* ☎787/721–5700 ☰*AE, MC, V* ☉*Closed Mon.*

CONTEMPORARY

$$$$ ✕**Pikayo.** Chef Wilo Benet is clearly the star here—a plasma television lets diners watch everything that's going on in his kitchen. The Puerto Rico native artfully fuses Caribbean cuisine with influences from around the world. Veal

is served in a swirl of sweet-pea couscous, for example, and beef medallions are covered with crumbled blue cheese and a red wine reduction. The regularly changing menu is a feast for the eye as well as the palate and might include perfectly shaped tostones stuffed with oven-dried tomatoes or ravioli filled with spinach and truffles. A changing selection of paintings wraps around the minimalist dining room—the restaurant is, after all, inside a museum. ⊠*Museo de Arte de Puerto Rico, 299 Av. José de Diego, Santurce* ☎787/721–6194 ═AE, MC, V ⊘*Closed Sun. and Mon.*

$$-$$$$ ✕**Chayote.** Slightly off the beaten path, this chic eatery is
★ definitely an "in" spot. The chef gives haute international dishes tropical panache. Starters include chayote stuffed with prosciutto and corn tamales with shrimp in a coconut sauce. Half the entrées are seafood dishes, including pan-seared tuna with a ginger sauce and red snapper served over spinach. The ginger flan is a must for dessert. Works by local artists add to the sophistication of the dining room. ⊠*Hotel Olimpo Court, 603 Av. Miramar, Miramar* ☎787/722–9385 ═AE, MC, V ⊘*Closed Sun. and Mon. No lunch Sat.*

$$-$$$ ✕**Zabó.** In a restored plantation surrounded by a quiet garden, this inventive restaurant seems as if it's out on the island somewhere rather than just off bustling Avenida Ashford. Make sure to order several of the tasty appetizers—such as breaded calamari in a tomato-basil sauce—so you can share them with your dinner companions. Of the notable main courses, try the veal chops stuffed with provolone and pancetta or the miso-marinated salmon served over lemony basmati rice. ⊠*14 Calle Candida, Condado* ☎787/725–9494 ═AE, D, DC, MC, V ⊘*Closed Sun. and Mon. No lunch Tues.–Thurs. and Sat.*

SEAFOOD

$$-$$$ ✕**La Dorada.** This fine seafood establishment in the middle of Condado's restaurant row is surprisingly affordable. The grilled seafood platter is the specialty, but there are plenty of other excellent dishes, including mahimahi in caper sauce and codfish in green sauce. The bland dining room is a bit off-putting, but the friendly staff makes you feel genuinely welcome. ⊠*1105 Av. Magdalena, Condado* ☎787/722–9583 ═AE, D, MC, V.

On the Menu

Adobo. A seasoning made of salt, onion powder, garlic powder, and ground black pepper, usually rubbed on meats before they are roasted.

Aji-li-mojili. A dressing combining garlic and sweet, seeded chili peppers, flavored further with vinegar, lime juice, salt, and olive oil; it's traditionally served with lechón asado.

Alcapurrias. Banana croquettes stuffed with beef or pork.

Amarillos. Fried ripe, yellow-plantain slices, a common side dish.

Arepas. Fried corn or bread cakes.

Asopao. A gumbo made with fish or chicken, flavored with spices, salt pork, cured ham, green peppers, chili peppers, onions, tomatoes, chorizo, and pimentos.

Bacalaítos. Deep-fried codfish fritters, which are often served as an appetizer for lunch or dinner.

Batido. A tropical fruit-and-milk shake.

Chimichurri. An herb sauce of finely chopped cilantro or parsley with garlic, lemon, and oil that is usually served with grilled meats.

Lechón Asado. A slow-roasted, garlic-studded whole pig, marinated in sour orange juice and coloring made from achiote, whose seeds are sometimes ground as a spice; it's traditionally served with aji-li-mojili.

Mofongo. A mix of plantains mashed with garlic, olive oil, and salt in a pilón, the traditional mortar and pestle used in the Puerto Rican kitchen.

Mojo or Mojito Isleño. A sauce made of olives and olive oil, onions, pimientos, capers, tomato sauce, vinegar, and a flavoring of garlic and bay leaves that is usually served with fried fish.

Pasteles. Corn or yucca wrapped in a plantain leaf with various fillings.

Picadillo. Spicy ground meat, which is used for stuffing or eaten with rice.

Pique. A condiment consisting of hot peppers soaked in vinegar, sometimes with garlic or other spices added.

Sofrito. A seasoned base made with pureed tomatoes, sautéed onions, bell peppers, tomatoes, sweet red chili peppers, herbs and spices, cilantro (coriander), recao, and garlic, and colored with achiote (annato seeds); it's used in rice, soups, and stews, giving them a bright yellow coloring.

Tembleque. A coconut custard sprinkled with cinnamon or nutmeg.

Tostones. Crushed fried-green plantains, usually served as an appetizer.

SPANISH

$$–$$$ ✕**Urdin.** The name of this restaurant comes from the Basque word for blue, which also happens to be the dining room's dominant color. The menu here consists mostly of Spanish dishes, but Caribbean touches abound. The soup and seafood appetizers are particularly good, and a highly recommended entrée is *chillo urdin de lujo* (red snapper sautéed with clams, mussels, and shrimp in a tomato, herb, and wine sauce). ✉*1105 Av. Magdalena, Condado* ☎*787/724–0420* ▭*AE, MC, V.*

OCEAN PARK

CAFÉS

¢–$ ✕**Kasalta.** Those who think coffee can never be too strong
★ will be very happy at Kasalta, which has an amazing inky-black brew that will knock your socks off. Make your selection from the display cases full of luscious pastries and other tempting treats. Walk up to the counter and order a sandwich, such as the savory Cubano, or such items as the meltingly tender octopus salad. ✉*1966 Calle McLeary, Ocean Park* ☎*787/727–7340* ▭*AE, MC, V.*

¢–$ ✕**Pinky's.** This tiny café near the beach is known for its gourmet wraps and sandwiches, as well as its freshly squeezed juices and fruity frappés. The pink sub is a blend of turkey, salami, and mozzarella, topped with black olives, chopped tomatoes, and basil. The surfer wrap is a mix of grilled turkey and mozzarella topped with pesto mayonnaise. Don't see what you want? You are free to make up your own. Seating is limited, but takeout is available. Or place your order from the beach, where speedy delivery people tend to your hunger pangs. ✉*51 Calle María Moczo, Ocean Park* ☎*787/727–3347* ▭*MC, V* ☉*Closed Mon. No dinner.*

CARIBBEAN

$$$ ✕**Pamela's.** For a quintessential tropical dining experience,
★ make a beeline here, the only city restaurant that offers outdoor seating on the sand, just steps away from the ocean, though it's also possible to dine indoors in air-cooled comfort. The contemporary Caribbean menu is as memorable as the alfresco setting; daily specials might include blackened salmon glazed with a Mandarin honey sauce or Jamaican jerk shrimp and coconut corn *arepas* (pancakes, of sorts) with guava coulis. ✉*Numero Uno Guesthouse, 1 Calle Santa Ana, Ocean Park* ☎*787/726–5010* ▭*AE, D, MC, V.*

MEDITERRANEAN

$$–$$$$ ✕**Uvva.** You might feel you're in the South Pacific or Bali when you take a seat at one of the bamboo tables at this romantic restaurant, especially when you see the oiled teak beams across the ceiling and the shutters that swing up to catch the breeze. The menu has a bit of a split personality—the appetizers lean toward Caribbean favorites, whereas the entrées are mostly Mediterranean staples. It all comes together with such dishes as seared tuna with a ginger and cilantro vinaigrette or sesame-crusted salmon served on a bed of Asian vegetables. There are always several vegetarian options on the menu. ⊠*Hostería del Mar, 1 Calle Tapia, Ocean Park* ☎787/727–0631 ⊟*AE, D, DC, MC, V.*

ISLA VERDE

CONTEMPORARY

$$–$$$$ ✕**Tangerine.** The dining room spills onto a terrace fronting the ocean, whose the steady breezes are as much a part of the dreamy scene as the muted-orange lighting and cream walls. This place is all about sensual pleasures, so it's no surprise that the descriptions of many of the dishes sound a bit risqué. (A plate with three types of marinated fish is named, quite simply, "Threesome.") Appetizers such as roasted pumpkin soup with lemongrass foam and crispy wild mushroom dumplings are seductive but overpriced. Artful entrées include chicken breast stuffed with eggplant puree and a pan-seared sea bass with sea-urchin butter sauce. ⊠*San Juan Water & Beach Club, 2 Calle Tartak, Isla Verde* ☎787/728–3666 ⊟*AE, MC, V.*

WHERE TO STAY

San Juan prides itself on its clean, comfortable, plentiful accommodations, and hoteliers, by and large, aim to please. Big hotels and resorts, several with casinos, and a few smaller establishments line the sandy strands along Condado and Isla Verde. Between these two neighborhoods, the Ocean Park area has homey inns, as do the districts of Miramar and Santurce, although the latter two areas aren't directly on the beach. Old San Juan has only a few noteworthy hotels, one of which has a casino.

APARTMENT RENTALS

Puerto Rico Vacation Apartments (✉*Calle Marbella del Caribe Oeste S-5, Isla Verde 00979* ☎*787/727–1591 or 800/266–3639* ⊕*www.sanjuanvacations.com*) represents some 200 properties in Condado and Isla Verde.

WHAT IT COSTS IN U.S. DOLLARS				
HOTELS FOR TWO PEOPLE				
$$$$	$$$	$$	$	¢
over $350	$250–$350	$150–$250	$80–$150	under $80

Prices are for a double room in high season, excluding 9% tax (11% for hotels with casinos, 7% for paradores) and 5%-12% service charge.

OLD SAN JUAN

$$$$ 🏨**El Convento.** Carmelite nuns once inhabited this 350-
★ year-old convent, but they never had high-tech gadgets like in-room broadband connections or plasma TVs. The accommodations here beautifully combine the old and the new. All the guest rooms have hand-hewn wood furniture, shuttered windows, and mahogany-beamed ceilings, but some have a little extra. Room 508 has two views of the bay, while rooms 216, 217, and 218 have private walled patios. Guests gather for the complimentary wine and hors d'oeuvres that are served before dinner. The streetside Café Bohemio, the second-floor El Picoteo, and the courtyard Café del Níspero are all good dining choices. ✉*100 Calle Cristo, Old San Juan* ⌂*Box 1048, 00902* ☎*787/723–9020 or 800/468–2779* 🖷*787/723–9260* ⊕*www.elconvento.com* 📑*63 rooms, 5 suites* ⌂*In-room: safe, refrigerator, DVD, Ethernet, Wi-Fi. In-hotel: 3 restaurants, room service, bars, pool, gym, concierge, laundry service, public Internet, public Wi-Fi, parking (fee), no-smoking rooms* ▤*AE, D, DC, MC, V* ⏐⊙*EP.*

$$-$$$ 🏨**Chateau Cervantes.** There's nothing like this hotel any-
★ where else in San Juan—or Puerto Rico, for that matter. The brainchild of local fashion icon Nono Maldonado, this luxury lodging has a look that's completely au courant. Bursts of color from red pillows or gold upholstery on the banquettes add considerable warmth. And the amenities are above and beyond other hotels. Splurge for

one of the larger suites and you get a butler who'll come to mix cocktails; the two-level presidential suite comes with a car and driver. The rooftop terrace has a bar, a hot tub, and an area for massages. Only one downside: this colonial-era building is on a side street, so it doesn't have a view of the water. But with such a gorgeous interior, you may not even notice. ⊠ *329 Calle Recinto Sur, Old San Juan 00901* ☎ *787/724–7722* ☎ *787/289–8909* ⊕ *www.cervantespr.com* ⇋ *6 rooms, 6 suites* ⚬ *In-room: safe, Wi-Fi. In-hotel: restaurant, bar, laundry service, concierge* ⊟ *AE, D, DC, MC, V* ⊺⊙⍝*EP.*

$$–$$$ ▦ **Gallery Inn.** You can shop from your bed at this 200-year-
★   old mansion, as owner Jan D'Esopo has filled the rooms with her own artworks. And not just the rooms—the hallways, staircases, and even the roof are lined with her fascinating bronze sculptures. Even if you aren't a guest, D'Esopo is pleased to show you around and may even offer you a glass of wine. (Just make sure that Campeche, one of her many birds, doesn't try to sneak a sip.) No two rooms are alike, but all have four-poster beds, hand-woven tapestries, and quirky antiques filling every nook and cranny. There are views of the coastline from several of the rooms, as well as from the spectacular rooftop terrace. The first-floor Galería San Juan displays artwork by D'Esopo and others. ⊠ *204–206 Calle Norzagaray, Old San Juan 00901* ☎ *787/722–1808* ☎ *787/724–7360* ⊕ *www.thegalleryinn. com* ⇋ *13 rooms, 10 suites* ⚬ *In-room: no TV. In-hotel: no elevator, no-smoking rooms* ⊟ *AE, DC, MC, V* ⊺⊙⍝*CP.*

$$ ▦ **Sheraton Old San Juan.** This hotel's triangular shape subtly echoes the cruise ships docked nearby. Rooms facing the water have dazzling views of these behemoths as they sail in and out of the harbor. Others have views over the rooftops of Old San Juan. The rooms have been plushly renovated and have nice touches like custom-designed beds. On the top floor you can find a sunny patio with a pool and whirlpool bath, as well as a spacious gym with the latest equipment; the concierge level provides hassle-free check-ins, Continental breakfasts, and evening hors d'oeuvres. ⊠ *100 Calle Brumbaugh, Old San Juan 00901* ☎ *787/721–5100 or 866/376-7577* ☎ *787/289–1910* ⊕ *www.sheratonoldsanjuan.com* ⇋ *200 rooms, 40 suites* ⚬ *In-room: safe, Ethernet. In-hotel: restaurant, room service, bar, pool, gym, laundry service, executive floor, public Internet, public Wi-Fi, parking (fee), no-smoking rooms* ⊟ *AE, D, DC, MC, V* ⊺⊙⍝*EP.*

PUERTA DE TIERRA

$$$-$$$$ ⚘ **Caribe Hilton San Juan.** How many hotels can claim
♻ to have their own fort? The 18th-century Fuerte San
Gerónimo, which once guarded the entrance to San Juan
Bay, is on the grounds of this sprawling resort, which also
has a private beach, a luxurious spa, and one of the best-
developed kids' programs on the island. The addition of
the Condado Lagoon Villas, a new wing of one- and two-
bedroom apartments, makes this one of the island's big-
gest resorts. Unfortunately, the sheer size of the property
means that some of the guest rooms are past their prime,
the staff can be disorganized, and the open-air lobby
is crowded, noisy, and free of any charm whatsoever.
✉*Calle Los Rosales, Puerta de Tierra 00901* 🕾*787/721–
0303 or 877/464–4586* 🖷*787/725–8849* ⊕*www.hilton
caribbean.com/sanjuan* 🛏*602 rooms, 44 suites, 168 vil-
las* ⚲*In-room: safe, Ethernet. In-hotel: 8 restaurants,
room service, bar, tennis courts, pool, gym, spa, beach-
front, concierge, children's programs (ages 4–12), laundry
service, public Wi-Fi, parking (fee), no-smoking rooms*
⊟*AE, D, DC, MC, V* ⦿*EP.*

★ **Fodor's**Choice ⚘ **Normandie Hotel.** One of the Caribbean's fin-
$$$-$$$$ est examples of art deco architecture, this ship-shape hotel
hosted high-society types back in the 1940s. After a stem-
to-stern renovation, it's ready to sail again. Egyptian motifs
in the grand ballroom and other period details have been
meticulously restored. Guest rooms, many of them as big
as suites, are decorated in sensuous shades of cream and
oatmeal. Business travelers will appreciate the huge desks
outfitted with broadband access. Relaxation-seekers need
not look further than the sparkling pool or the compact
spa with its massage area overlooking the ocean. N Bar,
on the second floor, has quickly become a see-and-be-seen
place for the city's trendy crowd. ✉*499 Av. Muñoz Rivera,
Puerta de Tierra 00901* 🕾*787/729–2929* 🖷*787/729–3083*
⊕*www.normandiepr.com* 🛏*58 rooms, 117 suites* ⚲*In-
room: safe, refrigerator, Wi-Fi. In-hotel: restaurant, room
service, bars, pool, gym, spa, beachfront, laundry service,
public Internet, parking (fee), no-smoking rooms* ⊟*AE,
MC, V* ⦿*EP.*

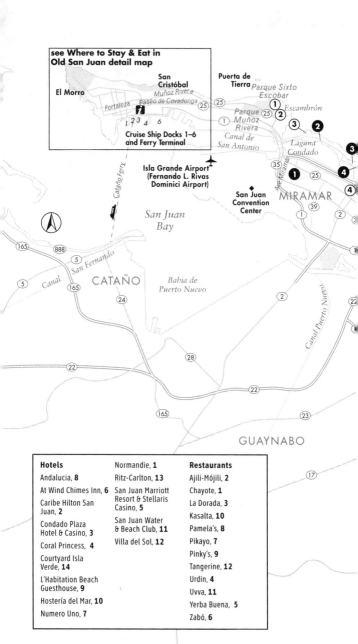

see Where to Stay & Eat in Old San Juan detail map

El Morro

San Cristóbal

Fortaleza

Muñoz Rivera
paseo de Covadonga

Cruise Ship Docks 1–6
and Ferry Terminal

Puerta de Tierra Parque Sixto Escobar

Parque Muñoz Rivera

Canal de San Antonio

Escambrón

Laguna Condado

Isla Grande Airport
(Fernando L. Rivas
Dominici Airport)

San Juan Convention Center

MIRAMAR

Cataño Ferry

San Juan Bay

San Fernando

Canal

CATAÑO

Bahía de Puerto Nuevo

Canal Puerto Nuevo

GUAYNABO

Hotels		Restaurants
Andalucia, **8**	Normandie, **1**	Ajili-Mójili, **2**
At Wind Chimes Inn, **6**	Ritz-Carlton, **13**	Chayote, **1**
Caribe Hilton San Juan, **2**	San Juan Marriott Resort & Stellaris Casino, **5**	La Dorada, **3**
Condado Plaza Hotel & Casino, **3**	San Juan Water & Beach Club, **11**	Kasalta, **10**
Coral Princess, **4**	Villa del Sol, **12**	Pamela's, **8**
Courtyard Isla Verde, **14**		Pikayo, **7**
L'Habitation Beach Guesthouse, **9**		Pinky's, **9**
Hostería del Mar, **10**		Tangerine, **12**
Numero Uno, **7**		Urdin, **4**
		Uvva, **11**
		Yerba Buena, **5**
		Zabó, **6**

Where to Stay & Eat in Greater San Juan

ATLANTIC OCEAN

Isla Verde

Punta
las Maias

Guerrero
Noble

Park Blvd
C Cacique

C Mc Leary

Loiza

Parque
Barbosa

Amapola

Rosa
Violeta

Luis Muñoz Marín
International Airport

SANTURCE

Avenida Eduardo Conde

C Sagrado Corazon
de Jesus

Calle Tapia

Avenida Rexach

RÍO PIEDRAS

Constitucion

Canal Martin Peña

Laguna
Los
Corozos

Teodoro
Moscoso Br.

CAROLINA

shford
etti

Taft

CONDADO

$$$–$$$$ ⊠**San Juan Marriott Resort & Stellaris Casino.** This hotel is
☾ a breath of fresh air—literally: it's the island's first hotel
to be entirely smoke-free. And after a $35 million renova-
tion, it's looking spiffier, too. The hangerlike lobby rever-
berates with the exceptionally loud music from the lounge
and the ringing of slot machines from the adjoining casino.
The rooms have tropical fabrics, and bright colors lighten
the mood considerably. And of course there's the view of
the ocean you have from most of the balconies. The high-
est point is undoubtedly the pair of pools, which add a
bit of whimsy with their gushing fountains and swirling
mural. ⊠*1309 Av. Ashford, Condado 00907 ☎787/722–
7000 or 800/465–5005 ☎787/722–6800 ⊕www.marriott.
com ⤹512 rooms, 17 suites ⚲In-room: safe, refrigerator,
Ethernet, Wi-Fi. In-hotel: 4 restaurants, room service, bar,
tennis courts, pool, gym, children's programs (ages 4–12),
laundry service, concierge, parking (fee), no-smoking
rooms ⊟AE, D, DC, MC, V ⦿EP.*

$$$–$$$ ⊠**Condado Plaza Hotel & Casino.** The Atlantic Ocean and
☾ the Laguna del Condado border this high-rise (once a
Wyndham), whose two wings—fittingly named Ocean and
Lagoon—are connected by a covered walkway. Standard
rooms have nice touches like walk-in closets and dressing
areas. A stay on the Plaza Club floor entitles you to 24-hour
concierge service, use of a private lounge, and complimen-
tary Continental breakfast. Find your own place in the sun
on the beach or beside one of four pools. Some rooms are
being renovated—make sure to ask for one of the newer
ones. ⊠*999 Av. Ashford, Condado 00902 ☎787/721–1000
or 800/468–8588 ☎787/722–7955 ⊕www.condadoplaza.
com ⤹570 rooms, 62 suites ⚲In-room: safe, refrigerator,
Ethernet, Wi-Fi. In-hotel: 7 restaurants, room service, bar,
tennis courts, pools, gym, children's programs (ages 4–12),
laundry service, concierge, parking (fee), no-smoking rooms
⊟AE, D, DC, MC, V ⦿EP.*

$ ⊠**At Wind Chimes Inn.** Hidden behind a whitewashed wall
covered with bougainvillea, this Spanish-style villa has
the feel of an exclusive retreat. So much about the place
invites you to relax: the patios shaded by royal palms, the
terra-cotta-tiled terraces, and the small pool with a built-in
whirlpool spa. The soft, ever-present jingle of wind chimes
reminds you that the beach is just a block away. Spacious
guest rooms maintain the tropical feel. The Boat Bar, open

only to guests, serves a light menu from 7 AM to 11 PM. ✉*1750 Av. McLeary, Condado 00911* ☎*787/727–4153 or 800/946–3244* 📠*787/728–0671* ⊕*www.atwindchimesinn. com* ⌨*17 rooms, 5 suites* ⌂*In-room: kitchen (some). In-hotel: bar, pool, parking (fee), no-smoking rooms* ☰*AE, D, MC, V* ⎮○⎮*EP*.

$ ⛾**Coral Princess.** This art deco building—one of the few left in Condado—has personality to spare. Ample guest rooms subtly reflect the hotel's heritage with crisp lines and simple furnishings. The hotel is a block from the neighborhood's main drag, so you don't have to fight the crowds every time you walk out the front door. If the five-minute walk to the beach is too much, you can always take advantage of the swimming pool on the palm-shaded terrace or the hot tub on the rooftop. ✉*1159 Av. Magdalena, Condado00911* ☎*787/977–7700* 📠*787/722–5032* ⊕*www.coralpr.com* ⌨*25 rooms, 1 apartment* ⌂*In-room: kitchen (some), Ethernet. In-hotel: bar, pool* ☰*AE, D, DC, MC, V* ⎮○⎮*CP.*

OCEAN PARK

$$ ⛾**Hostería del Mar.** Before you even walk in the door, this hotel manages to charm you. Pause to admire a pond filled with iridescent goldfish before continuing into the wood-paneled lobby. The decor might be described as South Seas meets South Beach. The spacious guest rooms continue the tropical theme, aided by colorful fabrics and rattan furnishings. Many rooms have views of the beach, which is only a few feet away. Make sure to enjoy the kitchen's creative cuisine, either in the dining room or at a table on the sand. The staff is courteous and helpful. ✉*1 Calle Tapia, Ocean Park 00911* ☎*787/727–3302 or 877/727–3302* 📠*787/268–0772* ⊕*www.hosteriadelmarpr.com* ⌨*8 rooms, 5 suites* ⌂*In-room: kitchen (some). In-hotel: restaurant, bar, beachfront, no elevator, parking (no fee), no-smoking rooms* ☰*AE, D, DC, MC, V* ⎮○⎮*EP.*

$–$$ ⛾**Numero Uno.** The name refers to the address, but Numero Uno is also how this small hotel rates with its guests. It's not unusual to hear people trading stories about how many times they've returned to this relaxing retreat. Behind a whitewashed wall is a patio where you can catch some rays beside the pool, dine in the restaurant, or enjoy a cocktail at the bar. A few steps away, a sandy beach beckons; guests are provided with beach chairs and umbrellas. Rooms are decorated in sophisticated shades of cream and taupe; several have ocean views. ✉*1 Calle Santa Ana, Ocean Park 00911* ☎*787/726–5010* 📠*787/727–5482* ⊕*www.numero1guest house.com* ↪*11 rooms, 2 apartments* ⚭*In-room: kitchen (some), refrigerator, Ethernet. In-hotel: restaurant, bar, pool, beachfront, no elevator* ▭*AE, MC, V* ⦿*CP.*

$ 🏨**Andalucia.** Living up to its name, this charming Spainsh-
★ style inn boasts details like hand-painted tiles and ceramic pots filled with greenery. The central courtyard has a kidney-shape hot tub big enough for you and four or five of your closest friends. Bamboo headboards and other nice touches give the rooms a beachy feel. Hosts Estaban Haigler and Emeo Cheung give you the warmest welcome imaginable. One of the prettiest beaches in the city is a five-minute walk away. ✉*2011 Calle McLeary, Ocean Beach 00911* ☎*787/309–3373* 📠*787/728–7838* ⊕*www. andalucia-puertorico.com* ↪*8 rooms* ⚭*In-room: kitchen (some), refrigerator, Wi-Fi. In-hotel: public Internet, public Wi-Fi, parking (no fee), no elevator* ▭*MC, V.*

¢–$ 🏨**L'Habitation Beach Guesthouse.** Don't let the name fool you—this oceanfront inn may have a French name, but its laid-back vibe is pure Caribbean. The primarily gay clientele is extremely loyal, coming back year after year. Those unlucky enough to find it fully booked often drop by anyway to recline on the sandy beach or sip a cocktail on the palm-shaded patio. (The margaritas here will knock your sandals off.) Rooms are simple and comfortable; numbers 8 and 9 are the largest and have ocean views. ✉*1957 Calle Italia, Ocean Park 00911* ☎*787/727–2499* 📠*787/727– 2599* ⊕*www.habitationbeach.com* ↪*10 rooms* ⚭*In-room: fans. In-hotel: bar, beachfront, laundry facilities, parking (free)* ▭*AE, D, MC, V* ⦿*CP.*

ISLA VERDE

$$$–$$$$ 🏨**Ritz-Carlton San Juan Hotel, Spa & Casino.** Elegant marble
� floors and gushing fountains don't undermine the feeling
★ that this is a true beach getaway. The hotel's sandy stretch is lovely, as is the cruciform pool, which is lined by statues of the hotel's signature lion. Works by Latin American artists adorn the lobby lounge and the hallways leading to the well-equipped business center. A full-service spa with 11 treatment rooms pampers you with aloe body wraps and *parcha* (passion-fruit juice) massages. Rooms have a mix of traditional wooden furnishings and wicker pieces upholstered in soft fabrics. Though most room windows

are sealed shut to muffle airport noise, many suites open onto terraces. Tastefully so, the casino has its own separate entrance. ⊠*6961 Av. Los Gobernadores, Isla Verde 00979* ☎*787/253–1700 or 800/241–3333* 🖷*787/253– 1777* ⊕*www.ritzcarlton.com* 🛏*403 rooms, 11 suites* ⚹*In-room: refrigerators, Ethernet. In-hotel: 3 restaurants, room service, bars, tennis courts, pool, gym, spa, concierge, children's programs (ages 4–12), laundry service, executive floor, public Wi-Fi, parking (fee), no-smoking rooms* ⊟*AE, D, DC, MC, V* |◎|*EP.*

$$$ ☷**Courtyard by Marriott Isla Verde Beach Resort.** This 12-story hotel tries to be all things to all people—and succeeds to a great degree. Harried business executives appreciate its location near the airport and the full-service business center. Families prefer the many dining options and the fact that the city's best beach is just outside. The place is buzzing during the day, especially around the three swimming pools. At night the action centers on the lobby bar, where live salsa music often has people dancing. (If you don't know how, you can take lessons.) Techies will love that wireless Internet is all over the property, including on the beach. ⊠*7012 Boca de Cangrejos, Isla Verde 00979* ☎*787/791–0404 or 800/791–2553* 🖷*787/791–1460* ⊕*www.sjcourtyard.com* 🛏*260 rooms, 33 suites* ⚹*In-room: safe, refrigerator, VCR (some), Ethernet, Wi-Fi. In-hotel: 3 restaurants, room service, bar, pools, gym, beachfront, laundry facilities, laundry service, public Internet, public Wi-Fi, parking (fee)* ⊟*AE, D, DC, MC, V* |◎|*BP.*

$$$ ☷**San Juan Water & Beach Club.** There's water everywhere at this boutique hotel, from the droplets that decorate the reception desk to the deluge that runs down the glass walls of the elevators. Guest rooms, all of which are decorated in a minimalist style, have an under-the-sea feel because of the soft glow of blue neon. Four rooms are equipped with telescopes for stargazing or people-watching along the beach. No matter which room you choose, you'll have a view of the ocean. The lobby's Liquid lounge is a popular stop along the party trail for hipsters. Wet, the rooftop bar, lets you recline on white leather sofas as you take in the view of the skyline. ⊠*2 Calle Tartak, Isla Verde 00979* ☎*787/728–3666 or 888/265–6699* 🖷*787/728–3610* ⊕*www.waterbeachclubhotel.com* 🛏*84 rooms* ⚹*In-room: safe, refrigerators, VCR (some), Ethernet. In-hotel: restaurant, room service, bars, pool, gym, beachfront, concierge,*

laundry service, public Wi-Fi, parking (fee), no-smoking rooms ⊟*AE, D, DC, MC, V* ⏏*EP.*

$ ⛱**Villa del Sol.** With stucco walls and a barrel-tile roof, this little hotel resembles the manor house of a hacienda. Swaying palm trees line the entrance, which takes you to an interior courtyard. Enjoy the sun from one of the chaise longues surrounding the pool or on the second-story terrace. The cheerful rooms are more spacious than you'd expect in a budget hotel. The only thing you're giving up by staying here is the beachfront, but the ocean is only a block away. ⊠*4 Calle Rosa, Isla Verde 00979* ☎*787/791–2600* 🖷*787/791–5666* ⊕*www.villadelsolpr.com* ⤣*24 rooms* ⌂*In-room: refrigerator. In-hotel: restaurant, bar, pool, parking (free)* ⊟*AE, D, MC, V* ⏏*EP.*

NIGHTLIFE & THE ARTS

Several publications will tell you what's happening in San Juan. *Qué Pasa,* the official visitor's guide, has current listings of events in the city and out on the island. For more up-to-the-minute information, pick up a copy of the English-language the *San Juan Star,* the island's oldest daily; the weekend section, which appears each Thursday, is especially useful. *Bienvenidos* and *Places,* both published by the Puerto Rico Hotel & Tourism Association, are also helpful. The English-language *San Juan City Magazine* has extensive calendars as well as restaurant reviews and cultural articles.

NIGHTLIFE

In Old San Juan, Calle San Sebastián is lined with bars and restaurants. Salsa music blaring from jukeboxes in cut-rate pool halls competes with mellow Latin jazz in top-flight nightspots. Evenings begin with dinner and stretch into the late hours (often until 3 or 4 in the morning) at the bars of the more upscale, so-called SoFo (south of Fortaleza) end of Old San Juan. Well-dressed visitors and locals alike often mingle in the lobby bars of large hotels, many of which have bands in the evening. An eclectic crowd heads to the Plaza del Mercado off Avenida Ponce de León at Calle Canals in Santurce after work to hang out in the plaza or enjoy drinks and food in one of the small establishments skirting the farmers' market. Condado and Ocean Park

BANANA

Marriott Courtyard
7012 Ave. Boca de Cangrejos
Isla Verde PR 00919
Tel. 787-791-0404

108 YAMINAH

Chk 4359   Oct25'10 09:34AM Gst 1

DINE IN

2 Latte @ 2.95   5.90
733037
8000/MICROS CASH

Cash   10.31

Beverage   5.90
STATE TAX   0.35
CITY TAX   0.06
PAYMENT   6.31
Change Due   4.00

------108 Check Closed------
------Oct25'10 09:36AM------

have their share of nightlife, too. Most are restaurant-and-bar environments.

BARS

El Batey. This wildly popular hole-in-the-wall bar won't win any prizes for its decor. Grab a marker to add your own message to the graffiti-covered walls, or add your business card to the hundreds that cover the lighting fixtures. The ceiling may leak, but the jukebox has the best selection of oldies in town. Join locals in a game of pool. ⊠ *101 Calle Cristo, Old San Juan* ☎ *787/725–1787.*

Karma. Music of all kinds, from *rock en español* to hip-hop to Latin rhythms, is played this popular, spacious bar-lounge in the heart of Santurce, and there's often a lively crowd. A menu of Spanish and Puerto Rican tapas is available when hunger strikes. ⊠ *1402 Av. Ponce de León, Santurce* ☎ *787/721–5925.*

Liquid. In the lobby of the San Juan Water & Beach Club Hotel, glass walls filled with undulating water surround fashionable patrons seated on stools that seem carved from gigantic, pale seashells. If the wild drinks and pounding music are too much, head upstairs to Wet, a less frenetic and more welcoming space on the penthouse floor, where you can relax at the bar or on a leather banquette. ⊠ *San Juan Water & Beach Club, 2 Calle Tartak, Isla Verde* ☎ *787/725–4664.*

CASINOS

By law, all casinos are in hotels, and the government keeps a close eye on them. They're allowed to operate from noon to 4 AM, but within those parameters individual casinos set their own hours. In addition to slot machines, typical games include blackjack, roulette, craps, Caribbean stud poker (a five-card stud game), and *pai gow* poker (a combination of American poker and the ancient Chinese game of pai gow, which employs cards and dice). That said, an easing of gaming regulations has set a more relaxed tone and made such perks as free drinks and live music more common. The range of available games has also greatly expanded. The minimum age is 18.

Condado Plaza Hotel & Casino. With its tentlike chandeliers and whirring slots, the Condado Plaza casino is popular with locals. A band performs at one on-site bar, and the TV is tuned in to sports at another. ⊠ *999 Av. Ashford, Condado* ☎ *787/721–1000.*

InterContinental San Juan Resort & Casino. You may feel as if you're in Las Vegas here, perhaps because this property was once a Sands. A torch singer warms up the crowd at a lounge-bar just outside the gaming room. Inside, a garish chandelier dripping with strands of orange lights runs the length of a mirrored ceiling. ⊠*5961 Av. Isla Verde, Isla Verde* ☎*787/791–6100.*

Ritz-Carlton San Juan Hotel, Spa & Casino. With its golden columns, turquoise and bronze walls, and muted lighting, the Ritz casino is refined by day or night. There's lots of activity, yet everything is hushed. ⊠*Av. Las Gobernadores, Isla Verde* ☎*787/253–1700.*

El San Juan Hotel & Casino. Slow-turning ceiling fans hang from a carved-wood ceiling, and neither the clangs of the slots nor the sounds of the salsa band disrupt the semblance of old world. The polish continues in the adjacent lobby, with its huge chandeliers and polished mahogany paneling. ⊠*6063 Av. Isla Verde, Isla Verde* ☎*787/791–1000.*

San Juan Marriott Resort & Stellaris Casino. The crowd is casual, and the decor is tropical and bubbly at this spacious gaming room. A huge bar, where Latin musicians usually perform, and an adjacent café are right outside. ⊠*1309 Av. Ashford, Condado* ☎*787/722–7000.*

Sheraton Old San Juan Hotel & Casino. It's hard to escape this ground-floor casino, the only place to gamble in Old San Juan. You can see it from the hotel's main stairway, from the balcony above, and from the lobby lounge. Light bounces off the Bahía de San Juan and pours through its many windows; passengers bound off their cruise ships and pour through its many glass doors. ⊠*101 Calle Brumbaugh, Old San Juan* ☎*787/721–5100.*

DANCE CLUBS

Candela. This lounge–art gallery housed in an historic building hosts some of the most innovative local DJs on the island and often invites star spinners from New York or London. This is the island's best showcase for experimental dance music. The festive, late-night haunt is open Tuesday through Saturday from 8 PM, and the conversation can be as stimulating as the dance floor. ⊠*110 San Sebastián, Old San Juan* ☎*787/977–4305.*

Pool Palace. No, there's no swimming pool here. The name refers to the 15 pool tables that are the centerpiece of this cavernous club. If a game of eight ball isn't your thing, there's also a dance floor the size of an airplace hangar and a lounge area with clusters of cozy leather sofas. ✉ *330 Calle Recinto Sur, Old San Juan* ☎ *787/725–8487.*

Rumba. With a large dance and stage area and smokin' Afro-Cuban bands, this is one of the best parties in town. ✉ *152 Calle San Sebastián, Old San Juan* ☎ *787/725–4407.*

GAY & LESBIAN BARS & CLUBS

Puerto Rico Breeze (⊕ *www.puertoricobreeze.com*) is a monthly newspaper covering Puerto Rico's gay and lesbian community. It's chock full of listings, articles, and advertisements on dining options, entertainment, and lodging alternatives.

Atlantic Beach. The oceanfront-deck bar of this hotel is famed in the gay community for its early-evening happy hours. But the pulsating tropical music, the wide selection of exotic drinks, and the ever-pleasant ocean breeze make it a hit regardless of sexual orientation. Good food is also served on deck. ✉ *1 Calle Vendig, Condado* ☎ *787/721–6100.*

Cups. This women-oriented bar in the middle of Santurce has been a mainstay of San Juan's nightlife since 1980. Karaoke on Thursday is especially popular. It's open Wednesday to Saturday. ✉ *1708 Calle San Mateo, Santurce* ☎ *787/268–3570.*

Eros. A balcony bar overlooks all the drama on the dance floor at this popular club. Most of the time DJs spin music ranging from house and hip hop to salsa and reggaetón, but there are occasional disco nights that send you back to the 1970s and '80s. It's open Wednesday to Sunday. ✉ *1257 Av. Ponce de León, Santurce* ☎ *787/722–1131.*

THE ARTS

San Juan is the epicenter of Puerto Rico's lively arts scene, and on most nights there's likely to be a ballet, a play, or an art opening somewhere in town. If you're in town on the first Tuesday of the month, take advantage of Old San Juan's **Noches de Galerias** (☎ *787/723–6286*). Galleries and select museums open their doors after hours for viewings that are accompanied by refreshments and music. Afterward, people head to bars and music clubs, and the area remains festive until well past midnight. The event is so popular that finding a parking space is difficult; it's best to take a cab.

The **Casals Festival** (☎787/723–9185 ⊕*www.festcasalspr. gobierno.pr*) has been bringing some of the most important figures in classical music to San Juan ever since Pablo Casals, the famous cellist, conductor, and composer, started the festival in 1957. He went on to direct it until his death in 1973. It has continued to serve as a vibrant stage for top-notch classical performers since then. The festival takes place from mid-February through mid-March. Tickets are available at the box office of the Centro de Bellas Artes Luis A Ferré.

Orquesta Sinfónica de Puerto Rico *(Puerto Rico Symphony Orchestra).* The island's orchestra is one of the most prominent in the Americas. Its 76 members perform a full 48-week season that includes classical-music concerts, operas, ballets, and popular-music performances. The orchestra plays most shows at Centro de Bellas Artes Luis A Ferré, but it also gives outdoor concerts at museums and university campuses around the island, and has an educational outreach program in island schools. ☎787/721–7727 ⊕*www.sinfonicapr.gobierno.pr.*

San Juan is a great place to hear jazz, particularly Latin jazz, and the annual **Puerto Rico Heineken Jazzfest** (☎866/994–0001 ⊕*www.prheinekenjazz.com*), which takes place in June, is one of the best opportunities for it. Each year's festival is dedicated to a particular musician. Honorees have included Chick Corea, Mongo Santamaria, and Tito Puente. Although the festival was born at the Tito Puente Amphiteatro, it has since moved to the Puerta de Tierra oceanside park and sports facility right outside Old San Juan.

SPORTS & THE OUTDOORS

Many of San Juan's most enjoyable outdoor activities take place in and around the water. With miles of beach stretching across Isla Verde, Ocean Park, and Condado, there's a full range of water sports, including sailing, kayaking, windsurfing, kiteboarding, Jet Skiing, deep-sea fishing, scuba diving, and snorkeling.

EACHES

★ **Balneario de brón.** In Puerta de Tierra, this government-run beach is just off Avenida Muñoz Rivera. This patch of honey-color sand has shade provided by coconut palms and surf that's generally gentle. There are also lifeguards, bathhouses, bathrooms, and restaurants. The park is open daily from 7 to 7, and parking is $3. ⊠ *Off Av. Muñoz Riviera, west of Normandie Hotel, Puerto de Tierra.*

★ **Balneario de Carolina.** A government-maintained beach, this balneario east of Isla Verde is so close to the airport that the leaves rustle when planes take off. The long stretch of sand, which runs parallel to Avenida Los Gobernadores, is shaded by palms and almond trees. There's plenty of room to spread out, and lots of amenities: lifeguards, restrooms, changing facilities, picnic tables, and barbecue grills. The gates are open daily from 8 to 6, and parking is $2. ⊠ *Av. Los Gobernadores, Isla Verde.*

Playa del Condado. East of Old San Juan and west of Ocean Park, this long, wide beach is overshadowed by an unbroken string of hotels and apartment buildings. Beach bars, water-sports outfitters, and chair-rental places abound (expect to pay $3 or $4 for a chair). You can access the beach from several roads off Avenida Ashford, including Calle Cervantes and Calle Candina. The stretch of sand near Calle Vendig (behind the Atlantic Beach Hotel) is especially popular with the gay community. If you're driving, on-street parking is your only option. ⊠ *Off Av. Asford, Condado.*

Playa de Isla Verde. The most popular beach within the city limits, Isla Verde is hidden from view by high-rise hotels and sprawling condo developments. There are plenty of places to rent beach chairs and water-sports equipment or grab a bite to eat. Unfortunately, there's not much street parking, so you might want to pay to park at a hotel. ⊠ *Off Av. Isla Verde, Isla Verde.*

Playa de Ocean Park. The residential neighborhood east of Condado and west of Isla Verde is home to this 1½-km-long (1-mi-long) stretch of golden sand. The waters are often choppy but still swimmable—take care, however, as there aren't any lifeguards. Windsurfers say the conditions here are nearly perfect. The beach is popular with young people, particularly on weekends, as well as gay men. Parking is a bit difficult, as many of the streets are restricted to residents. ⊠*Ocean Park*.

BIKING

As a visitor, your best bet is to look into a bike tour offered by an outfitter. One popular 45-minute trip travels from Old San Juan's cobblestone streets to Condado. It passes El Capitolio and runs through either Parque del Tercer Milenio (ocean side) or Parque Luis Muñoz Rivera, taking you past the Caribe Hilton Hotel and over Puente Dos Hermanos (Dos Hermanos Bridge) onto Avenida Ashford.

At **Hot Dog Cycling** (⊠*5916 Av. Isla Verde, Isla Verde, San Juan* ☎*787/982–5344* ⊕*www.hotdogcycling.com*), Raul del Río and his son Omar rent mountain bikes for $30 a day. They also organize group excursions to El Yunque and other places out on the island.

DIVING & SNORKELING

The waters off San Juan aren't the best places to scuba dive, but several outfitters conduct short excursions to where tropical fish, coral, and sea horses are visible at depths of 30 to 60 feet. Escorted half-day dives range from $45 to $95 for one or two tanks, including all equipment; in general, double those prices for night dives. Packages that include lunch and other extras start at $100; those that include accommodations are also available.

Eco Action Tours (☎*787/791–7509* ⊕*www.ecoactiontours. com*) offers diving trips for all skill levels. **Ocean Sports** (⊠*1035 Av. Ashford, Condado* ☎*787/723–8513* ⊠*77 Av. Isla Verde, Condado* ☎*787/268–2329* ⊕*www.osdivers. com*) offers certified scuba dives; airtank fill-ups; and equipment repairs, sales, and rentals. It also rents surfboards by the day.

FISHING

Puerto Rico's waters are home to large game fish such as snook, wahoo, dorado, tuna, and barracuda; as many as 30 world records for catches have been set off the island's shores. Prices for fishing expeditions vary, but they tend to include all your bait and tackle, as well as refreshments, and start at $500 (for a boat with as many as six people) for a half-day trip to $1,000 for a full day. Other boats charge by the person, starting at $150 for a full day.

Half-day and full-day excursions can be arranged through **Mike Benítez Sport Fishing** (⊠*Club Náutico de San Juan, Miramar,* ☎*787/723–2292* ⊕*www.mikebenitezfishingpr. com*). From the 45-foot *Sea Born* you can fish for sailfish, white marlin, and blue marlin.

SHOPPING

In Old San Juan, you can find everything from T-shirt emporiums to jewelry stores to shops that specialize in made-to-order Panama hats. With many stores selling luxury items and designer fashions, the shopping spirit in Condado is reminiscent of that in Miami. Avenida Ashford is considered the heart of San Juan's fashion district.

MARKETS & MALLS

Look for vendors selling crafts from around the island at the **Artesanía Puertorriqueña** (⊠*Plaza de la Dársena, Old San Juan* ☎*787/722–1709*). It's convenient for cruise-ship passengers, as it's across from Pier 1. Several vendors also sell handbags, hats, and other items along nearby Calle San Justo. For a mundane, albeit complete shopping experience, head to **Plaza Las Américas** (⊠*525 Av. Franklin Delano Roosevelt, Hato Rey* ☎*787/767–1525*), which has 200 shops, including the world's largest JCPenney store, the Gap, Sears Roebuck, Macy's, Godiva, and Armani Exchange, as well as restaurants and movie theaters.

FACTORY OUTLETS

With no sales tax, Old San Juan has turned into an open-air duty-free shop for people pouring off the cruise ships. With only a few hours in port, they pass by more interesting shops and head directly for the factory outlets on and around Calle Cristo. The prices aren't particularly good, but nobody seems to mind. Designer bags can be had at **Coach** (⊠*158 Calle Cristo* ☎*787/722–6830*). There's clothing for men and women at **Gant** (⊠*Calle Cristo and Calle Fortaleza* ☎*787/724–4326*). The staff is eager to please. **Guess** (⊠*213 Calle Cristo*) stocks clothing that appeals to a ★ slightly younger crowd. Taking up several storefronts, **Ralph Lauren** (⊠*Calle Cristo and Calle Fortaleza* ☎*787/722–*

2136) has perhaps the best deals around. Stop here toward the end of your trip, as there are plenty of items such as pea coats and scarves that you won't be wearing until you get home.

SPECIALTY SHOPS

ART

★ **Galería Botello** (✉*208 Calle Cristo, Old San Juan* ☎*787/723–9987*), a gorgeous gallery, displays the works of the late Angel Botello, who as far back as 1943 was hailed as the "Caribbean Gaugin." His work, which often uses the bright colors of the tropics, often depicts island scenes. Among those who have displayed their works at

★ **Galería Petrus** (✉*726 Hoare St., Miramar* ☎*787/289–0505* ⊕*www.petrusgallery.com*) are Dafne Elvira, whose surreal oils and acrylics tease and seduce; Marta Pérez, another surrealist, whose bewitching paintings examine such themes as how life on a coffee plantation might have been; and Elizam Escobar, a former political prisoner whose oil paintings convey the often-intense realities of human experience. Half a block from the Museo de Arte de Puerto

★ Rico, **Galería Raíces** (✉*314 Av. José de Diego, Santurce* ☎*787/723–8909*) is dedicated to showing work by such emerging Puerto Rican artists as Nayda Collazo Llorens.

CLOTHING

ACCESSORIES

Louis Vuitton (✉*1054 Av. Ashford, Condado* ☎*787/722–2543*) carries designer luggage and leather items, as well as scarves and business accessories. Aficionados of the famous Panama hat, made from delicately hand-woven straw, should stop at **Olé** (✉*105 Calle Fortaleza, Old San Juan* ☎*787/724–2445*). The shop sells top-of-the-line hats for as much as $1,000. There are plenty for women, as well.

MEN'S CLOTHING

Clubman (✉*1351 Av. Ashford, Condado* ☎*787/722–1867*), after many years of catering to a primarily local clientele, is still the classic choice for gentlemen's clothing. **Otto** (✉*69 Av. Condado, Condado* ☎*787/722–4609*), owned by local designer Otto Bauzá, stocks his own line of casual wear for younger men. **Pedro Serranor** (✉*1110 Av. Ashford, Condado* ☎*787/722–0662*) designs eye-catching swimwear for men.

WOMEN'S CLOTHING

Prolific designer **David Antonio** (⊠*69 Av. Condado, Condado* ☎*787/725–0600*) runs a small shop that's full of surprises. His joyous creations include fluid chiffon tunics for women. **Lisa Cappalli** (⊠*151 Av. José de Diego, Condado* ☎*787/724–6575*) sells her lacey designs from a boutique in Condado. The window displays at **Nativa** (⊠*55 Calle Cervantes, Condado* ☎*787/724–1396*) are almost as daring as the clothes its sells.

HANDICRAFTS

★ **Arte & Máscaras** (⊠*222 Calle San José, Old San Juan* ☎*787/724–9020*) has walls covered with festival masks made all over Puerto Rico. Exotic *mariposas* cover the walls of **Butterfly People** (⊠*257 Calle de la Cruz, Old San Juan* ☎*787/732–2432*). It's a lovely place, with clear plastic cases holding everything from a pair of common butterflies to dozens of rarer specimens. **Mi Pequeño San Juan** (⊠*107 Calle Cristo, Old San Juan* ☎*787/977–1636*) specializes in tiny versions of the doorways of San Juan. These ceramics, all done by hand right in the shop, are a wonderful souvenir of your stay. You might even find the hotel where you stayed reproduced in plaster.

JEWELRY

For a wide array of watches and jewelry, visit **Bared** (⊠*264 Calle Fortaleza, Old San Juan* ☎*787/722–2172*), with a charmingly old-fashioned ambience. **Joyería Cátala** (⊠*Plaza de Armas, Old San Juan* ☎*787/722–3231*) is distinguished for its large selection of pearls. **Joyería Riviera** (⊠*257 Calle Fortaleza, Old San Juan* ☎*787/725–4000*) sells fine jewelry by David Yurman and Rolex watches.

N. Barquet Joyeros (⊠*201 Calle Fortaleza, Old San Juan* ☎*787/721–3366*), one of the bigger stores in Old San Juan, has Fabergé jewelry, pearls, and gold as well as crystal and watches. **Portofino** (⊠*250 Calle San Francisco, Old San Juan* ☎*787/723–5113*) has an especially good selection of watches.

SAN JUAN ESSENTIALS

To research prices, get advice from other travelers, and book travel arrangements, visit www.fodors.com.

TRANSPORTATION

BY AIR

San Juan's busy Aeropuerto Internacional Luis Muñoz Marín (SJU), 20 minutes east of Old San Juan in the neighborhood of Isla Verde, is the Caribbean hub of American Airlines and the busiest airport in Puerto Rico. San Juan's other airport is the small Fernando L. Ribas Dominicci Airport in Isla Grande (SIG), near the city's Miramar section. From either airport you can catch flights to Culebra, Vieques, and other destinations on Puerto Rico and throughout the Caribbean. If you are flying to many other islands, you are likely to make a connection here. A taxi from the international airport to most parts of San Juan costs $10 to $16. For more information on flying to San Juan, see Transportation by Air in Puerto Rico Essentials, at the end of this book.

Information **Aeropuerto Fernando L. Rivas Dominici** (☎ 787/729–8711). **Aeropuerto Internacional Luis Muñoz Marín** (☎ 787/791–4670).

BY BOAT & FERRY

Cruise ships pull into the city piers on Calle Gilberto Concepción de Gracia. There are often hundreds of people fighting over the handful of taxis lined up along the street. Save yourself the hassle and walk the few blocks to Old San Juan. If you're headed to other neighborhoods, take a taxi from nearby Plaza Colón.

The Autoridad de los Puertos (Port Authority) ferry between Old San Juan (Pier 2) and Cataño costs a mere 50¢ one-way. It runs every half hour from 6 AM to 10 PM and every 15 minutes during peak hours.

Information The **Autoridad de los Puertos** (☎ 787/788–1155).

BY BUS

The Autoridad Metropolitana de Autobuses (AMA) operates buses that thread through San Juan, running in exclusive lanes on major thoroughfares and stopping at signs marked PARADA. Destinations are indicated above the windshield. Bus B-21 runs through Condado all the way to Plaza Las Américas in Hato Rey. Bus A-5 runs from San Juan through Santurce and the beach area of Isla Verde. Fares are 50¢ or 75¢, depending on the route, and are paid in exact change upon entering the bus. Most buses are air-conditioned and have wheelchair lifts and lock-downs.

Information AMA (☎ 787/767-7979).

BY CAR

Although car rentals in Puerto Rico are inexpensive (rates can start at $39 a day), we don't recommend that you rent a car if you're staying only in San Juan (at most, you might want to rent a car for a day to explore more of the island). Parking is difficult in San Juan—particularly in Old San Juan—and many hotels charge; also, traffic can be very heavy at times. With relatively reasonable taxi rates, it simply doesn't pay to rent a car unless you're going out of the city.

Major Agencies Avis (☎ 787/774-3556). **Budget** (☎ 787/791-0600). **Hertz** (☎ 787/654-3131). **National** (☎ 787/791-1805). **Thrifty** (☎ 787/367-2277).

Local Agencies AAA Car Rental (☎ 787/726-7350 ⊕ www.aaa carrentalpr.com). **Charlie Car Rental** (☎ 787/791-1101 ⊕ www. charliecars.com). **L&M Car Rental** (☎ 787/725-8307).

BY TAXI

The Puerto Rico Tourism Company oversees a well-organized taxi program. Taxis turísticos, which are painted white and have the *garita* (sentry box) logo, charge set rates based on zones; they run from the airport and the cruise-ship piers to Isla Verde, Condado, Ocean Park, and Old San Juan, with rates ranging $10 to $19. Make sure to agree on a price before you get inside. City tours start at $30 per hour.

Information Major Taxi (☎ 787/723-2460). **Metro Taxi** (☎ 787/725-2870).

CONTACTS & RESOURCES

BANKS & EXCHANGE SERVICES

Banks are generally open weekdays from 9 to 5. The island's largest bank is Banco Popular de Puerto Rico, which has currency-exchange services and branches and ATMs all over the island. Other banks include Citibank, which has a branch across the street from the Radisson Ambassador

Plaza in Condado and another convenient branch near the cruise-ship pier in Old San Juan.

Information **Banco Popular de Puerto Rico** (✉ *1060 Av. Ashford, Condado* ☎ *787/725-4197* ✉ *Plaza Las Américas, 525 Av. Franklin Delano Roosevelt, Hato Rey* ☎ *787/753-4590* ✉ *1818 Av. Loíza, Ocean Park* ☎ *787/721-5557*). **Citibank** (✉ *206 Calle Tanca, Old San Juan* ☎ *787/721-0108* ✉ *1358 Av. Ashford, Condado* ☎ *787/721-5656*).

EMERGENCIES

General Emergencies **Ambulance, police, and fire** (☎ *911*).

Hospitals **Ashford Presbyterian Memorial Community Hospital** (✉ *1451 Av. Ashford, Condado* ☎ *787/721-2160*). **Clínica Las Américas** (✉ *400 Av. Franklin Delano Roosevelt, Hato Rey* ☎ *787/765-1919*).

Pharmacies **Puerto Rico Drug Company** (✉ *157 Calle San Francisco, Old San Juan* ☎ *787/725-2202*). **Walgreens** (✉ *1130 Av. Ashford, Condado* ☎ *787/725-1510* ✉ *1963 Av. Loíza, Ocean Park* ☎ *787/728-0083*).

INTERNET, MAIL & SHIPPING

In San Juan, Internet cafés are few and far between. If that weren't bad enough, many hotels have yet to install high-speed Internet access in their rooms. Your best bet is to use your hotel business center.

In Condado and Isla Verde, branches of Cyber Net are open weekdays until 10 and weekends until midnight. In Isla Verde, try Internet Active, in a small shopping center across the street from the Hampton Inn. It's open daily 11 to 11.

San Juan post offices offer Express Mail next-day service to the U.S. mainland and to Puerto Rican destinations. Post offices are open weekdays from 7:30 to 4:30 and Saturday from 8 to noon.

Internet Cafés **Cyber Net** (✉ *1128 Av. Ashford, Condado* ☎ *787/724-4033* ✉ *5980 Av. Isla Verde, Isla Verde* ☎ *787/728-4195*). **Internet Active** (✉ *Av. Isla Verde and Calle Rosa, Isla Verde* ☎ *787/791-1916*).

Post Offices **Old San Juan Branch** (✉ *100 Paseo Colón, Old San Juan* ☎ *787/723-1277*). **Puerta de Tierra Branch** (✉ *163 Av. Fernandez Juncos, Puerta de Tierra* ☎ *787/722-4134*).

TOUR OPTIONS

In Old San Juan free trolleys can take you around, and the tourist board can provide you with a copy of *Qué Pasa*, which contains a self-guided walking tour. The Caribbean Carriage Company gives tours of Old San Juan in horse-drawn carriages. It's a bit hokey, but it gets you off your feet. Look for these buggies at Plaza de la Dársena near Pier 1; the cost is $35 to $75 per couple.

Wheelchair Getaway offers city sightseeing trips as well as wheelchair transport from airports and cruise-ship docks to San Juan hotels. Colonial Adventure at Old San Juan offers group tours of the city's historic buildings. Legends of Puerto Rico has tours of Old San Juan as well as the modern neighborhoods that few travelers ever visit.

Information **Caribbean Carriage Company** (☎787/797–8063). **Colonial Adventure at Old San Juan** (☎787/793–2992 or 888/774–9919). **Legends of Puerto Rico** (☎787/605–9060 ⊕www. legendsofpr.com). **Wheelchair Getaway** (☎787/883–0131 or 800/868–8028).

VISITOR INFORMATION

You'll find Puerto Rico Tourism Company information officers (identified by their caps and shirts with the tourism company patch) near the baggage-claim areas at Luis Muñoz Marín International Airport. It's open daily from 9 AM to 10 PM in high season and daily from 9 AM to 8 PM in low season.

In San Juan the tourism company's main office is at the old city jail, La Princesa, in Old San Juan. It operates a branch in a pretty yellow colonial building in Plaza de la Dársena. It's open Thursday and Friday 9 to 5:30, Saturday to Wednesday 9 to 8. Be sure to pick up a free copy of *Qué Pasa*, the official visitor guide. Information officers are posted around Old San Juan (look for them at the cruise-ship piers and at the Catedral de San Juan Bautista) during the day.

La Oficina de Turismo del Municipio de San Juan, run by the city, has offices in Old San Juan (at the Alcaldía) and in Condado (in front of the Condado Plaza Hotel on Avenida Ashford). Both are open weekdays from 8 to 4.

Information **Oficina de Turismo del Municipio de San Juan** (✉Alcaldía, 153 Calle San Francisco, Old San Juan ☎787/724–7171 ✉999 Av. Ashford, Condado ☎787/740–9270). **Puerto**

Rico Tourism Company (✉ Box 902-3960, Old San Juan Station, San Juan 00902-3960 ☎ 787/721–2400 ✉ Plaza de la Dársena, near Pier 1, Old San Juan ☎ 787/722–1709 ✉ Luis Muñoz Marín International Airport ☎ 787/791–1014 or 787/791–2551 ⊕ www. gotopuertorico.com).

El Yunque & the Northeast

WORD OF MOUTH

"We enjoyed a hike in [El Yunque] down to the waterfall. That alone gave us a nice feel for the rain forest. We rented a car, [and it] was about 45 minutes from San Juan. Your hotel can set you up with a tour if you don't feel like renting a car."

—lv2trvl

TREE FROGS, RARE PARROTS, and wild horses only start the list of northeastern Puerto Rico's offerings. The backdrops for encounters with an array of flora and fauna include the 28,000-acre El Yunque, the only tropical rain forest in the U.S. National Forest system; the seven ecosystems in the Reserva Natural Las Cabezas de San Juan; and Laguna Grande, where tiny sea creatures appear to light up the waters.

The natural beauty and varied terrain continue in the area's towns as well. Loíza, with its strong African heritage, is tucked among coconut groves. Río Grande—which once attracted immigrants from Austria, Spain, and Italy—sits on the island's only navigable river. Naguabo overlooks what were once immense cane fields as well as Cayo Santiago, where the only residents are monkeys.

You can golf, ride horses, hike marked trails, and plunge into water sports throughout the region. In many places along the coast, green hills cascade down to the ocean. On the edge of the Atlantic, Fajardo serves as a jumping-off point for diving, fishing, and catamaran excursions. Luquillo is the site of a family beach so well equipped that there are even facilities enabling wheelchair users to enter the sea.

If you wish to get away from it all with a neatly packaged trip, eastern Puerto Rico has some of the island's top resorts: the El Conquistador Resort and the Wyndham Río Mar. You can also find the island's only all-inclusive resort, the Grand Meliá Puerto Rico. The extensive facilities and luxury services at these large, self-contained complexes make the list of regional offerings more than complete.

EXPLORING EL YUNQUE & THE NORTHEAST

As the ocean bends around the northeastern coast, it laps onto beaches of soft sand and palm trees, crashes against high bluffs, and almost magically creates an amazing roster of ecosystems. Beautiful beaches at Luquillo are complemented by more rugged southeastern shores. Inland, green hills roll down toward plains that once held expanses of coconut trees, such as those still surrounding the town of Loíza, or sugarcane, as evidenced by the surviving plantations near Naguabo and Humacao. Most notable, however, is the precipitation-fed landscape: green is the dominant color here.

EL YUNQUE & THE NORTHEAST TOP 5

■ Hiking past the waterfalls of El Yunque, the only tropical rain forest within the U.S. National Forest system.

■ Taking a dip at the Balneario de Luquillo, one of the prettiest beaches in Puerto Rico.

■ Sitting elbow-to-elbow with locals at one of the dozens of outdoor seafood shacks on the highway before you get to the the Balnea de Luquillo.

■ Gasping at the eye-popping views from the lighthouse at Reserva Natural Las Cabezas de San Juan.

■ Hitting the tree-lined fairways of the courses at Palmas del Mar.

ABOUT THE RESTAURANTS

Some restaurants carry the tourist board's *meson gastronómico* designation. Such establishments specialize in typical island food. The eastern region has both formal restaurants, where reservations are necessary, and casual beach-side eateries, where you can walk in unannounced in beach attire and have a fine meal of fresh fish. Bills generally don't include service charges, so a 15% tip is customary and expected. Most restaurants are open for dinner from late afternoon until at least 10 PM.

WHAT IT COSTS IN U.S. DOLLARS

		AT DINNER		
$$$$	$$$	$$	$	¢
over $30	$20–$30	$12–$20	$8–$12	under $8

Prices are per person for a main course at dinner, excluding service charges or taxes.

ABOUT THE HOTELS

The east coast has a wide variety of lodgings, from government-approved paradores to small lodges in the mountains to large, lavish resorts along the coast. The Wyndham Río Mar Beach Golf Resort & Spa is a good option, as is the El Conquistador Resort & Golden Door Spa. The Gran Meliá Puerto Rico is less polished than it should be for the high cost.

WHAT IT COSTS IN U.S. DOLLARS				
HOTELS FOR TWO PEOPLE				
$$$$	$$$	$$	$	¢
over $350	$250– $350	$150– $250	$80– $150	under $80

Prices are for a double room in high season, excluding 9% tax (11% for hotels with casinos, 7% for paradores) and 5%-12% service charge.

TIMING

In general, the island's northeast coast—preferred by those seeking abandoned beaches and nature reserves over casinos and urban glitz—tends to be less in demand than San Juan. The exception is Easter and Christmas, when Luquillo and Fajardo become crowded with local sun lovers, merrymakers, and campers. Island festivals also draw crowds, but planning a trip around one of them will give you a true sense of the region's culture. Be sure to make reservations well in advance if you're visiting during high season, which runs from December 15 through April 15.

Numbers in the margin correspond to numbers on the Eastern Puerto Rico and El Yunque maps.

EL YUNQUE

11 km (7 mi) southeast of Río Grande; 43 km (26 mi) southeast of San Juan.

★ **Fodor'sChoice** More than 28,000 acres of verdant foliage and often rare wildlife make up El Yunque, the only rain forest within the U.S. National Forest system. Formally known as the Bosque Nacional del Caribe (Caribbean National Forest), El Yunque's colloquial name is believed to be derived from the Taíno word yukiyú (good spirit), although some people say it comes directly from yunque, the Spanish word for "anvil," because some of the forest's peaks have snub shapes.

Rising to more than 3,500 feet above sea level, this protected area didn't gain its "rain forest" designation for nothing: more than 100 billion gallons of precipitation fall over it annually, spawning rushing streams and cascades, 240 tree species, and oversized impatiens and ferns. In the evening millions of inch-long *coquís* (tree frogs) begin their calls. El Yunque is also home to the *cotorra*, Puerto

IF YOU LIKE

BEACHES

The Atlantic east coast is edged with sandy, palm-lined shores that are occasionally cut by rugged stretches. Some of these beaches are quiet, isolated escapes. Others—such as Luquillo and Seven Seas near Fajardo—are jammed with water-loving families, especially on weekends and during the Easter holidays.

GREAT FOOD

Puerto Ricans love sybaritic pleasures, and that includes fine dining—whether it be on Continental, Nueva Latina, or authentically native cuisine. In the east you can find fine fare of all types. On the traditional side, look for the deep-fried snacks (often stuffed with meat or fish) known as *frituras*, as well as numerous dishes laced with coconut. Plantains appear as the starring ingredient in the hearty *mofongo*, a seafood-stuffed dish, or as *tostones* (fried plantain chips). Fresh fish is commonly prepared with tomatoes, onions, and garlic, or some combination of the three.

GOLF

There's something to be said for facing a rolling, palm-tree-lined fairway with the distant ocean at your back. And then there are the ducks, iguanas, and pelicans that congregate in the mangroves near some holes. That's what golf in eastern Puerto Rico is all about. The Arthur Hills–designed course at El Conquistador is one of the island's best. The Flamboyán course, a Rees-Jones creation at Palmas del Mar Country Club, consistently gets raves, as do the courses at the Wyndham Río Mar. An old-time favorite is the Bahía Beach Plantation course, which was developed on a former coconut plantation.

Rico's endangered green parrot, as well as 67 other types of birds.

The forest's 13 hiking trails are extremely well maintained; many of them are easy to navigate and less than 1 mi long. If you prefer to see the sights from a car, as many people do, simply follow Route 191 as it winds into the mountains. Several observation points are along this often narrow road, which is the park's main thoroughfare. Las Cabezas observation point is at Km 7.8; Cascada La Coca, one of two waterfalls where you can take a refreshing dip (the other, La Mina, is to the south), lies just past Km 8.1; and the Torre Yokahú observation point sits at Km 8.9.

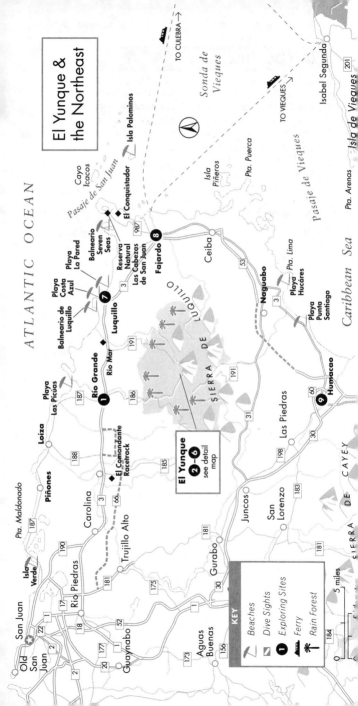

El Yunque & the Northeast

KEY

- Beaches
- Dive Sights
- Exploring Sites
- Ferry
- Rain Forest

ATLANTIC OCEAN

Caribbean Sea

Sonda de Vieques

Pasaje de Vieques

Isla de Vieques

SIERRA DE LUQUILLO

SIERRA DE CAYEY

El Yunque ❷–❻ see detail map

San Juan
Old San Juan
Isla Verde
Pta. Maldonado
Piñones
Loíza
Playa Las Picúas
Río Grande
Río Mar
Luquillo
Balneario de Luquillo
Playa Costa Azul
Playa La Pared
Balneario Seven Seas
Reserva Natural Las Cabezas de San Juan
El Conquistador
Fajardo
Cayo Icacos
Pasaje de San Juan
Isla Palominos
Isla Piñeros
Pta. Puerca
Ceiba
Naguabo
Playa Hucares
Pta. Lima
Playa Punta Santiago
Humacao
Las Piedras
Las Piedras
Juncos
San Lorenzo
Gurabo
Aguas Buenas
Guaynabo
Trujillo Alto
Río Piedras
Carolina
El Comandante Racetrack
Isabel Segunda
Pta. Arenas

TO CULEBRA →
TO VIEQUES →

Roads: 22, 1, 2, 17, 18, 177, 20, 173, 156, 52, 30, 181, 1, 175, 66, 181, 188, 190, 187, 3, 187, 186, 185, 191, 191, 198, 183, 181, 184, 31, 30, 60, 53, 3, 987, 201

5 miles

When hurricanes and mud slides haven't caused portions of the road to be closed, you can drive straight from the entrance to Km 13, the base of Pico El Yunque, the peak that forms the centerpiece of this amazing park.

Arrive early and plan to stay the entire day. The road into El Yunque opens at 7:30 AM and closes at 6 PM. You'll be charged an admission fee if you visit El Portal, the information center that has an interesting movie and interactive exhibits, but everything else is free. There are picnic areas with sheltered tables and bathrooms, as well as several basic eateries along the way.

② A lizard's tongue darts across three movie screens, a forest erupts in flames, a tiny seedling pushes up from the ground and flourishes. Before you begin exploring El Yunque, check out the high-tech, interactive displays—explaining rain forests in general and El Yunque in particular—at **El Portal,** the information center near the northern entrance. The beautifully designed facility is a good stop for families, as many of the exhibits are geared toward youngsters. Kids especially like a short film narrated by actor Jimmy Smits (whose mother is Puerto Rican) about efforts to save the endangered Puerto Rican parrot. All exhibits are in English and Spanish. This is also a good place to pick up a map of the park and talk to rangers about which trails are open. You can also stock up on water, snacks, film, and souvenirs at the small gift shop. ⊠*Rte. 191, Km 4.3, off Rte. 3* ☎*787/888–1880* ⊕*www.fs.fed.us/r8/caribbean* ⊠*$3* ☉*Daily 9–4:30.*

③ The first spectacular sight you're likely to see in El Yunque is **Cascada La Cola** (*La Cola Falls*), which plunges 85 feet down a rocky cliff. The waterfall is inches from the road, so it's visible even to those who don't want to navigate the trails. The gate to the park, which opens at 7:30 AM and closes at 6 PM, is just before the falls. ⊠*Rte. 191, Km 8.1.*

④ Resembling the turret of a castle, **Torre Yokahú** (*Yokahú Observation Tower)* rises unexpectedly from a little hill not far from the road. A peek through the windows of its circular stairway gives you a hint of the vistas awaiting you at the top: 1,000-year-old trees, exotic flowers in brilliant hues, birds in flight. Postcards and books on El Yunque are sold in the small kiosk at the tower's base. The parking lot has restrooms. ⊠*Rte. 191, Km 8.9.*

❺ Just beyond the halfway point along the road into El Yunque, the **Centro de Información Sierra Palm** is a great place to stop for trail updates. El Yunque's steep slopes, unstable wet soil, heavy rainfall, and exuberant plant life result in the need for intensive trail maintenance; some trails must be cleared and cleaned at least twice a year. Rangers at the office here have information on closures, conditions of open trails, what flora and fauna to look for, and any activities planned that day. There are rest rooms and water fountains near the parking lot. ⊠*Rte. 191, Km 11.6.*

❻ Palo Colorado, the red-bark tree in which the endangered
☾ cotorra nests, dominates the forest surrounding the **Centro de Información Palo Colorado.** The center—which is home to Forest Adventure Tours and its two-hour, ranger-led hikes (reservations are required)—is the gateway for several walks. The easy Baño del Oro Trail loops 2 km (1 mi) through an area dubbed the Palm Forest. The even shorter El Caimitillo Trail starts at the same place and runs for about 1 km (½ mi). Although it begins as asphalt, the challenging El Yunque–Mt. Britton Trail turns to gravel as it climbs Pico El Yunque. At a higher elevation you can follow the Mt. Britton spur to an observation tower built in the 1930s. Without detours onto any of the side trails, El Yunque Trail takes about three hours round-trip and includes some mild ascents. Signs clearly mark each turn-off, so it's hard to get lost if you stay on the path. All the trails here are edged by giant ferns, bamboo, and oversized impatiens. There are rest rooms and parking at the center and a picnic area nearby. ⊠*Rte. 191, Km 11.9* ☎*787/888– 5646* ⊕*www.fs.fed.us/r8/caribbean* ⊡*Free* ☉*Daily 8–5.*

RÍO GRANDE

❶ *5 km (3 mi) east of Canóvanas; 13 km (8 mi) southeast of Loíza; 35 km (21 mi) southeast of San Juan.*

This urban cluster of about 50,000 residents proudly calls itself "The City of El Yunque," as it's the closest community to the rain forest, and most of the reserve falls within its district borders. Two images of the rare green parrot, which makes its home in El Yunque, are found on the city's coat of arms; another parrot peeks out at you from the town's flag. The city is also near the posh Wyndham Río Mar Beach Golf Resort & Spa, known for its seaside golf courses, lovely beach, and first-class restaurants.

CLOSE UP

Be Prepared

When you come to El Yunque, you need to remember that while the forest is not far from San Juan (just 45 minutes), it's still a wilderness area, despite the extensive development. Prepare yourself as if you were going to explore any national park. Bring binoculars, a camera with a zoom lens, bottled water, and sunscreen; wear a hat or visor, good walking shoes, and comfortable clothes. Although daytime temperatures rise as high as 80°F (27°C), wear long pants, because some plants can cause skin irritations. There are no poisonous snakes in the forest (or on the island as a whole), but bugs can be ferocious, so a strong repellent is a must. And remember: this is a rain forest, so be prepared for frequent showers.

Río Espíritu Santo, which runs through Río Grande, begins in El Yunque's highest elevations and is the island's only navigable river. It was once used to transport lumber, sugar, and coffee from plantations. Immigrants flocked to the region to take advantage of the employment opportunities; many of today's residents can trace their families to Spain, Austria, and Italy.

BEACHES

Playa Las Picúas is northeast of Río Grande, on a bay close to where Río Espíritu Santo meets the Atlantic. There are no facilities, but the water is fine. ⊠ *Northeast of Río Grande.*

WHERE TO EAT

$$$–$$$$ ✕**Palio.** Northern Italian dishes such as rack of lamb with
★ olive tapenade and poached salmon with spinach are the star attractions at this award-winning restaurant. The friendly staff serves everything with a flourish, whipping up the salads and other dishes beside your table. The arrival of the specialty coffees, served in mugs engulfed in blue flames, is such a showstopper that people at neighboring tables applaud. The dining room, with its black-and-white checkerboard floor and its dark-wood paneling, is gently curved, so it never feels cramped. ⊠ *Wyndham Río Mar Beach Golf Resort & Spa, 6000 Río Mar Blvd., Río Grande* ☎ *787/888–6000* ⚞ *Reservations essential* ⚌ *AE, D, DC, MC, V* ⚘ *No lunch.*

$-$$ ✕**Antojitos Puertorriqueñas.** The menu here couldn't be simpler—dishes like fried pork with plantains or stewed crab with beans and rice are your best options. The premises are just as straightforward, just a covered patio with plastic tables and chairs. But at these prices, who can complain? ⊠*160 Río Mar Blvd.* ☎*787/888–7378* ▭*No credit cards.*

WHERE TO STAY

★ **Fodor's**Choice ⊡**Wyndham Río Mar Beach Golf Resort & Spa.**
$$$$ With more than 500 acres, this sprawling resort—formerly
☾ a Westin—is geared toward outdoor activities. Many people come to play the championship golf courses or hike in the nearby rain forest, but the biggest draw is the 2-mi-long stretch of sand just steps from the door. There's a kiosk near the swimming pools that rents sailboats and other equipment; a dive shop organizes excursions to nearby sites. Even the extensive programs for children are mostly outdoors. The seven-story hotel, which wraps around lush gardens, never feels overwhelming. Some of the rooms are on the small side, but all are cleverly designed to make use of all the available space. The Mandara Spa echos the South Pacific with its hand-carved wood furnishings from Bali. ⊠*6000 Río Mar Blvd., Río Grande 00745* ☎*787/888–6000* ⊟*787/888–6235* ⊕*www.wyndham.com* ⤵*528 rooms, 72 suites, 59 villas* ⌂*In-room: safe, refrigerator, Ethernet. In-hotel: 7 restaurants, bars, golf courses, tennis courts, pools, gym, spa, beachfront, diving, water sports, bicycles, concierge, children's programs (ages 4– 12), laundry service, public Internet, public Wi-Fi, airport shuttle, no-smoking rooms* ▭*AE, D, DC, MC, V* ⏐⎊*EP.*

$$$ ⊡**Gran Meliá Puerto Rico.** This sprawling resort, to the east of Río Mar, is on an enviable stretch of pristine coastline. The open-air lobby, with its elegant floral displays, resembles a Japanese garden, while the swimming pool's columns call to mind ancient Greece. If it sounds like there's an identity crisis here, you're right. But the hotel, run by Sol Meliá, does fairly well at being all things to all people. The 500 suites, many with their own hot tubs, are spread among two-story bungalows. In the works is an 11,000-square-foot spa. The remote location is fine if you plan on staying put, but not if you want to see the rest of the island. ⊠*Rte. 968, Km 5.8, Coco Beach* ☎*787/657–1026 or 800/336–3542* ⊟*787/657–1055* ⊕*www.solmelia.com* ⤵*500 suites, 5 villas* ⌂*In-room: safe, refrigerator, Ethernet. In-hotel: 6 restaurants, bars, golf courses, tennis courts, pool, gym, spa, beachfront, diving, water sports,*

concierge, children's programs (ages 4–12), laundry service ⊟*AE, D, MC, V* ⊠I*AI.*

SPORTS & THE OUTDOORS

Activities in Río Grande region are mostly oriented around the two big resorts, the Wyndham Río Mar Beach Golf Resort & Spa and the newer Gran Meliá Puerto Rico, but only guests can use the facilities at Gran Meliá.

GOLF

The 18-hole **Bahía Beach Plantation Course** (⊠*Rte. 187, Km 4.2* ☎787/256–5600) skirts the north-coast beaches. A public course, it was carved out of a long-abandoned coconut grove, and coconut palms and other native trees and tropical vegetation dominate the scene. Giant iguanas roam the premises, as hawks, waterfowl, and tropical birds fly overhead. The course also offers views of El Yunque, and most greens run either along lakes or the untamed Río Grande coastline. Greens fees range from $65 to $85, depending on day of the week and the time of day. The Bahía Cantina, an on-site bar-restaurant, offers refreshments and sustenance.

The **Berwind Country Club** (⊠*Rte. 187, Km 4.7* ☎787/876–3056) has an 18-hole course known for its tight fairways and demanding greens. It's open for nonmembers from Tuesday through Friday, with greens fees of $65, which includes a cart and bucket of balls. On Sunday afternoons nonmembers can play if they make arrangements in advance.

★ The spectacular **Wyndham Río Mar Country Club** (⊠*Wyndham Río Mar Beach Golf Resort & Spa, 6000 Río Mar Blvd., Río Grande* ☎787/888–6000 ⊕*www.wyndham. com*) has a clubhouse with a pro shop and two restaurants between two 18-hole courses. The River Course, designed by Greg Norman, has challenging fairways that skirt the Mameyes River. The Ocean Course has slightly wider fairways than its sister; iguanas can usually be spotted sunning themselves near its fourth hole. If you're not a resort guest, be sure to reserve tee times at least 24 hours in advance. Greens fees range from $100 to $165 for hotel guests and $135 to $190 for nonguests, depending on tee time.

HORSEBACK RIDING

Hacienda Carabalí (⊠*Rte. 992, Km 4, at Mameyes River Bridge, Barrio Mameyes* ☎787/889–5820 *or* 787/889–4954), a family-run operation, is a good place to jump in the saddle and ride one of Puerto Rico's Paso Fino horses. Riding excursions ($45 an hour) include a one-hour jaunt along Río Mameyes and the edge of El Yunque and a two-hour ride along Balneario de Luquillo.

KAYAKING

Percy Rier and Dalberto Arce of **Kayaking Puerto Rico** (⊠*Río Grande* ☎*787/435–1665* ⊕*www.kayakpuertorico.com*) take you on trips that let you explore the coast by kayak, then drop into the water to see what's under the sea. Trips range from $55 to $74 per person.

LUQUILLO

❼ *13 km (8 mi) northeast of Río Grande; 45 km (28 mi) east of San Juan.*

Known as the "Sun Capital" of Puerto Rico, Luquillo has one of the island's best-equipped family beaches. It's also a community where fishing traditions are respected. On the east end of Balneario de Luquillo, past the guarded swimming area, fishermen launch small boats and drop nets in open stretches between coral reefs.

Like many other Puerto Rican towns, Luquillo has its signature festival, in this case the Festival de Platos Típicos (Festival of Typical Dishes), a late-November culinary event that revolves around one ingredient: coconut. During the festivities, many of the community's 18,000 residents gather at the main square to sample treats rich with coconut or coconut milk. There's also plenty of free entertainment, including folk shows, troubadour contests, and salsa bands.

BEACHES

★ **Fodor's**Choice Just off Route 3, gentle, shallow waters lap the edges of palm-lined **Balneario de Luquillo,** which is a magnet for families. It's well equipped with dressing rooms and restrooms, lifeguards, guarded parking, food stands, picnic areas, and even cocktail kiosks. Its most distinctive facility, though, is the Mar Sin Barreras (Sea Without Barriers), a low-sloped ramp leading into the water that allows wheelchair users to take a dip. The beach is open every day but Monday from 9 to 5. Admission is $2 per car. ⊠*Off Rte. 3.*

Waving palm trees and fishing boats add charm to the small **Playa Costa Azul,** although the ugly residential buildings along the water make an unattractive backdrop. The water here is good for swimming, and the crowds are thinner than elsewhere, but there are no facilities. ⊠*Off Rte. 193, near Rte. 3.*

Playa La Pared, literally "The Wall Beach," is a surfer haunt. Numerous local competitions are held here throughout the year, and several surfing shops are close by just in case you need a wet suit or a wax for your board. The waves here are medium-range. It's very close to Balneario de Luquillo, but has a separate entrance. ⊠*Off Rte. 3.*

WHERE TO EAT

¢ ╳**La Parrilla.** There are more than 50 *kioskos,* or food stands, along the highway on the way to Luquillo Beach. They all serve basically the same thing—fried seafood. This place, true to its name, also has a grill, so there are burgers and other meat dishes in addition to the fish. There's even a comfortable patio in the rear that let's you escape the traffic noise. ⊠*Luquillo Beach, Kiosk #2* ☎787/889–0590 ⊟*No credit cards.*

WHERE TO STAY

$–$$ ▦ **Luquillo Beach Inn.** This five-story, white-and-pink hotel is within walking distance of the public beach and caters to families—children stay free with their parents. The modest one- or two-bedroom suites have sofa beds, kitchenettes, and living rooms equipped with TVs and VCRs; the largest sleep up to six people. It's a good jumping-off point for visits to El Yunque. Transportation (about $45) can be arranged from San Juan if you don't wish to rent a car. ⊠*701 Ocean Dr., 00773* ☎787/889–1063 or 787/889–3333 ⊟787/889–1966 ⊕*home.coqui.net/jcdiaz/fotos3. html* ⇆*20 rooms* ⚭*In-room: kitchens, VCR. In-hotel: bar, pool, laundry service, parking (free)* ⊟*AE, MC, V* ◎*EP.*

FAJARDO

❽ *11 km (7 mi) southeast of Luquillo; 55 km (34 mi) southeast of San Juan.*

Fajardo, founded in 1772, has historical notoriety as a port where pirates stocked up on supplies. It later developed into a fishing community and an area where sugarcane flourished. (There are still cane fields on the city's fringes.) Today it's a hub for the yachts that use its marinas; the divers who head to its good offshore sites; and the day-trippers who travel by catamaran, ferry, or plane to the off-islands of Culebra and Vieques. With the most significant docking facilities on the island's eastern side, Fajardo is a bustling city of 37,000—so bustling, in fact, that its unremarkable downtown is often congested and difficult to navigate.

The 316-acre **Reserva Natural Las Cabezas de San Juan,** on a headland north of Fajardo, is owned by the nonprofit Conservation Trust of Puerto Rico. You ride in open-air trolleys and wander down boardwalks through seven ecosystems, including lagoons, mangrove swamps, and dry-forest areas. Green iguanas skitter across paths, and guides identify other endangered species. A half-hour hike down a wooden walkway brings you to the mangrove-lined **Laguna Grande,** where bioluminescent microorganisms glow at night. The restored **Fajardo lighthouse** is the final stop on the tour; its Spanish-colonial tower has been in operation since 1882, making it Puerto Rico's second-oldest lighthouse. The first floor houses ecological displays; a winding staircase leads to an observation deck. A few miles past the reserve is the fishing area known as **Las Croabas,** where seafood snacks are sold along the water-front. The only way to see the reserve is on a mandatory guided tour; reservations are required. ⊠ *Rte. 987, Km 6* ☎ *787/722–5882 or 787/860–2560* ⊕ *www.fideicomiso. org* ⊇ *$7* ⊙ *Tours Fri.–Sun.*

BEACHES

⟳ A long stretch of powdery sand near the Reserva Natural Las Cabezas de San Juan, **Balneario Seven Seas** may turn out to be the best surprise of your trip. Facilities include food kiosks, picnic tables, changing areas, restrooms, and showers. On weekends the beach attracts crowds keen on its calm, clear waters—perfect for swimming and other water sports. If you've never tried out a sea kayak, this is a good place to learn. ⊠ *Rte. 987.*

WHERE TO EAT

$$$–$$$$ ✕ **Blossoms.** Hung with elaborate lanterns, this dining room is a fanciful version of the Far East. The first thing you'll notice is the sound of meats and vegetables sizzling on the large teppanyaki tables. The chefs here know they're on stage, and they perform with a flourish. Hunan and Szechuan specialties round out the menu. Despite the abundance of fresh fish, it's not so easy to find a sushi bar in this part of Puerto Rico. The one here, with a seemingly endless array of dishes, is excellent. ⊠ *El Conquistador Resort & Golden Door Spa, Rte. 987, Km 3.4*

☎787/863–1000 ⚓*Reservations essential* ▭*AE, D, DC, MC, V* ⊗*No lunch Mon.–Sat.*

$$–$$$ ✕**Anchor's Inn.** Seafood is the specialty at this restaurant perched high on a hill near the marine. (Alas, there's no view.) This is a great place to sample specialties such as *chillo entero* (fried whole red snapper). The convenient location, down the road from El Conquistador Resort, lures travelers who have had enough hotel food. ⊠*Rte. 987, Km 2.7, Fajardo* ☎787/863–7200 ⚓*Reservations not accepted* ▭*AE, MC, V* ⊗*Closed Tues.*

WHERE TO STAY

$$–$$$$ ▨**El Conquistador Resort & Golden Door Spa.** The name means ★ "The Conqueror," and this sprawling resort has claimed the northeastern tip of the island for itself. Perched on a bluff overlooking the ocean, it has some of the island's best views. The resort's beach is on Palomino Island, just offshore; a free shuttle boat takes you there in about 15 minutes. (There's no beach at the hotel itself.) Its branch of the Japanese-influenced Golden Door Spa is widely considered among the Caribbean's best spas. A new owner is investing $100 million to spruce up the tired design and add a new conference center. ⊠*1000 Av. El Conquistador, Box 70001, 00738* ☎787/863–1000 *or* 800/468–0389 🖷787/863–6500 ⊕*www.elconresort.com* ⊷*750 rooms, 17 suites, 155 villas* ⚭*In-room: safe, refrigerator, Ethernet, Wi-Fi. In-hotel: 17 restaurants, bars, golf course, tennis courts, pools, gym, spa, beachfront, diving, water sports, children's programs (ages 4–12), laundry service, airport shuttle, public Wi-Fi, parking (fee), no-smoking rooms* ▭*AE, MC, V* ⊺◎*EP.*

$ ▨**Fajardo Inn.** The whitewashed buildings that make up this hilltop resort have lovely views of the Atlantic Ocean and El Yunque. A bit closer are the lush gardens, part of the hotel's efforts to begin reforestation on this part of the island. All rooms have simple furnishings and white-tile floors; some have balconies that let you enjoy the sunrise. Two restaurants, Starfish and Blue Iguana, are so good that they attract locals. The closest beach is the public Balneario Seven Seas, about a five-minute drive away. ⊠*Rte. 195, 52 Parcelas, Beltran Sector, 00740* ☎787/860–6000 *or* 888/860–6006 🖷787/860–5063 ⊕*www.fajardoinn. com* ⊷*54 rooms* ⚭*In-room: kitchens (some), refrigerators (some). In-hotel: 2 restaurants, bar, 2 pools, parking (free)* ▭*AE, MC, V* ⊺◎*EP.*

SPORTS & THE OUTDOORS

DIVING

The waters off eastern Puerto Rico are probably the best suited for scuba diving and snorkeling and compare favorably to other Caribbean diving destinations. Most operators will take you on dives up to 65 feet down, where visibility averages 40 feet to 60 feet and the water is still warm. The east has bountiful coral reefs, with a good variety of hard and soft coral, as well as a large variety of marine life. Fine snorkeling and diving spots can be found immediately offshore from Fajardo, and there are many small, uninhabited islets from which to dive just off the coast. Experienced divers will find more than enough variety to fulfill themselves, and those just starting out will find eastern Puerto Rico a perfect place, with easy dives that offer a taste of the real beauty of life underwater.

At **Sea Ventures Pro Dive Center** (⊠*Puerto del Rey Marina, Rte. 3, Km 51.4, Fajardo* ☎787/863–3483 ⊕*www. divepuertorico.com*) you can get PADI certified, arrange dive trips to 20 offshore sites, or organize boating and sailing excursions. A two-tank dive for certified divers, including equipment, is $99.

GOLF

★ The 18-hole Arthur Hills–designed course at **El Conquistador Resort & Golden Door Spa** (⊠*1000 Av. El Conquistador* ☎787/863–6784) is famous for its 200-foot changes in elevation. From the highest spot, on the 15th hole, you have great views of the surrounding mountains. The trade winds make every shot challenging. Greens fees for resort guests range from $100 to $165 and are even higher for nonguests.

KAYAKING

Several tour operators, including some based in San Juan, offer nighttime kayaking tours in the bioluminescent bay at the Reserva Natural Las Cabezas de San Juan, just north of Fajardo.

Eco Action Tours (☎787/791–7509 *or* 787/640–7385 ⊕*www.ecoactiontours.com*) provides transportation and gives tours of the Fajardo shimmering bay by kayak every night, with pickup service in Fajardo area and San Juan hotels. The outfit also offers sailing tours to Culebra, daylong snorkeling trips, and Jet Ski rentals.

Las Tortugas Adventures (☎787/725–5169 or 787/889–7734 ⊕*www.kayak-pr.com*) provides transportation from San Juan for a one-day kayaking trip in the Reserva Natural Las Cabezas de San Juan. Rates include transportation from San Juan, but it's possible to join up with the group from Fajardo.

2

HUMACAO

❾ *15 km (9 mi) southwest of Naguabo; 55 km (34 mi) south-east of San Juan.*

Humacao is known for the sprawling resort called Palmas del Mar and its two world-class golf courses, the Flamboyán and the Palm, which draw golfers from all over the world. Although it's not thought of as a tourist destination, Humacao does have some interesting neocolonial buildings along its crowded downtown streets.

The former residence of sugar baron Antonio Roig Torruellas, **Museo Casa Roig** was built in 1919. Czech architect Antonio Nechodoma designed the facade, unusual for its wide eaves, mosaic work, and stained-glass windows with geometric patterns. This was Puerto Rico's first 20th-century building to go on the register of National Historic Places. The Roig family lived in the home until 1956; it was then abandoned before being turned over to the University of Puerto Rico in 1977. It's currently a museum and cultural center, with historical photos, furniture, and rotating exhibits of works by contemporary island artists. ✉*66 Calle Antonio López* ☎*787/852–8380* ⊕*www.uprh. edu/~museocr* 🎟*Free* ☉*Wed.–Fri. and Sun. 10–4.*

Plaza de Humacao, downtown's broad square, is anchored by the pale pink Catedral Dulce Nombre de Jesús (Sweet Name of Jesus Cathedral), which dates from 1869. It has a castlelike facade, and even when its grille door is locked, you can peek through to see the sleek altar, polished floors, and stained-glass windows dominated by blues. Across the plaza, four fountains splash under the shade of old trees. People pass through feeding the pigeons, children race down the promenade, and retirees congregate on benches to chat. Look for the little monument with the globe on top; it's a tribute to city sons who died in wars. ✉*Av. Font Martel at Calle Ulises Martinez.*

As you travel from Naguabo to Humacao, there are stretches of beach and swaths of undeveloped land, including the swamps, lagoons, and forested areas of the **Refugio de Vida Silvestre de Humacao.** This nature reserve has an information office, restrooms, and campsites. ⊠*Rte. 3, Km 74.3* ☎*787/852–4440* ☑*Free* ⊙*Weekdays 7:30–4:30.*

BEACHES

Right beside the Refugio de Vida Silvestre de Humacao, **Playa Punta Santiago** is a long strand with closely planted palm trees that are perfect for stringing up hammocks. The beach, one of 12 government-operated public beaches, has changing facilities with showers and restrooms, food kiosks, and lifeguard stations. Parking is $3. ⊠*Rte. 3, northeast of Humacao.*

WHERE TO EAT

★ **Fodor'sChoice** ✕**Chez Daniel.** When the stars are out, there
$$$–$$$$ could hardly be a more romantic setting than this restaurant in the Anchor's Village Marina. The casual atmosphere belies the elegance of Daniel Vasse's culinary creations. His French country–style dishes are some of the best on the island. The Catalan-style *bouillinade,* full of fresh fish and bursting with the flavor of a white garlic sauce, is exceptional. Pair it with a bottle from the extensive wine cellar. Sunday brunch, with its seemingly endless seafood bar, draws people from all over the island. ⊠*Anchor's Village Marina, Rte. 906, Km 86.4* ☎*787/850–3838* ⚓*Reservations essential* ▭*AE, MC, V* ⊙*Closed Tues. No lunch Mon.–Thurs.*

WHERE TO STAY

$$ ☵**Four Points by Sheraton Palmas del Mar Resort.** The only hotel in Palmas del Mar, this hotel sits amid acres and acres of condo developments. It's surprisingly modest in scale, given its opulent surroundings. Rooms have a luxurious feel, with lovely wood furnishings and rich fabrics. None has a view of the ocean, but they all have balconies overlooking the pool or the lush grounds. Since you have access to the facilities at Palmas del Mar, you can stroll around the marina or hit the links at the two championship golf courses. ⊠*170 Candelero Dr., 00792* ☎*787/850–6000* ☎*787/850–6001* ⊕*www.starwoodhotels.com* ☛*107 rooms* ⟋*In-room: safe, refrigerator, Ethernet. In-hotel: restaurant, room service, bar, golf courses, tennis courts, pool, gym, public Internet, public Wi-Fi, airport shuttle* ▭*AE, D, DC, MC, V* ⊺⊙*EP.*

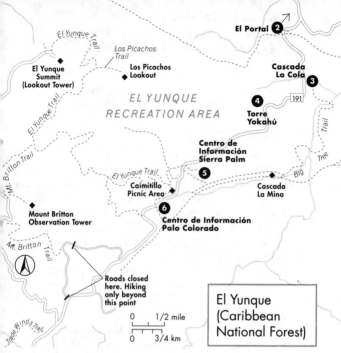

El Yunque (Caribbean National Forest)

SPORTS & THE OUTDOORS

GOLF

★ **Palmas del Mar Country Club** (✉*Rte. 906* ☎*787/285–2256* ⊕*www.palmascountryclub.com*) has two good golf courses: the Rees Jones–designed Flamboyán course, named for the nearly six dozen flamboyant trees that pepper its fairway, winds around a lake, over a river, and to the sea before turning toward sand dunes and wetlands. It's been rated one of the top five in the world. The older, Gary Player–designed Palm course has a challenging par 5 that scoots around wetlands. Greens fees are $70 to $100.

EL YUNQUE & THE NORTHEAST ESSENTIALS

To research prices, get advice from other travelers, and book travel arrangements, visit www.fodors.com.

TRANSPORTATION

BY AIR

Air Flamenco, Isla Nena Air Service, and Vieques Air Link offer several daily flights between Fajardo and San Juan, as well as between Fajardo and Vieques and Culebra. Trips to any of these destination are between 10 and 15 minutes; the cost ranges from $40 to $100 round-trip.

Information **Air Flamenco** (☎787/724–1105 ⊕www.airflamenco. net). **Cape Air** (☎800/525–0280 ⊕www.flycapeair.com). **Isla Nena Air Service** (☎787/741–6362 or 877/812–5144 ⊕www.islanena.8m. com). **Vieques Air Link** (☎787/722–3266 or 888/901–9247 ⊕www. vieques-island.com/val).

AIRPORTS

Fajardo is served by the one-room Aeropuerto Diego Jiménez Torres, which is just southwest of the city on Route 976. The landing field at Aeropuerto Regional de Humacao is used mostly by private planes.

Information **Aeropuerto Diego Jiménez Torres** (☎787/860–3110). **Aeropuerto Regional de Humacao** (☎787/852–8188).

BY BUS

Públicos travel between San Juan and Fajardo, stopping en route at the ferry terminal. The full journey can take up to two hours, depending on where you board and where you are dropped off. However, the fare is a huge bargain at $5 (pay the driver as you board). To get to Fajardo, you simply flag públicos down anywhere along Route 3.

BY CAR

Unless you're planning to hop directly onto a ferry to Vieques or Culebra, you should consider renting a car in eastern Puerto Rico. Even the destination resorts are fairly isolated, and you may appreciate the mobility if you want to get out and have a meal away from the resort, if not to explore El Yunque or some of the great beaches on your own. Rates generally start about $35 a day, but it's sometimes possible to rent directly from your lodging, so ask about packages that include lodging and a car rental.

Agencies **Avis** (✉ *El Conquistador Resort & Golden Door Spa, 1000 Av. El Conquistador, Fajardo* ☎ *787/863–2735* ✉ *170 Candelero Dr., Humacao* ☎ *787/285–1376* ✉ *Wyndham Río Mar Beach Golf Resort & Spa, 6000 Río Mar Blvd., Río Grande* ☎ *787/888–6638* ⊕ *www.avis. com*). **L & M** (✉ *Rte. 3 Marginal, Km 43.8, Fajardo* ☎ *787/860–6868* ⊕ *www.lmcarrental.com*). **Leaseway of Puerto Rico** (✉ *Rte. 3, Km 44.4, Fajardo* ☎ *787/860–5000*).

BY FERRY

The Fajardo Port Authority's 400-passenger ferries run between that east-coast town and the out-islands of Vieques and Culebra; both trips take about 90 minutes. The vessels carry cargo and passengers to Vieques three times daily ($2 one-way) and to Culebra twice a day Sunday through Friday and three times a day on Saturday ($2.25 one-way). Get schedules for the Culebra and Vieques ferries by calling the Port Authority in Fajardo, Vieques, or Culebra. You buy tickets at the ferry dock. Be aware that there may be a line, particularly on the weekend.

Information **Fajardo ferry terminal** (*Fajardo Port Authority* ☎ *787/863–4560*).

BY TAXI

You can flag cabs down on the street, but it's faster and safer to have your hotel call one for you. Either way, make sure the driver is clear on whether he or she will charge a flat rate or use a meter to determine the fare. In most places the cabs are metered. Instead of renting a car, some people opt to take a taxi to Fajardo. The cost from the San Juan area should be about $80 for up to five people.

Information **Fajardo Taxi Service** (☎ *787/860–1112*). **Humacao Taxi** (☎ *787/852–6880*).

CONTACTS & RESOURCES

BANKS & EXCHANGE SERVICES

Banks and ATMs (or ATHs, as they're known here) are plentiful. Banks are usually open weekdays from 9 to 5; very few open on Saturday, and those that do are open only until noon.

Information **Banco Popular** (✉ *Rte. 3, Km 42.4, Fajardo* ☎ *787/860–1570*). **Banco Roig** (✉ *55 Calle Antonio Lopez, Humacao* ☎ *787/852–8601*).

EMERGENCIES

Emergency Numbers **General** (☎911). **Medical Clinics** (☎787/823–2550, 787/887–2020 in Río Grande, 787/889–2620, 787/889–2020 in Luquillo, 787/863–2550, 787/863–2020 in Fajardo).

Hospitals **Hospital Dr. Dominguez** (✉300 Font Martelo, Humacao ☎787/852–0505). **Hospital Gubern** (✉110 Antonio Barcelo, Fajardo ☎787/863–0669). **Hospital San Pablo del Este** (✉Av. General Valero, Km 2.4, Fajardo ☎787/863–0505). **Ryder Memorial Hospital** (✉Salida Humacao-Las Piedras, Humacao ☎787/852–0768).

Pharmacies **Walgreens** (✉Fajardo Plaza, Fajardo ☎787/860–1060 ✉Oriental Plaza, Humacao ☎787/852–1868).

INTERNET, MAIL & SHIPPING

Puerto Rico is part of the U.S. postal system, and most communities of any size have multiple branches of the post office. Some aren't open on Saturday, however. Big hotels and resorts also have postal drop boxes.

There are very few Internet cafés in this part of the country, but all of the larger hotels have in-room Internet access.

Vieques & Culebra

WORD OF MOUTH

"[Vieques] is a beautiful island that hasn't been overdeveloped, and the beaches haven't been taken over by Hyatts and Hiltons. Thank goodness!! BYOE–bring your own everything."

—BeachGirl247

"Most of the islands have pretty shades of blue and green. But I was in Culebra, and the water there sparkled like I never saw water sparkle before. It was like looking at diamonds!!!!!"

—noonema

ALTHOUGH THEY'RE JUST A FEW MILES off the coast of Puerto Rico, the islands of Vieques and Culebra feel like another world. While the rest of the mainland rings with the adrenaline rush of Latin America, this pair of palm-ringed islands have the laid-back vibe of the Caribbean. Not surprising, as St. Thomas and St. Croix are clearly visible from the eastern edges of Culebra.

Vieques and Culebra are alike in many ways. Neither has much traffic—in fact, you won't find a single traffic light on either island. High-rise hotels haven't cast a shadow on the beautiful beaches. And there are no casinos, fast-food chains, strip malls, or most other trappings of modern life. "Barefoot" is often part of the dress code at the casual restaurants, and the hum you hear in your room is more likely than not coming from a ceiling fan rather than an air-conditioner.

But each island has its own personality. Vieques is the biggest of the siblings, so it gets the most attention. The island, 21 mi long and 4 mi wide, has two small communities. Isabel Segunda, the town on the northern shore where the ferry docks, is a knot of one-way streets. It's not pretty, but it has a couple of interesting sights, including a hilltop fortress. On the southern shore is the town of Esperanza, little more that a string of low-cost restaurants and hotels along a waterfront promenade. Nearby is the world-famous Bahía Mosquito, a bioluminescent bay that twinkles like the night sky. The bulk of the island is a national park, the Vieques National Wildlife Refuge. Within the park you can find dozens of beaches with names like Red, Green, and Blue, as well as many more that have no official name.

At 7 mi long and 4 mi wide, Culebra is much smaller. There's only one community, the tiny town of Dewey. People come to Culebra to see Playa Flamenco, consistently rated as one of the two or three best beaches in the world, as well as many lesser-known but equally beautiful beaches. The island is mostly unspoiled, a quality that brings many people back year after year.

Getting to the islands is much easier than in years past. Both are accessible from Fajardo—either on 90-minute ferry trips or 10-minute puddle-jumper flights. There are also flights from either of San Juan's airports that take between 20 and 30 minutes. The flights are scenic, skirting the main island's northern coast before heading out over the azure waters of the Caribbean.

VIEQUES & CULEBRA TOP 5

■ Swimming after dark in Bahía Mosquito, the astounding bioluminscent bay on Vieques.

■ Catching some rays on Culebra's Playa Flamenco, consistently ranked as one of the world's best beaches.

■ Hiking to the deserted lighthouse on one of the islands that make up the Refugio Nacional de Vida Silvestre de Culebra.

■ Watching the sunset from the cantilevered deck at Al's Mar Azul, the best happy hour spot on Vieques.

■ Discovering Playa Media Luna, or one of the dozens of other deserted beaches that fringe Vieques.

XPLORING VIEQUES & CULEBRA

It's nearly impossible to see either island without renting a car. Sure, you could stay at one of the small hotels along the waterfront in Vieques, eating at the handful of restaurants within walking distance, but you'd miss out on most of what the island has to offer. Scooters are another option for getting around, especially on tiny Culebra, but they aren't a good idea if you're headed to the beach. Roads are dusty, paved with loose gravel, and riddled with huge potholes.

ABOUT THE RESTAURANTS

Most of the restaurants on Vieques and Culebra are extremely casual, meaning that the dress code doesn't get much stricter than No SHOES, NO SHIRT, NO SERVICE. Because even the most formal restaurants on the islands are on covered terraces or in open-air dining rooms, there's not a single establishment where you'll be frowned on for wearing shorts. Pack a couple of nice shirts and you'll be set.

WHAT IT COSTS IN U.S. DOLLARS				
AT DINNER				
$$$$	$$$	$$	$	¢
over $30	$20–$30	$12–$20	$8–$12	under $8

Prices are per person for a main course at dinner.

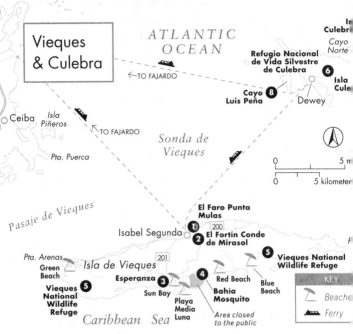

ABOUT THE HOTELS

Vieques has a wide variety of lodgings, from surf shacks across from the beach to boutique hotels high up on secluded hillsides. There's something here for everyone. Looking for tropical splendor? Try Hacienda Tamarindo or the Inn on the Blue Horizon. Interesting architecture? There's Hix Island House or Bravo Beach Resort. An intimate inn where you can meet all of your fellow travelers? Head to Casa de Amistad.

Culebra has fewer options. Dewey, the island's only town, has a handful of small inns that are easy on the wallet. Scattered around the island are a couple of more luxurious lodgings. There's nothing here that remotely resembles a chain hotel, and that's how the locals like it.

TIMING

High season runs from December 15 through April 15. The crowds are the most unbearable at Christmas and Easter, when Vieques and Culebra are packed with families enjoying the sun and sand. Be sure to make reservations well in advance if you're visiting during the holidays. The shoulder season, when prices are a bit lower, is a good option.

Remember, however, that some restaurants and hotels are only open during the high season. The only time you might want to avoid is late August through late October, when most hurricanes roll through the area.

WHAT IT COSTS IN U.S. DOLLARS				
HOTELS FOR TWO PEOPLE				
$$$$	$$$	$$	$	¢
over $350	$250–$350	$150–$250	$80–$150	under $80

Prices are for a double room in high season, excluding 9% tax (11% for hotels with casinos, 7% for paradores) and 5%-12% service charge.

Numbers in the margins correspond to numbers on the Vieques and Culebra maps.

VIEQUES

13 km (8 mi) southeast of Fajardo.

Looking for a place to play Robinson Crusoe? Then head to Vieques, where you can wander along almost any stretch of sand and never see another soul. You can while away the hours underneath the coconut palms, wade in the warm water, or grab a mask and snorkel and explore the coral reefs that ring the island.

For many years the island was known mostly for the conflict between angry islanders and aloof federal officials. Over the course of six decades, the U.S. Navy used two-thirds of Vieques, mostly on the island's eastern and western tips, as a bombing range. Residents complained that their mighty neighbor stifled economic development and harmed the environment. After an April 1999 bombing accident took the life of one resident, waves of protests that brought the maneuvers to a standstill, and political pressure from the island's government, the military reluctantly agreed to leave on May 1, 2003.

Ironically, the military's presence helped to keep the island pristine by limiting the land available for rambling resorts. Today, most of the military's holdings have been turned into the Vieques National Wildlife Refuge. The western end of the island has the most public access. Here you can

IF YOU LIKE

BEACHES

Beautiful beaches abound on Vieques and Culebra. Many of the best stretches of sand on Vieques—Red Beach, Blue Beach, and Green Beach, to name a few—are on land that was once part of a naval base. This means that development hasn't reared its ugly head. It also means there are few, if any, amenities at most of these beaches, so make sure to bring plenty of water and a picnic lunch. The beaches on Culebra are just as unspoiled. Playa Flamenco, on the island's northern coast, is considered one of the best in the world.

SEAFOOD

Hopefully you like seafood, since that's what you can get at almost every eatery on Vieques and Culebra. The good news is that the fish is as fresh as you can find anywhere, since that red snapper was probably splash-ing around in the Caribbean that very morning. Unlike some other parts of Puerto Rico, here you can order it in any number of ways. Chefs are experimenting with European and Asian cooking techniques, so you may find your fish smoked or even in a sushi roll.

WATER SPORTS

Some of the best snorkel-ing and diving can be found in the waters surrounding Vieques and Culebra. You can sign up for a half-day or full-day excursion to nearby coral reefs, which are teem-ing with colorful fish. It's also possible to grab a mask and snorkel, then simply wade out for a few yards to see what you can see. Playa Esperanza, on the southern coast of Vieques, is a good place for beginners. More experienced snorkelers will prefer Blue Beach or Green Beach.

find Monte Pirata, the island's highest peak. (At 987 feet, it isn't much of a mountain, but it looks impressive.) More and more of the eastern part of the island is being opened every year. The park is your gateway to some of the island's best beaches, including Green Beach in the west and Red and Blue beaches in the east.

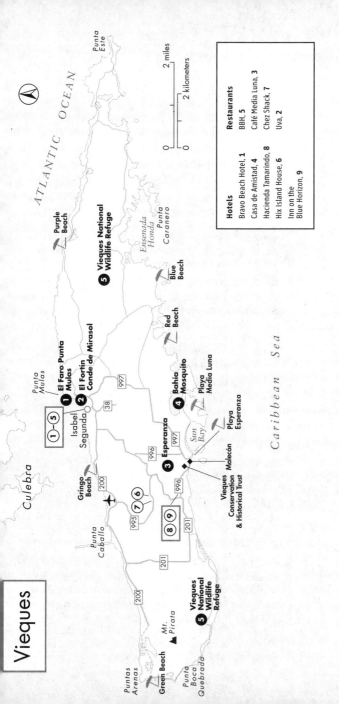

Vieques

ATLANTIC OCEAN

Caribbean Sea

Culebra

Hotels
Bravo Beach Hotel, 1
Casa de Amistad, 4
Hacienda Tamarindo, 8
Hix Island House, 6
Inn on the
Blue Horizon, 9

Restaurants
BBH, 5
Café Media Luna, 3
Chez Shack, 7
Uva, 2

Punta Este

Punta Mulas

Punta Caballo

Puntas Arenas

Punta Boca Quebrada

Punta Caranero

Ensenada Honda

Purple Beach

Vieques National Wildlife Refuge

Blue Beach

Red Beach

El Faro Punta Mulas

El Fortín Conde de Mirasol

Isabel Segunda

Gringo Beach

Bahía Mosquito

Playa Media Luna

Esperanza

Playa Esperanza

Sun Bay

Malecón

Vieques Conservation & Historical Trust

Mt. Pirata

Vieques National Wildlife Refuge

Green Beach

200
997
38
996
997
995
996
201
201
200

0   2 miles
0   2 kilometers

EXPLORING VIEQUES

Just because Vieques is sleepy doesn't mean there's nothing to do besides hit the beach. There are two communities—Isabel Segunda and Esperanza—where you can dine at an open-air eatery, stock up on supplies, or book a trip to the astonishing Bahía Mosquito, perhaps the world's most luminous bioluminescent bay.

ISABEL SEGUNDA
29 km (18 mi) southeast of Fajardo by ferry.

Since it's the transportation hub of Vieques, you won't be able to avoid Isabel Segunda. The ferry drops off passengers at the town's dock, and propeller planes deposit passengers at the tiny airport to the west. If you want to rent a car, or gas up the one you already have, you need to make a trip to Isabel Segunda.

But Isabel Segunda (or Isabel II, as it's often labeled on maps) has some charms that are not immediately apparent. There's a lovely lighthouse on the coast just east of the ferry dock, and on the hill above town you can find the last fort the Spanish constructed in the New World. Some of the best bars and restaurants are found here, as well as lodgings ranging from funky to fancy.

① **El Faro Punta Mulas,** a Spanish-built lighthouse beside the ferry dock in Isabel Segunda, dates from 1895. It was built to guide vessels into the harbor, which is surrounded by a chain of dangerous reefs. It's said that the red light can be seen from as far away as St. Croix and St. Thomas. In 1992 the elegant structure was carefully restored and transformed into a maritime museum that traces much of the island's history, including the visit by South American liberation leader Simón Bolívar. Sadly, the museum had been closed for more than a year when this book was updated, and there were no plans to reopen it. The lighthouse itself is worth a look, however. ✉*At end of Rte. 200* ☎*787/741–0060.*

② On a hilltop overlooking Isabel Segunda is **El Fortín Conde de Mirasol** *(Count of Mirasol Fort),* the last military structure begun by the Spanish in the New World. It was erected on Vieques's northern coast in 1840 at the order of Count Mirasol, then governor of Puerto Rico. It took more than a decade to complete, which meant Mirasol had to repeatedly ask for more money. (Queen Isabel, on being petitioned yet again, asked Mirasol whether the walls were made of gold.) The fort helped solidify Spanish control of the area, keeping British, French, Dutch, and Danish colonists away and dissuading pirates from attacking Isabel Segunda. After sitting empty for several decades, it was transformed into a museum in 1991. The museum has an impressive collection of artifacts from the Taíno Indians and other cultures that thrived on this and nearby islands before the arrival of the Spanish. There are also exhibits on the island's years as a sugar plantation and its occupation by the U.S. Navy. ✉ *471 Calle Magnolia, Isabel Segunda* ☎ *787/741–1717* ⊕ *www.enchanted-isle.com/elfortin* 🎫 *$2* ⊙ *Wed.–Sun. 10–4.*

ESPERANZA

❸ *10 km (6 mi) south of Isabel Segunda*

The only time there's a traffic jam in Esperanza is when one of the wild horses frequently seen on the nearby beaches wanders into the road. This community, once a down-at-heel fishing village, is now a string of budget bars, restaurants, and hotels. All of them overlook Playa Esperanza, a shallow stretch of sand made all the more picturesque by the presence of a tiny islet called Cayo Afuera.

In the evening, there's not a better way to enjoy the sunset than a stroll along Esperanza's **Malecón,** a waterfront walkway running the length of the beach.

☪ The **Vieques Conservation & Historical Trust** was established to help save Bahía Mosquito, one of the last remaining bioluminescent bays in the world. The small museum, on the main drag in Esperanza, has interesting information about the bay, as well as the island's flora and fauna. A little pool lets kids get acquainted with starfish, sea urchins, and other denizens of the not-so-deep. There's also a tiny gift shop where the profits are funneled back into the foundation. ✉ *138 Calle Flamboyán, Esperanza* ☎ *787/741–8850* ⊕ *www.vcht.com* 🎫 *Free* ⊙ *Tues.–Sun. 11–4.*

ELSEWHERE ON VIEQUES

Isabel Segunda and Esperanza are just a tiny portion of Vieques. Most of the island—more than two-thirds of it, in fact—was commandeered by the military until 2003. It's now a nature preserve that draws thousands of visitors each year.

★ Fodor'sChoice East of Esperanza, **Bahía Mosquito** *(Mosquito* **❹** *Bay)* is also known as Bioluminescent Bay or Phosphorescent Bay. It's one of the world's best spots to have a glow-in-the-dark experience with undersea dinoflagellates. Tour operators offer kayak trips or excursions on nonpolluting boats to see the bay's tiny microorganisms that appear to light up when their water is agitated. Dive into the bay and you'll emerge covered in sparkling water. Look behind your boat, and you'll see a twinkling wake. Even the fish that jump from the water will bear an eerie glow. The high concentration of dinoflagellates sets the bay apart from the other spots (including others in Puerto Rico) that are home to these tiny organisms. The bay is at its best when there's little or no moonlight; rainy nights are beautiful, too, because the raindrops splashing in the water produce ricochet sparkles. Some of the best excursions to the bay are offered by Sharon Grasso of Island Adventures. ⊠*Reach via unpaved roads off Rte. 997.*

❺ A portion of the west and the entire eastern end of the island is being administered as the **Vieques National Wildlife Refuge,** comprising 18,000 acres—about 14,900 acres on the eastern end and 3,100 acres on the west—making it the biggest protected natural reserve in Puerto Rico. Most of eastern Vieques is being administered by the U.S. Fish & Wildlife Service as a nature reserve, except for the 900-acre bombing range on the far eastern end, which will be permanently closed off, a consequence of its contamination by the ordnance shot over its 60-year existence. But most of the rest of eastern Vieques is pristine nature, astonishingly beautiful and well-forested, with a hilly center region overlooking powder-white sandy beaches and a coral-ringed coastline; it served mainly as a buffer zone between the military maneuvers and civilian population. The vast majority of this acreage remains off-limits to visitors as a search for unexploded munitions and contaminants is carried out. Cleanup plans, which the Puerto Rico government hopes will allow much more public access to the island, were still being drawn up at this writing. ✏️*Box 1527, 00765* ☎*787/741–2138* ⊕*southeast.fws. gov/caribbean/vieques.*

BEACHES

Many of the beaches around the island have oddly similar names: Red Beach, Blue Beach, and Green Beach. The U.S. Navy, lacking any imagination, simply assigned them random colors. Some beaches are known by one name by tourists, another by locals. Islanders know Sun Bay as Sombé.

Underwater Fireworks

On most moonless nights strings of kayaks float along the surface of Bahía Mosquito. People come to this otherwise unremarkable bay on the island of Vieques to witness one of nature's most eye-popping events. As a paddle skims the top of the water, thousands of points of light appear just below the surface. Behind each kayak is a blue-green glow that slowly fades. Those who trail their fingers in the water can see the outline of every digit.

This glow is produced by dinoflagellates, single-celled organisms that are found everywhere. But the species found in the Caribbean, called Pyrodinium bahamense, happens to glow when the surrounding water is disturbed in any way. The concentration of dinoflagellates in Bahía Mosquito is an astounding 720,000 per gallon—more than anywhere else on earth. This accounts for the nightly display of underwater fireworks.

The conditions at Bahía Mosquito are perfect for growing dinoflagellates. A mangrove forest surrounding the bay constantly drops leaves and branches into the water. As bacteria eat the decaying matter, they produce prodigious amounts of vitamin B12—an essential part of the dinoflagellate diet.

There are other bioluminescent bays in Puerto Rico, such as Fajardo's Laguna Grande and La Parguera's Bahía de Fosforescente, but many are losing their luster. Light pollution is one of the main causes, as the dinoflagellates can't compete with the glare of headlights or the glow of street lamps. (Even the moon makes the glow difficult to discern.) On Vieques, conservation-minded citizens constantly remind their neighbors to make sure their outdoor lights are shaded so they point downward.

Water pollution is another problem. Ironically, spillage from the gas- and diesel-powered boats that take tourists to see the spectacle is often the culprit. The smoke-belching boats that depart for La Parguera's Bahía de Fosforescente every night are slowly putting themselves out of business. The display in La Parguera, once as dazzling as the one in Vieques, is dismal.

On Vieques these boats are banned from Bahía Mosquito. Instead, there are kayaks and electric-powered pontoon boats that barely cause a ripple on the surface. But there are plenty of waves when the passengers dive into the inky black water, leaving behind them a trail of light that reminds many people of the tail of a comet.

Blue Beach. Beyond Red Beach, you can find a handful of covered cabanas here. There can be strong surf in some spots, making swimming here difficult at times. ✉ *Off Rte. 997, east of Red Beach.*

Green Beach. On the western edge of the island is this beach, which is reached via a dirt road. Miles of coral reef just off shore attract snorkelers and divers. From the shore you can catch a glimpse of El Yunque on the mainland. ✉ *At western end of Rte. 200.*

★ **Playa Media Luna.** An unpaved road east of Playa Sun Bay leads to a pretty little beach that's ideal for families because the water is calm and shallow. This is a good spot to try your hand at snorkeling. Take note, though, that there are no facilities. ✉ *Off Rte. 997, east of Playa Sun Bay.*

Red Beach. On former U.S. Navy land on the eastern end of Vieques, this beautiful beach is reached via a well-maintained dirt road. It's open daily from sunrise to sunset. The water is crystal-clear, and its location in Bahía Corcho means that the waves are usually not so strong. ✉ *Off Rte. 997, east of Playa Media Luna.*

★ **Sun Bay.** Of Vieques's more than three dozen beaches, this one east of Esperanza is easily the most popular. Its 1-mi-long white sands skirt a crescent-shape bay. You can find food kiosks, picnic tables, and changing facilities. On weekdays, when the crowds are thin, you might also find wild horses grazing among the palm trees. Parking is $3, but there's often nobody at the gate to take your money. ✉ *Rte. 997, east of Esperanza.*

WHERE TO EAT

★ **Fodor's**Choice ✕**Uva.** On Vieques, Carlos Alzogaray has
$$$–$$$$ single-handedly changed how people approach seafood. The chef at this "Caribbean-fusion" eatery serves mahimahi, as does everyone else, but he turns it into ceviche with a lemon-passionfruit sauce. His tuna steak is marinated in a soy-ginger sauce and served over soba noodles. Even his lobster is completely rethought, appearing as a carpaccio with avocado ragout. Meat dishes include a huge rib eye with lobster mashed potatoes. And there's a great wine list, as you might guess from the pillars covered with thousands of corks. For lunch, you can pick up wraps and other items at the less expensive Uva Next Door. ✉ *359 Calle Antonio Mellado, at Calle Luis Muñoz*

Rivera, Isabel Segunda ☎787/741–2050 ☖*Reservations essential* ⊟*AE, MC, V* ☾*Closed Tues. No lunch.*

$$–$$$ ✕**Café Media Luna.** Tucked into a beautifully restored building in Isabel Segunda, this eatery has been a favorite for many years. Its popularity might be due to the convenient downtown location, or the intimate tables on the balconies that surround the second-floor dining room. More likely, however, it's the creativity of the cooks. (You can watch all the action, as the kitchen is in full view.) Try the cornish hen in a sweet-spicy coconut sauce or the seared yellowfin tuna served with vegetable tempura. Not so hungry? Then share one of the tasty pizzas. Half a dozen are on offer at any given time. ⊠*351 Calle Antonio Mellado, Isabel Segunda, Vieques* ☎787/741–2594 ☖*Reservations essential* ⊟*AE, MC, V* ☾*Closed Mon. and Tues. No lunch.*

$$–$$$ ✕**Chez Shack.** This restaurant is not a shack—but it's close. It's in a delightfully ramshackle building on a one-lane road winding through the hills. The dining room is inches from the pavement, but it's unlikely a single car will pass by while you're enjoying your meal. Chicken, beef, and seafood are grilled to tender perfection. The restaurant is justifiably famous for its weekly barbecue night with a steel band, but there's usually some good jazz or island rhythms on the sound system. The restaurant is on Route 995, off Route 201. ⊠*Rte. 995, Km 1.8* ☎787/741–2175 ☖*Reservations essential* ⊟*AE, MC, V.*

$–$$ ✕**BBH.** In this stylish dining room there's not a bad seat in the house. Choose one of the comfortable couches near the door, a stool at the bar, or a banquette overlooking the swimming pool. A few choice tables are outside on the covered terrace. Just as good is the wide array of small dishes created by chef Christopher Ellis. Not content to stay in Spain, his tapas travel the globe. Some, like the chipotle barbecued pork, are clearly from Mexico. The mussels, in red coconut-curry broth, have an Asian flair. If there's a wait for a table, your server will suggest you enjoy a cocktail at the Palms, which is just around the corner. ⊠*North Shore Rd., Isabel Segunda* ☎787/741–1128 ☖*Reservations essential* ⊟*AE, D, MC, V.*

WHERE TO STAY

PRIVATE VILLA RENTALS

One good way to visit Vieques is to rent one of the beautiful vacation homes that have been built in the hilly interior or along the coasts. These are concentrated in three major areas: Bravos de Boston, Esperanza, and Pilón. Several local real-estate agents deal in short-term rentals of at least a week. A list of properties is available from gay-friendly **Rainbow Realty** (☎787/741–4312 ⊕www.enchanted-isle.com/rainbow). There are some high-end properties available through **Vieques Villa Rental** (☎787/721–0505 ⊕www.viequesvillarental.com).

HOTELS & GUESTHOUSES

$$-$$$$ ⓣ**Inn on the Blue Horizon.** This inn, consisting of six Mediterranean-style villas, was the tiny island's first taste of luxury. A favorite since it opened in 1994, it's still one of the most sought-after accommodations, mostly because of its breathtaking setting on a bluff overlooking the ocean. The entire place is often booked months in advance by weddings and other big groups. Everything is geared toward upping the romance quotient, from the intimate guest rooms to the open-air bar, where the staff will make any cocktail you can name—or create a new one and name it after you. Sadly, the popular Blue Macaw restaurant closed for good in 2005. ⊠*Rte. 996, Km 4.2, Esperanza, Vieques* ⊕*Box 1556, Vieques 00765* ☎787/741–3318 ☎787/741–0522 ⊕*www.innontthebluehorizon.com* ⌁*10 rooms* ⌂*In-room: no phone, no TV. In-hotel: restaurant, bar, tennis courts, pool, gym, beachfront, bicycles, no kids under 14, no elevator* ⊟*AE, MC, V* ⊺◯⌁*BP.*

★ **Fodor's**Choice ⓣ**Hix Island House.** Constructed entirely of con-
$$-$$$ crete—wait, keep reading! This award-winning hotel, set on 13 secluded acres, is one of the most striking in Puerto Rico. The idea, according to architect John Hix, was to design a place that echoed the gray granite boulders strewn around Vieques. He was successful, as his three buildings blend beautifully into the environment. A minimalist aesthetic runs through the rooms, which avoid the blockiness of most concrete buildings through the use of sinewy lines and sexy curves. Sunny terraces, unglazed windows, and showers that are open to the stars (yet still very private) make sure nature is never far away. And the resort's embrace of the environment goes beyond form into function, with the use of recycled water and even solar-power

systems. Even the swimming pool is ecofriendly, avoiding the use of excess chemicals. The hotel is on Route 995, off Route 201. ⊠*Rte. 995, Km 1.5, Box 1556, 00765* ☎*787/741–2302* 🖶*787/741–2797* ⊕*www.hixislandhouse. com* ⇆*13 rooms* ⬦*In-room: no phone, kitchens, refrigerators, no TV. In-hotel: pool* ⊟*AE, MC, V* ⊚*CP.*

★ **Fodors**Choice ▭**Bravo Beach Hotel.** If this boutique hotel were
$$ plopped down into the middle of South Beach, no one would raise an eyebrow. What was once a private residence has been expanded to include four different buildings, all with views of nearby Culebra from their balconies. The guest rooms have a minimalist flair, brightened by splashes of red and yellow. High-tech offerings include an iPod docking station and a Sony Playstation in every room. If you're traveling with an entourage, the two-bedroom villa has plenty of space to entertain. One of the pools is the setting for the Palms, a chic lounge; the other is the backdrop for the not-to-be-missed tapas bar. The hotel is on a pretty stretch of beach, several blocks north of the ferry dock in Isabel Segunda. ⊠*North Shore Rd., Isabel Segunda, Vieques 00765* ☎*787/741–1128* 🖶*787/741–3908* ⊕*www. bravobeachhotel.com* ⇆*9 rooms, 1 villa* ⬦*In-room: refrigerator, no phone. In-hotel: restaurant, bar, pools, public Wi-Fi, no kids under 14* ⊟*AE, D, MC, V* ⊚*BP.*

$$ ▭**Hacienda Tamarindo.** The century-old tamarind tree
★ rising through the center of the main building gives this plantation-style house its name. With its barrel-tile roof and wood-shuttered windows, it's one of the most beautiful hotels on the island. Finding a spot all to yourself is easy, whether it's on a shady terrace or beside the spectacular pool. The guest rooms were individually decorated by Linda Vail, who runs the place along with her husband, Burr. "Caribbean chic" might be the best way to describe her effortless way of combining well-chosen antiques, elegant wicker furniture, and vintage travel posters. The nicest room might be Number One, which is in a separate building and has a private terrace overlooking the ocean. The beach is nearby, but you'll need a car to get there. ⊠*Rte. 996, Km 4.5, Esperanza, Vieques* ⬠*Box 1569, Vieques 00765* ☎*787/741–8525* 🖶*787/741–3215* ⊕*www.haciendatamarindo.com* ⇆*16 rooms* ⬦*In-room: no phone, no TV. In-hotel: pool, public Wi-Fi, no kids under 15, no elevator* ⊟*AE, MC, V* ⊚*BP.*

¢–$ ⛱**Casa de Amistad.** A groovy vibe permeates this small guesthouse not far from the ferry dock in Isabel Segunda. Citrus colors and wicker furnishings give the place a tropical feel. It's hard not to feel at home here, especially when you can use the common kitchen to pack a picnic lunch or borrow an umbrella for your trip to the beach. The rooftop terrace is a great place to chill out. There's a gift shop on the premises that sells original art by the owners. ⊠*27 Calle Benito Castano, Isabel Segunda 00765* ☎*787/741–3758* 🖷*787/741–4782* ⊕*www.casadeamistad.com* ⇨*7 rooms* ⚭*In room: regrigerator. In hotel: public Internet, public Wi-Fi, pool* ⊟*MC, V* ⦿*EP.*

NIGHTLIFE

Not far from the ferry terminal, **Al's Mar Azul** (⊠*Calle Plinio Peterson, Isabela Segunda* ☎*787/741–3400*) is where everyone gathers to watch the sunset. The main virtue of this open-air bar is a deck overlooking the ocean. You can find dart boards, pool tables, and a juke box.

Bananas (⊠*142 Calle Flamboyán, Esperanza* ☎*787/741–8700*) is the place for burgers and beer—not necessarily in that order. There's sometimes live music and dancing.

La Nasa (⊠*Calle Flamboyán, Esperanza* ☎*No phone*) is the only establishment on the waterfront side of the street in Esperanza. This simple wooden shack, decorated with strings of Christmas lights the entire year, serves up cheap and very cold beer and rum drinks. Locals congregate on plastic chairs out front or stare off into the placid Caribbean from an open-air back room.

SPORTS & THE OUTDOORS

BIKING

The friendly folks at **La Dulce Vida** (☎*787/741–0495* ⊕*www.bikevieques.com*) can set you up with mountain bikes and all the equipment you need for $25 to $35 a day. They'll even bring the bikes to wherever you happen to be staying. Customized tours of the island—which range from easy rides on country roads to muddy treks into the hills—are $30 to $65 per hour. But you need to book the tours far in advance.

BOATING & KAYAKING

Any number of companies offer trips to Bahía Mosquito, the most famous of the island's bioluminescent bays. Most are trips in single-person kayaks, which can be a challenge if you don't have experience or if you aren't in the best shape. A better option for most people is a boat. Make sure it's an electric-powered model, as the gas-powered ones are bad for the environment.

Aqua Frenzy Kayaks (✉ *At dock area below Calle Flamboyán, Esperanza, Vieques* ☎787/741–0913) rents kayaks and arranges kayak tours of Bahía Mosquito and other areas. Reservations for the excursion to glowing Bahía Mosquito cost $30. Make reservations at least 24 hours in advance.

Blue Caribe Kayaks (✉ *149 Calle Flamboyán, Esperanza, Vieques* ☎787/741–2522 ⊕*www.enchanted-isle.com/bluecaribe*) offers kayak trips to Bahía Mosquito for about $30, as well as trips to deserted parts of the coast and to nearby islets. You can also rent a kayak and set off on your own.

★ **Island Adventures** (✉ *Rte. 996, Esperanza, Vieques* ☎787/741–0720 ⊕*www.biobay.com*), owned by former school teacher Sharon Grasso, will take you to Bahía Mosquito aboard nonpolluting, electrically powered pontoon boats. The best part is leaping into the water, where the outline of your body will be softly illuminated thanks to bioluminescent organisms. The cost is about $30 per person.

DIVING & SNORKELING

Nan-Sea Charters (☎787/741–3224), run by affable "Chipper the Skipper," promises to take you snorkeling at a beach so remote that it doesn't have a name. The cost is $60 per person for groups up to six people.

Blue Caribe Kayaks (✉ *149 Calle Flamboyán, Esperanza* ☎787/741–2522 ⊕*www.enchanted-isle.com/bluecaribe*) will rent you snorkels, masks, and fins for $12 a day. The efficient staff can also arrange snorkeling trips to nearby islets.

SHOPPING

Most residents do their shopping on the mainland, so there are very few shops on Vieques. You can find mostly clothing shops that lean toward beach attire, as well as a few art galleries.

Kim's Cabin (✉*136 Calle Flamboyán, Esperanza* ☎*787/741–0520*), which has been in business on Vieques since the early 1990s, is a local institution. There's jewelry in the front room and two other rooms with clothing for men and women.

★ **Siddhia Hutchinson Fine Art Studio & Gallery** (✉*15 Calle 3, Isabel Segunda* ☎*787/741–8780*) is north of the ferry dock. The artist has lived on Vieques since the early 1990s, creating pastel watercolor prints of Caribbean scenes, as well as limited-edition ceramic dinnerware. The gallery is open Monday through Saturday, 10 to 4.

Taína Pottery Workshop (☎*787/741–1556*) is a local female artisans collective that makes beautiful ceramics, pottery, and other artwork. Visits to the studio are by appointment only.

CULEBRA

28 km (17 mi) east of Fajardo by ferry.

Culebra is known around the world for its curvaceous coastline. Playa Flamenco, the tiny island's most famous stretch of sand, is considered one of the two or three best beaches in the world. If Playa Flamenco gets too crowded, as it often does around Easter or Christmas, there are many other beaches that will be nearly deserted. And if you crave complete privacy, hire a motorboat to take you to one of the nearby islets such as Isla Culebrita or Cayo Luis Peña. It won't be difficult to find a little cove that you will have all to yourself.

There's archaeological evidence that Taíno and Carib peoples lived on Culebra long before the arrival of the Spanish in the late 15th century. The Spanish didn't bother laying claim to it until 1886; its dearth of fresh water made it an unattractive location for a settlement. The U.S. Navy, however, thought it was a valuable piece of real estate. It used this island, as well as nearby Vieques, for target practice beginning in the early 20th century. Despite their smaller

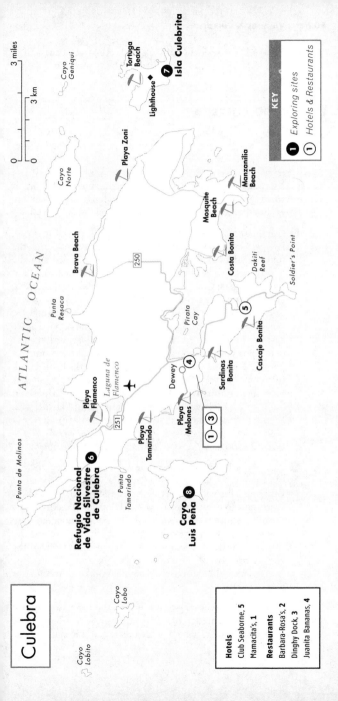

Culebra

ATLANTIC OCEAN

Cayo Lobito

Cayo Lobo

Punta de Molinos

Refugio Nacional de Vida Silvestre de Culebra **6**

Cayo Luis Peña **8**

Punta Tamarindo

Playa Tamarindo

Playa Flamenco

Laguna de Flamenco

251

Dewey

Playa Melones

1—3

Juanita Bananas **4**

Sardinas Bonita

Pirata Cay

Punta Resaca

Brava Beach

250

Mosquite Beach

Costa Bonita

Cascaje Bonita

Dakiti Reef

Soldier's Point

Club Seaborne **5**

Manzanilia Beach

Cayo Norte

Playa Zoni

Cayo Geniqui

Tortuga Beach

Lighthouse

Isla Culebrita **7**

0   3 km

0   3 miles

KEY

1 Exploring sites

① Hotels & Restaurants

Hotels
Club Seaborne, 5
Mamacita's, 1

Restaurants
Barbara-Rosa's, 2
Dinghy Dock, 3
Juanita Bananas, 4

numbers, the residents of Culebra were more successful in their efforts to oust the military. The troops left Culebra in 1975.

EXPLORING CULEBRA

Almost everything about Culebra is diminutive. The island's only community, named in honor of U.S. Admiral George Dewey, is set along a single street leading from the ferry dock. You can explore all the shops along Calle Pedro Márquez in a half-hour. The one-room airport is a mile or so to the north. Except for one sprawling resort, there are no hotels with more than a dozen rooms.

❻ Commissioned by President Theodore Roosevelt in 1909, **Refugio Nacional de Vida Silvestre de Culebra** is one of the nation's oldest wildlife refuges. Some 1,500 acres of the island make up a protected area. It's a lure for hikers and bird-watchers: Culebra teems with seabirds, from laughing gulls and roseate terns to red-billed tropic birds and sooty terns. Maps of trails in the refuge are hard to come by, but you can stop by the U.S. Fish & Wildlife Service office east of the airport to find out about trail conditions and determine whether you're headed to an area that requires a permit. The office also can tell you whether the leatherback turtles are nesting. From mid-April to mid-July, volunteers help to monitor and tag these creatures, which nest on nearby beaches, especially Playa Resaca and Playa Brava. If you'd like to volunteer, you must agree to help out for at least three nights. ⊠ *Rte. 250, north of Dewey* ☎ *787/742–0115* ⊕ *southeast.fws.gov* ☜ *Free* ☉ *Daily dawn–dusk.*

❼ Part of the Refugio Nacional de Vida Silvestre de Culebra, **Isla Culebrita** is clearly visible from the northeast corner of Culebra. This islet is a favorite destination for sunbathers who want to escape the crowds at Playa Flamenco. On the northern shore there are several tide pools; snuggling into one of them is like taking a warm bath. Snorkelers and divers love the fact that they can reach the reef from the shore. You can also hike around the island and visit the ruins of an old lighthouse. To get there, take a dive boat or hire a water taxi.

❽ A kayak is a great way to reach **Cayo Luis Peña,** an islet just off the western edge of Culebra. There are a handful of protected beaches where you can soak up the sun and not run into a single soul. Cayo Luis Peña is also part of the Refugio Nacional de Vida Silvestre de Culebra.

BEACHES

★ **Fodor'sChoice Playa Flamenco.** On the island's north coast is an amazingly lovely stretch of white sand. This beach, with its almost perfect half-moon shape, is consistently ranked as one of the two or three best in the world. Once you see it, you'll know why. Mountains rise up on all sides, making it feel miles away from civilization. It's only when the propeller planes fly low over the beach that you remember that the airport in just over the ridge. During the week Playa Flamenco is pleasantly uncrowded; on the weekend, though, it fills up fast with day-trippers. This is the only beach on Culebra with amenities such as restrooms, showers, and kiosks selling simple fare. ⊠*Rte. 251, west of the airport.*

Playa Melones. Just west of Dewey, this beach is a favorite spot for snorkelers. The reef that runs around the rocky point is easy to reach from shore. To get here, head uphill on the unmarked road behind the church. ⊠*Off Rte. 251, west of Dewey.*

Playa Tamarindo. North of Playa Melones, this beach is another good destination for snorkelers. It's a little hard to find, which means you'll probably have the place to yourself. To find it, head west on Route 251. When you see the signs pointing toward Tamarindo Estates, take a left. ⊠*Off Rte. 251, north of Playa Melones.*

Playa Zoni. On the island's northeastern end, this beach is far more isolated than Playa Flamenco, and it's just as beautiful. From the shore you can catch a glimpse of Isla Culebrita, not to mention St. Thomas and St. Croix. ⊠*At end of Rte. 250, 11 km (7 mi) northeast of Dewey.*

WHERE TO EAT

$–$$$ ✕**Juanita Bananas.** Trees overflowing with bananas, papa-
★ yas, and passion fruit line the walkway that leads to one of Culebra's best eateries. Chef Jennifer Daubon, whose parents also ran a restaurant on the island, focuses on the freshest local produce, which is why about an acre of land on the surrounding hillside is used for growing vegetables and herbs. The menu changes with the seasons, but look

for dishes like lobster limonjili, which is medallions of lobster in a fresh lime and garlic sauce. The dining room, with its low lights and soft music, is the most romantic in Culebra. ⊠*Calle Melones, Km 1* ☎*787/742–3855* ⌖*Reservations essential* ▭*MC, V.*

¢–$ ✕**Barbara-Rosa's.** Her husband chats with the customers, but Barbara Petersen does everything else: takes your order, cooks it up, and serves it with a flourish. You won't find better food anywhere on the island, and that includes the places that charge twice as much. Locals swear by her tender, flaky fish-and-chips. (The secret, her husband proudly points out, is using red snapper.) Finish with key lime pie or peach and pineapple cobbler. ⊠*Calle Escudero, Dewey, Culebra* ☎*787/742–3271* ▭*MC, V* ⊙*Closed Sun. and Mon.*

WHERE TO STAY

VILLA RENTALS

Lovely vacation homes are available all over the island. **All Vacation Reservations** (⊠*Calle Pedro Marquez, Dewey* ☎*787/742–3112* ⊕*www.allvacationreservations.com*) has a complete list of all the homes available for rental, ranging from studios to three-bedroom houses.

HOTELS & GUESTHOUSES

$$ ⊡**Club Seaborne.** The prettiest place to stay in Culebra, this cluster of plantation-style cottages sits on a hilltop overlooking Fulladoza Bay. It feels completely isolated, but it's only a mile or so from the center of town. Opt for one of the rooms surrounding the pool or one of the spacious villas. The largest sleeps five, making it a favorite of families. Specializing in seafood, the terrace restaurant ($$–$$$) is one of the best on the island. The friendly staff is happy to help you set up snorkeling and diving trips. Beaches, including Playa Flamenco, are a few miles away. ⊠*Calle Fulladoza, Km 1.5, Box 357, Culebra 00775* ☎*787/742–3169* ⊟*787/742–3176* ⊕*www.club seabourne.com* ◔*3 rooms, 8 villas, 1 cottage* ⌕*In-room: kitchen (some). In-hotel: restaurant, bar, pool, no elevator* ▭*AE, MC, V* ⍒*CP.*

$ ✕⊡**Mamacita's.** PLEASE DON'T FEED THE IGUANAS reads a sign hanging on the terrace of this longtime favorite. Set beneath lazily turning ceiling fans, the disarmingly charming restaurant ($–$$$) overlooks a canal filled with fishing boats.

The menu, which is scribbled on a chalkboard, includes dishes like pork tenderloin with pineapple or salmon with a cilantro sauce. The bar gets crowded during happy hour, which starts early in these parts. If you like it so much you don't want to leave, there are guest rooms upstairs with tropical furnishings. The best have balconies overlooking the canal. ⊠66 Calle Castelar, Dewey 00775 ☎787/742–0090 🖷787/742–0301 ⊕www.mamacitaspr.com ➩10 rooms, 1 suite ♿In-room: kitchens, refrigerators. In-hotel: restaurant, bar ➡AE, MC, V ⓘⓞⓘEP.

NIGHTLIFE

Dinghy Dock (⊠Calle Fulladoza, Dewey ☎787/742–0581) is the spot where the island's expat community begins piling into the bar around sunset. It can be a raucous scene, especially when there's a band. The party continues into the wee hours, even during the week.

El Batey (⊠Calle Escudero ☎787/742–3828) is popular on the weekends, when locals dance to salsa music. It's in a cement-block building halfway between the airport and the town.

Happy Landings (⊠Rte. 250 and Rte. 251 ☎787/742–0135), at the end of the airport's runway, might just as accurately have been called Happy Hour. The open-air bar is popular with locals.

SPORTS & THE OUTDOORS

DIVING & SNORKELING
Culebra Divers (⊠4 Calle Pedro Marquez, Dewey, Culebra ☎787/742–0803 ⊕www.culebradivers.com), run by Monica and Walter Rieder, caters to those who are new to scuba diving. You travel to dive sites on one of the company's pair of 26-foot cabin cruisers. One-tank dives are $60, while two-tank dives are $95. You can also rent a mask and snorkel to explore on your own. The office is in downtown Dewey, across from the ferry terminal.

SHOPPING
Culebra is smaller than Vieques but has much better shopping. Dewey has several shops on its main drag that sell trendy jewelry, fashionable clothing, and a range of souvenirs from tacky to terrific.

In a wooden shack painted vivid shades of yellow and red,
★ **Fango** (⊠*Calle Castelar s/n, Dewey* ☎787/556–9308) is the
island's best place for gifts. Jorge Acevedo paints scenes of
island life, while Hannah Staiger designs sophisticated jewelry. The shop is no bigger than a walk-in closet, but you
could easily spend an hour or more browsing among their
one-of-a-kind works.

On Island (⊠*4 Calle Pedro Marquez, Dewey* ☎787/742–
0439) has a selection of block prints of the island's flora and
fauna. There's also a nice display of handmade jewelry.

Paradise (⊠*6 Calle Salisbury, Dewey* ☎787/742–3565) is
a good spot for souvenirs ranging from wrought-iron iguanas to hand-carved seagulls to plush baby turtles.

VIEQUES & CULEBRA ESSENTIALS

*To research prices, get advice from other travelers, and
book travel arrangements, visit www.fodors.com.*

TRANSPORTATION

BY AIR

It used to be that travelers arriving at San Juan's Aeropuerto Internacional Luis Muñoz Marín had to transfer
to nearby Aeropuerto Fernando L. Rivas Dominici to take
a flight to Vieques or Culebra. This is no longer the case,
as all carriers servicing the islands now have flights from
Aeropuerto Internacional Luis Muñoz Marín.

Air Flamenco, Isla Nena Air Service, and Vieques Air Link
offer daily flights from both airports in San Juan to Vieques
and Culebra. Cape Air flies between the international airport and Vieques. Trips from either airport in San Juan
last between 20 and 30 minutes, whereas those from Fajardo last about 10 minutes. Fares vary quite a bit, but are
between $120 and $150 from San Juan and between $40
and $50 from Fajardo. These companies use small propel-
ler planes that hold a maximum of nine passengers.

Information Air Flamenco (☎787/724–1105 ⊕www.airflamenco.
net). . **Cape Air** (☎800/525–0280 ⊕www.flycapeair.com). **Isla
Nena Air Service** (☎787/741–6362 or 877/812–5144 ⊕www.
islanena.8m.com). **Vieques Air Link** (☎787/722–3266 or 888/901–
9247 ⊕www.vieques-island.com/val).

AIRPORTS

Most international travelers fly to Vieques and Culebra from San Juan's Aeropuerto Internacional Luis Muñoz Marín (SJU) or San Juan's Aeropuerto Fernando L. Rivas Dominici (SIG; also known as Aeropuerto Isla Grande). A smaller number fly from Fajardo's Aeropuerto Diego Jiménez Torres (FAJ), which is just southwest of the city on Route 976.

Aeropuerto Antonio Rivera Rodríguez (VQS), on Vieques's northwest coast, is a 10-minute cab ride from Isabel Segunda or a 15-minute taxi ride from Esperanza. The airlines have offices on the top floor of the octagonal main terminal, and the single gate is on the lower level. There are no amenities to speak of, although there's an open-air eatery across the road. At this writing, American Eagle had broken ground on an addition to the main terminal that will have a separate gate for its flights. The new addition will also have car-rental agency.

Culebra's Aeropuerto Benjamin Rivera Noriega (CPX) is at the intersection of Route 250 and Route 251. The one-room facility has two car-rental agencies and a scooter-rental kiosk. There's a small café inside the terminal, and several others are across the road. The airport is about three minutes from downtown Dewey.

Information Aeropuerto Antonio Rivera Rodríguez (☒ *Vieques* ☎ *787/741–0515*). **Aeropuerto Benjamin Rivera Noriega** (☒ *Culebra* ☎ *787/742–0022*).

BY BUS

There is no public bus system around Puerto Rico. If you're planning to take a ferry to Vieques or Culebra, you can take a *público* (a privately operated, shared minivan) from San Juan to Fajardo. The two-hour journey costs about $6, depending on where you board and where you're dropped off; if you take this inexpensive mode of transportation, expect things to be a bit crowded. There are no central terminals: you simply flag públicos down anywhere along the route.

Vieques and Culebra are served by their own inexpensive públicos, whose drivers often speak English. Just flag them down along their routes. Rates vary depending on your destination, but are usually under $5.

BY CAR

Think about getting around on Vieques or Culebra without a car? Think again. If you plan on staying in a town, there's no need for a car. If you want to do anything else—say, go to the beach—you need a way to get there. And don't think about taking that car you rented in San Juan to the off-islands. The main roads are in great shape, but the secondary roads are so riddled with potholes that an SUV is a must.

On Vieques and Culebra you can find local agencies, including several that specialize in SUVs. Rates are between $40 and $80 a day, depending on the age of the car. It's sometimes possible to rent directly from your hotel or guesthouse, so ask about packages that include lodging and a car rental. If you plan to head out to remote beaches, seriously consider a four-wheel-drive vehicle. On Vieques, try Island Car Rental, Maritza Car Rental, or Martineau Car Rental. On Culebra, Carlos Jeep Rental has an office in the airport.

Agencies Carlos Jeep Rental (⊠*Aeropuerto Benjamin Rivera Noriega, Culebra* ☎*787/742–3514* ⊕*www.carlosjeeprental.com*). **Island Car Rental** (⊠*Rte. 201, Vieques* ☎*787/741–1666* ⊕*www. enchanted-isle.com/islandcar*). **Maritza's Car Rental** (⊠*Rte. 201, Vieques* ☎*787/741–0078*). **Martineau Car Rental** (⊠*Rte. 200, Km 3.4, Vieques* ☎*787/741–0087* ⊕*www.martineaucarrental.com*).

BY FERRY

The Puerto Rico Ports Authority runs passenger ferries from Fajardo to Culebra and Vieques. Service is from the ferry terminal in Fajardo, about a 90-minute drive from San Juan. A municipal parking lot next to the ferry costs $5 a day—handy if you're going to one of the islands for the day. On Culebra the ferry pulls right into a dock in downtown Dewey. The Vieques ferry dock is in downtown Isabel Segunda. These ferries can be very crowded on weekends and will often sell out early in the day, but you can't buy tickets in advance.

A more convenient way to get to Vieques and Culebra, especially if you're departing from San Juan, is the catamaran operated by Island High-Speed Ferry. It departs from Pier 2, next to the cruise-ship docks in Old San Juan.

FARES & SCHEDULES

The Fajardo Port Authority's 400-passenger ferries run between that east-coast town and the out-islands of Vieques and Culebra; both trips take about 90 minutes. The vessels carry cargo and passengers to Vieques three times daily ($2 one-way) and to Culebra twice a day Sunday through Friday and three times a day on Saturday ($2.25 one-way). Get schedules for the Culebra and Vieques ferries by calling the Port Authority in Fajardo, Vieques, or Culebra. You buy tickets at the ferry dock. Be aware that there may be a line, particularly on the weekend.

Information Puerto Rico Ports Authority (☎787/863–0705).

Ferry Terminals Culebra Terminal (☎787/742–3161). **Fajardo Terminal** (☎787/863–4560). **Vieques Terminal** (☎787/741–4761).

BY TAXI

You can flag down taxis on the street, but it's faster and safer to have your hotel call one for you. Either way, agree on how much the trip will cost before you get inside the taxi.

Information Lolo Felix Tours (✉Vieques ☎787/485–5447). **Willy's Taxi** (✉Culebra ☎787/742–3537).

CONTACTS & RESOURCES

BANKS & EXCHANGE SERVICES

There are only a handful of banks on Vieques and Culebra, but they have 24-hour ATMs (or ATHs, as they're known here). The local branches of Banco Popular are open weekdays from 9 to 5.

Information Banco Popular (✉115 Calle Muñoz Rivera, Isabel Segunda, Vieques ☎787/741–2071 ✉15 Calle Pedro Marquez, Dewey, Culebra ☎787/742–0220)

EMERGENCIES

Vieques has a pharmacy and a hospital, but there are neither on Culebra. Make sure you stock up on all supplies—such as allergy medications, contact-lens solution, or tampons—before heading to the island.

EMERGENCY NUMBERS

Hospitals Hospital Susana Centeno (✉Rte. 997, Isabel Segunda, Vieques ☎787/741–3283).

Pharmacies Farmacia Isla Nena (✉Calle Muñoz Rivera, Isabel Segunda, Vieques ☎787/741–1906).

INTERNET, MAIL & SHIPPING

Internet cafés are a rare commodity once you leave San Juan. On Culebra there are a few terminals at Excétera. You can get online for $15 an hour.

Vieques has a post office on the main street in Isabel Segunda, and Culebra has one on the main street in Dewey. Culebra's post office functions as a town center, and usually has a group of locals out front chewing the fat. It's in an older building with a hand-carved front door.

Internet Café **Excétera** (✉ *126 Calle Escudero, Dewey* ☎ *787/742–0844*).

VISITOR INFORMATION

The island's tourism offices are hit and miss when it comes to helpful material. The Vieques Tourism Office, across from the main square in Isabel Segunda, has a friendly staff that will give you armloads of brochures. If you need more, they'll print out a complete list of local businesses. It's open Monday to Saturday 8 to 4:30.

The Culebra Tourism Office, near the ferry dock, has little information on hand. The staffers will help you as best they can, even recommending restaurants that are off the beaten path. The office is open weekdays 9 to 5.

WEB SITES

The Web site Enchanted Isle has plenty of information about Vieques and Culebra; the Web site Isla Vieques has information about Vieques only.

Information **Enchanted Isle** (⊕ *www.enchanted-isle.com*). **Isla Vieques** (⊕ *www.isla-vieques.com*).

Ponce & the Southern Coast

WORD OF MOUTH

"San Germán, Guánica, and La Parguera are all no more than an hour's drive from each other. San Germán can be just a half-day stop. Walk a little around the center of town to enjoy the architecture and stop for a meal."

—PRnative

FROM LUSH TROPICAL MOUNTAINS to arid seacoast plains, Puerto Rico's southern region lets you sample the island from a local's perspective. The south is where San Juan families escape the hustle and bustle of the city for weekends on the beach. Though rich in history, the area also provides ample opportunities for golf, swimming, hiking, and cave exploration. Snaking roads between major highways reveal a glimpse of how rural Puerto Ricans enjoy life. Every mile or so you can see a café or bar, which is the local social center. The only traffic jams you'll likely encounter will be caused by slow-moving farmers taking their goods to the local market.

At the center of everything is Ponce, a city called the "Pearl of the South." Ponce was founded in 1692 by farmers attracted to the rich soil, which was perfect for growing sugarcane. Evidence found at the Tibes Indian ceremonial site, just north of Ponce, suggests that people have been living here as far back as 400 BC. Many residents still carry the last names of the dozens of European pioneer families who settled here during the 19th century. The region's largest city, Ponce is home to some of the island's most interesting architecture and one of its most important art museums. Nearby San Germán, the second-oldest city in Puerto Rico, is known for its two historic main squares well preserved in a wide variety of architectural styles.

EXPLORING PONCE & THE SOUTHERN COAST

The southeastern part of the island has a rugged shoreline, where cliffs drop right into the water. This is a little-explored section of the coast, which means that on one hand the beaches aren't crowded, but on the other there aren't many places to find a decent meal or a place to bed down for the night. Covered with dry vegetation, the southwest's ragged coast has wonderful inlets and bays and jagged peninsulas that make for breathtaking views. This region is a popular destination for Puerto Rican families, so expect crowds on weekends.

ABOUT THE RESTAURANTS

Not all the culinary hot spots are in San Juan. In fact, people from the capital drive to Ponce or Guánica to see what's new on the horizon. Some of the more ambitious restaurants in this part of Puerto Rico are experimenting with fusion cuisine, which means you might find pork with tamarind glaze or guava sauce or snapper in a plantain

SOUTHERN COAST TOP 5

■ Marvel at the Parque de Bombas, a century-old firehouse whose red-and-black color scheme has inspired thousands of photographers.

■ Hike through the Bosque Estatal de Guánica, where the cactus may make you think you're in the American Southwest.

■ Sample a cup of the local brew at historic Hacienda Buena Vista, a beautifully restored coffee plantation outside of Ponce.

■ Stroll around San Germán, whose cobblestone streets are lined with architectural treasures.

■ Step back in time at Casa Wiechers-Villaronga, a neoclassical treasure in the heart of Ponce.

4

crust. But what you can mostly find is open-air eateries serving simple, filling fare. The southern coast is known for seafood. A 15% to 20% tip is customary; most restaurants won't include it in the bill, but it's wise to check.

WHAT IT COSTS IN U.S. DOLLARS				
AT DINNER				
$$$$	$$$	$$	$	¢
over $30	$20–$30	$12–$20	$8–$12	under $8

Prices are per person for a main course at dinner.

ABOUT THE HOTELS

Modest, family-oriented establishments near beaches or in small towns are the most typical accommodations. Southern Puerto Rico doesn't have the abundance of luxury hotels and resorts found to the north and east; however, the Hilton Ponce & Casino and the Copamarina Beach Resort are self-contained complexes with a dizzying array of services.

TIMING

The resort towns of Guánica and La Parguera are also popular with Puerto Ricans during Easter and Christmas and in summer, when children are out of school. Ponce's spirited pre-Lenten Carnival, held the week before Ash

Wednesday, draws many visitors. Note that during busy times some *paradores* and hotels require a minimum two- or three-night stay on weekends.

Numbers in the text correspond to numbers in the margin and on the Southern Puerto Rico, Ponce Centro, Greater Ponce, and San Germán maps.

WHAT IT COSTS IN U.S. DOLLARS				
HOTELS FOR TWO PEOPLE				
$$$$	$$$	$$	$	¢
over $350	$250–$350	$150–$250	$80–$150	under $80

Prices are for a double room in high season, excluding 9% tax (11% for hotels with casinos, 7% for paradores) and 5%-12% service charge.

PONCE

34 km (21 mi) southwest of Coamo.

"Ponce is Ponce and the rest is parking space" is the adage used by the residents of Puerto Rico's second-largest city (population 194,000) to express their pride in being a *ponceño*. The rivalry with the island's capital began in the 19th century, when European immigrants from England, France, and Spain settled here. Because the city's limits extend from the Caribbean to the foothills of the Cordillera Central, it's a lot hotter in climate than San Juan. Another contrast is the architecture of the elegant homes and public buildings that surround the main square.

Many of the 19th-century buildings in Ponce Centro, the downtown area, have been renovated, and the Museo de Arte de Ponce—endowed by its late native son and for- mer governor Luis A. Ferré—is considered one of the Caribbean's finest art museums. Just as famous is Ponce's pre-Lenten carnival. The colorful costumes and *vejigante* (mischief maker) masks worn during the festivities are famous throughout the world. The best dining in Ponce is just west of town. Seafood restaurants line the highway in an area known as Las Cucharas, named for the spoon- shape bay you can overlook as you dine.

IF YOU LIKE

BEACHES

On Puerto Rico's southern coast you can find surfing beaches and calm bays for swimming. Ballena Bay, near Guánica, has oft-deserted sandy stretches. Boat operators make trips to such uninhabited cays as Gilligan's Island off the coast of Guánica and Caja de Muertos off Ponce.

DIVING & SNORKELING

Southern Puerto Rico is an undiscovered dive destination, which means unspoiled reefs and lots of fish. You can arrange for dive boats at Caribe Playa Beach Resort in the southeast, Ponce's La Guancha, and the Copama-

rina Beach Resort in the southwest. Shore diving and snorkeling are best around islands or cays or along the southwestern coast.

HIKING

Vegetation in the region is dramatically different from that of the rest of the island. Near Guánica is the 9,900-acre Bosque Estatal de Guánica, a rare dry tropical forest. With more than 100 species of birds, it's known for its excellent bird-watching. There are good trails throughout the area, but printed guides and trail maps are hard to come by. Ask locals for directions to their favorite paths.

EXPLORING PONCE

Las Delicias Plaza (Plaza of Delights) with its trees, benches, and famous lion fountain is a perfect people-watching square in which to spend an hour or two on a Sunday afternoon. The old red-and-black firehouse is right on the plaza and has a fire-fighting museum on its second floor. Ponce is known for its museums and has several dedicated to music, art, history, sports, and architecture. Ponceños are proud of their city, called the "Pearl of the South," and offer all visitors a warm welcome.

PONCE CENTRO

At the heart of Ponce Centro is the Plaza las Delicias, with trees, benches, and the famous lion fountain. Several interesting buildings are on this square or the adjacent streets, making the area perfect for a leisurely morning or afternoon stroll.

TIMING

Although it's possible to see Ponce Centro in one morning or afternoon, it's best to devote a full day and evening to

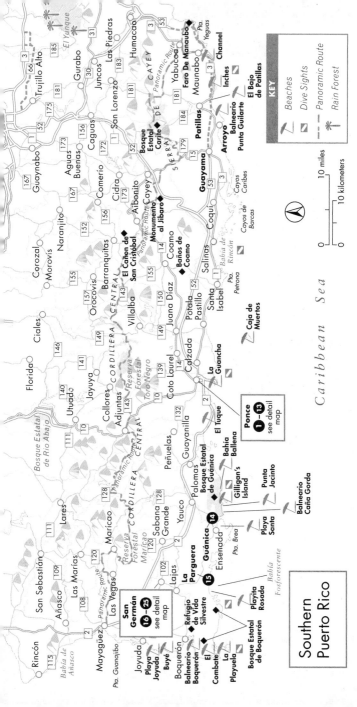

Southern Puerto Rico

KEY

↗ Beaches
⬛ Dive Sights
--- Panoramic Route
✳ Rain Forest

0   10 miles
0   10 kilometers

Caribbean Sea

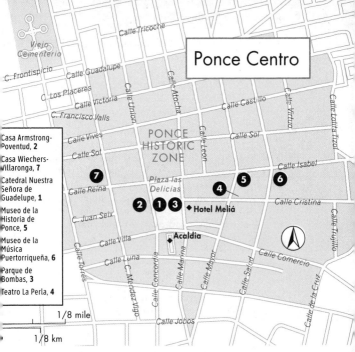

Ponce Centro

1/8 mile

1/8 km

it. Explore the streets and museums during daylight, then head for the plaza at night when the lion fountain and street lamps are lighted and townspeople stroll the plaza.

WHAT TO SEE

② **Casa Armstrong-Poventud.** Banker and industrialist Carlos Armstrong and his wife Eulalia Pou lived in this neoclassical house designed and built for them in 1901 by Manuel V. Domenech. The house is known for its ornate facade, which is chock-full of columns, statues, and intricate moldings. It now houses the offices of the Institute of Puerto Rican Culture. Note the high, pressed-tin ceilings and the decorative glass doors in the foyer. ⊠*Calle Union at Catedral, Ponce Centro* ☎*787/844–2540 or 787/840–7667* ✆*Free* ⊙ *Weekdays 8–4:30.*

★ **Fodor'sChoice** **Casa Wiechers-Villaronga.** In a city filled with
⑦ neoclassical confections, this is one of the most elaborate. It was designed by Alfredo B. Wiechers, who returned to his native Ponce after studying architecture in Paris. This house, though small in scale, makes a big impression with details like huge arched windows and a massive rooftop gazebo. No wonder that soon after it was completed in

1911 the Villaronga-Mercado family decided to make it their own. Check out the stained-glass windows and other fanciful touches. Inside you can find original furnishings and exhibits on Wiechers and other Ponce architects of his era. ⊠*Calle Reina and Calle Meléndez Vigo, Ponce Centro* ☎787/843–3363 *Free* ☉*Wed.–Sun. 8:30–4:30.*

❶ **Catedral de Nuestra Señora de Guadalupe.** This cathedral dedicated to the Virgin of Guadalupe is built on the site of a 1670 chapel destroyed by earthquakes. Part of the current structure, where mass is still held, dates from 1835. After another earthquake in 1918, new steeples and a roof were put on and neoclassical embellishments were added to the facade. Inside you can see stained-glass windows, chandeliers, and two alabaster altars. ⊠*Plaza las Delicias, Ponce Centro* ☎787/842–0134 ☉*Services daily* 6 AM *and* 11 AM.

❺ **Museo de la Historia de Ponce.** Housed in two adjoining buildings, this museum has 10 exhibition halls covering Ponce's development from the Taíno Indians to the present. Hour-long guided tours in English and Spanish give an overview of the city's history. ⊠*51–53 Calle Isabel, Ponce Centro* ☎787/844–7071 *or* 787/843–4322 *$3* ☉*Weekdays 9–5, weekends 10–6.*

❻ **Museo de la Música Puertorriqueña.** At this museum you can learn how Puerto Rican music has been influenced by African, Spanish, and Native American cultures. On display are instruments, such as the *triple* (a small string instrument resembling a banjo), and memorabilia of local composers and musicians. The small museum takes up several rooms in a neoclassical former residence. ⊠*Calle Isabel and Calle Salud, Ponce Centro* ☎787/848–7016 *Free* ☉*Wed.–Sun. 8:30–4:30.*

★ **Fodor's**Choice **Parque de Bombas.** After El Morro, this dis-
❸ tinctive red-and-black-striped building may be the most
☺ photographed building in Puerto Rico. Built in 1882 as a pavilion for an agricultural and industrial fair, it was converted the following year into a firehouse. Today it's a museum tracing the history—and glorious feats—of Ponce's fire brigade. Kids love the antique fire trucks. Short tours in English and Spanish are given on the half hour. There's a small tourist information desk just inside the door. ⊠*Plaza las Delicias, Ponce Centro* ☎787/284–3338 *Free* ☉*Wed.–Mon. 9:30–6.*

❹ Teatro La Perla. This theater was restored in 1941 after an earthquake and fire damaged the original 1864 structure. The striking interior contains seats for 1,047 and has excellent acoustics. It's generally open for a quick look on weekdays. ⊠*Calle Mayor and Calle Cristina, Ponce Centro* ☎*787/843–4322* ☏*Free* ⊙*Weekdays 8–4:30.*

GREATER PONCE

The greater Ponce area has some of Puerto Rico's most notable cultural attractions, including one of the island's finest art museums and its most important archaeological site.

WHAT TO SEE

⓫ Castillo Serrallés. This lovely Spanish-style villa—such a massive house that people in the town below referred to it as a castle—was built in the 1930s for Ponce's wealthiest family, the makers of Don Q rum. Guided tours give you a glimpse into the lifestyle of a sugar baron. A highlight is the dining room, which has the original hand-carved furnishings. A permanent exhibit explains the area's sugarcane and rum industries. The extensive garden, with sculptured bushes and a shimmering reflection pool, is considered the best kept on the island. ⊠*17 El Vigía, El Vigía* ☎*787/259–1774* ⊕*www.castilloserralles.org* ☏*$6, $9 includes admission to Cruceta El Vigía* ⊙*Tues.–Thurs. 9:30–5, Fri.–Sun. 9:30–5:30.*

⓬ Centro Ceremonial Indígena de Tibes. The Tibes Indian Ceremonial Center, discovered after flooding from a tropical storm in 1975, is the island's most important archaeological site. The pre-Taíno ruins and burial grounds date from AD 300 to 700. Be sure to visit the small museum before taking a walking tour of the site, which includes nine ceremonial playing fields used for a ritual ball game that some think was similar to soccer. The fields are bordered by smooth stones, some engraved with petroglyphs that researchers believe might have ceremonial or astronomical significance. Enough mutilated corpses have been found here for researchers to speculate that the residents practiced human sacrifice. A village with several thatch huts has been reconstructed in an original setting. ⊠*Rte. 503, Km 2.8, Barrio Tibes* ☎*787/840–2255 or 787/840–5685* ⊕*ponce. inter.edu/tibes/tibes.html* ☏*$2* ⊙*Tues.–Sun. 9–4.*

❿ Cruceta El Vigía. At the top of Cerro Vigía—a hill where the Spanish once watched for ships, including those of maraud-

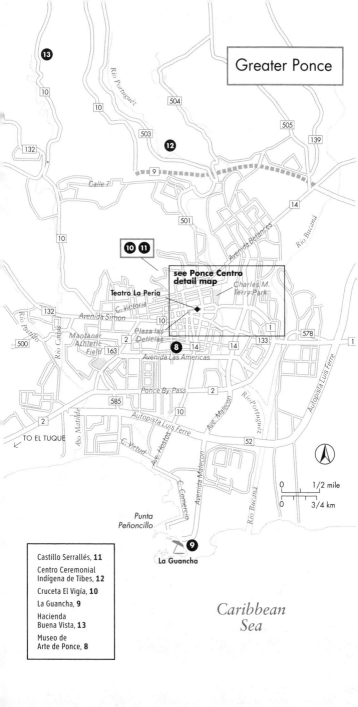

Greater Ponce

13

10

Río Portugués

504

10

12

505

139

10

503

132

9

Calle 7

14

501

Río Bucaná

Avenida Betances

10

10 11

see Ponce Centro detail map

Charles M. Terry Park

Teatro La Perla

C. Victoria

132

Avenida Simón

10

1

Río Cañas

Río Pastillo

Maotaner Athletic Field

2

163

Plaza las Delicias

8

14

14

133

578

1

500

Avenida Las Américas

Ponce By-Pass

2

585

10

Río Matilde

Autopista Luis Ferré

Ave. Matecon

Río Portugués

52

Autopista Luis Ferré

2

TO EL TUQUE

C. Virtud

Ave. Hostos

Avenida Matecon

Río Bucaná

N

0   1/2 mile

0   3/4 km

Punta Peñoncillo

C. Comercio

9

La Guancha

Caribbean Sea

Castillo Serrallés, **11**
Centro Ceremonial Indígena de Tibes, **12**
Cruceta El Vigía, **10**
La Guancha, **9**
Hacienda Buena Vista, **13**
Museo de Arte de Ponce, **8**

ing pirates—is this colossal concrete cross. You can climb the stairs or take an elevator to the top of the 100-foot cross for a panoramic view across the city. Purchase tickets at the nearby Castillo Serrallés. ⊠*Across from Castillo Serrallés, El Vigía* ☎787/259–3816 ⊕*home.coqui.net/castserr* 🖃*$4* ⊗*Tues.–Sun. 9–5:30.*

❾ La Guancha. Encircling the cove of a working harbor, the ℭ seaside boardwalk features kiosks where vendors sell local food and drink. The adjacent park has a large children's area filled with playground equipment and on weekends, live music. The nearby public beach has restrooms, changing areas, a medical post, and plenty of free parking. ⊠*End of Rte. 14, La Guancha* ☎787/844–3995.

★ **Fodor'sChoice Hacienda Buena Vista.** Built by Salvador de ⓭ Vives in 1838, Buena Vista was one of the area's larg-ℭ est coffee plantations. It's a technological marvel—water from the nearby Río Canas was funneled into narrow brick channels that could be diverted to perform any number of tasks, including turning the waterwheel. (Seeing the two-story wheel slowly begin to turn is thrilling, especially for kids.) Nearby is the two-story manor house, filled with furniture that gives a sense of what it was like to live on a coffee plantation nearly 150 years ago. Make sure to take a look in the kitchen, dominated by a massive hearth. In 1987 the plantation was restored by the Puerto Rican Conservation Trust. Tours, which are by reservation only, commence at 8:30, 10:30, 1:30, and 3:30. Make sure to call several days ahead to reserve a spot with an English-language guide. ⊠*Rte. 123, Km 16.8, Sector Corral Viejo* ☎787/722–5882 *weekdays, 787/284–7020 weekends* ⊕*www.fideicomiso.org/english/index.asp* 🖃*$5* ⊗*Wed.–Sun., by reservation only.*

★ **Fodor'sChoice Museo de Arte de Ponce.** This interesting ❽ building—designed by Edward Durrell Stone, who designed the original Museum of Modern Art in New York City and the Kennedy Center in Washington, D.C.—is easily identified by the hexagonal galleries on the second floor. It has one of the best art collections in Latin American, which is why residents of San Juan frequently make the trip down to Ponce. The 3,000-piece collection includes works by famous Puerto Rican artists such as Francisco Oller, represented by a lovely landscape called *Hacienda Aurora*. There are plenty of European works on display, including paintings by Peter Paul Rubens and Thomas Gainsborough. The highlight of the European collection is the pre-Raphaelite paintings, particularly the mesmerizing *Flaming June,* by Frederick Leighton, which has become the museum's unofficial symbol. Watch for special exhibits, such as a recent one examining the work of Frida Kahlo. ⊠*2325 Av. Las Américas, Sector Santa María* ☎*787/848–0505* ⊕*www. museoarteponce.org* ☜*$5* ⊙*Daily 10–5.*

BEACHES

Caja de Muertos *(Coffin Island).* This island a few miles off the coast has the best beaches in the Ponce area and is, perhaps, the second-best area in southern Puerto Rico for snorkeling, after La Parguera. Ask one of the many boatmen at La Guancha to take you out for about $30 round-trip. ⊠*Boats leave from La Guancha, at end of Rte. 14, Ponce.*

La Guancha. Ponce's public beach is small, but the shallow water makes it nice for children. There's some shade under thatched umbrellas, but bring sunscreen. ⊠*At end of Rte. 14, Ponce.*

El Tuque. This beach has a swimming area and picnic tables. ⊠*Rte. 2, approx. 5 km (3 mi) west of Ponce.*

WHERE TO EAT

★ Fodor'sChoice ✕**Mark's at the Meliá.** Hidden behind an etched-
$$–$$$$ glass door, this discreet restaurant is one of the best on the island. Chef Mark French has won praise for his creative blend of European cooking techniques and local ingredients. That skill results in appetizers like terrine of foie gras with dried cherry compote and smoked salmon topped with caramelized mango. The menu changes often, but you're likely to see such entrées as plantain-crusted dorado and rack of lamb with a goat cheese crust. The chocolate truffle cake draws fans from as far away as San Juan. This is a family-run business, so Mark's wife, Melody, is likely to greet you at the door. ⊠*Hotel Meliá, 75 Calle Cristina, Ponce Centro, Ponce* ☎*787/284–6275* ⌲*Reservations essential* ⊟*AE, MC, V* ⊙*Closed Mon.*

$$–$$$$ ✕**Rincón Argentina.** Housed in a beautifully restored criollo-style house, Rincón Argentina is one of the city's most popular restaurants. Completely unpretentious, this is the kind of steak house you find all over South America. The spe-

cialty of the house is *parrilladas,* meaning just about anything that comes off the grill. Don't pass up the skirt steak, served here with the best chimichurri you'll find anywhere. On cool evenings take a table on the terrace. Otherwise, wander through the maze of dining rooms until you find a table you like. ⊠*69 Calle Salud, at Calle Isabel, Ponce Centro, Ponce* ☎*787/840–3768* ⚓*Reservations essential* ▭*AE, MC, V.*

$-$$$ ✕**El Ancla.** Families favor this laid-back restaurant, whose
♻ dining room sits at the edge of the sea. The kitchen serves generous and affordable plates of fish, crab, and other fresh seafood with tostones, french fries, and garlic bread. Try the shrimp in garlic sauce, salmon fillet with capers, or the delectable mofongo. Finish your meal with one of the fantastic flans. The piña coladas—with or without rum—are exceptional. ⊠*9 Av. Hostos Final, Ponce Playa, Ponce* ☎*787/840–2450* ▭*AE, MC, V.*

$-$$$ ✕**Pito's Seafood.** Choose from the waterfront terrace or one of the enclosed dining rooms at this longtime favorite east of Ponce in Las Cucharas. No matter where you sit, you'll have a view of the ocean. The main attraction is the freshly caught seafood, ranging from lobster and crab to salmon and red snapper. To indulge yourself, try the shrimp wrapped in bacon—a specialty of the house. There's also a wide range of chicken and beef dishes. From the expansive wine cellar you can select more than 25 different wines by the glass. There's live music on Friday and Saturday nights. ⊠*Rte. 2, Sector Las Cucharas* ☎*787/841–4977* ▭*AE, MC, V.*

¢ ✕**Café Tompy.** The prices are right at this no-frills cafeteria, which draws a lot of locals for lunch. You can sample such down-home Puerto Rican cuisine as roasted chicken marinated with local spices or slices of roast pork in a honey-sweet glaze. You can pile on the side dishes, which include toasted plantains and creamy potato salad. There's also a selection of sandwiches piled high with meats and cheeses. It's open daily for lunch and dinner, and for breakfast every day except Sunday. ⊠*56 Calle Isabel, Ponce Centro* ☎*787/840–1965* ▭*MC, V.*

WHERE TO STAY

$$–$$$ ⊞**Hilton Ponce Golf & Casino Resort.** The south coast's biggest resort sits on a black-sand beach about 6 km (4 mi) south of Ponce. Everything on this 80-acre property is massive, beginning with the open-air lobby. Constructed of reinforced concrete, like the rest of the hotel, it requires huge signs to point you in the right direction. All of its bright, spacious rooms are decorated in a lush, tropical motif and have balconies overlooking the sea. A large pool is surrounded by palm trees and has a spectacular view of the Caribbean. Golf lovers will appreciate the 27-hole course at the adjacent Costa Caribe Resort, which has a clubhouse with its own restaurant and lounge. ⊠*1150 Av. Caribe, La Guancha* ⊕*Box 7419, Ponce 00732* ☎*787/259–7676 or 800/445–8667* ⊟*787/259–7674* ⊕*www.hiltoncaribbean. com* ⟿*253 rooms* ⚘*In-room: safe, refrigerator, Ethernet. In-hotel: 4 restaurants, room service, bars, golf courses, tennis courts, pool, gym, spa, beachfront, bicycles, public Wi-Fi, children's programs (ages 8–12), parking (fee)* ⊟*AE, D, DC, MC, V* ⊺❍❙*EP.*

$ ⊞**Hotel Meliá.** In the heart of the city, this family-owned
★ hotel has long been a local landmark. Its neoclassical facade, with flags from a dozen countries waving in the breeze, will remind you of a small lodging in Spain. The lobby, with wood-beamed ceilings and blue-and-beige tile floors, is well worn but extremely charming. The best rooms have French doors leading out to small balconies; the six suites have terrific views of the main square. Breakfast is served on the rooftop terrace, which overlooks the mountains. From an eye-catching tile wall, a waterfall drops into the beautiful tiled swimming pool. The restaurant, Mark's at the Meliá, is one of the best on the island. ⊠*75 Calle Cristina, Ponce Centro* ⊕*Box 1431, Ponce 00733* ☎*787/842–0260 or 800/448–8355* ⊟*787/841–3602* ⊕*www.hotelmeliapr.com* ⟿*72 rooms, 6 suites* ⚘*In-hotel: restaurant, bar, pool, public Internet, parking (fee)* ⊟*AE, MC, V* ⊺❍❙*CP.*

¢ ⊞**Hotel Bélgica.** Near the central square, this hotel is both comfortable and economical. A stairway off the large 1940s-era lobby leads to clean rooms with wrought-iron headboards and other furnishings. Those on the front of the building have balconies with wooden shutter-style doors. The rooms vary widely in size (Room 3 is one of the largest), so ask to see a few before you decide. The friendly staff makes up for the lack of amenities. The hotel has no restaurant, but there are plenty of options in the neighborhood. ⊠*122 Calle Villa, Ponce Centro 00731* ☎*787/844–3255* ⊕*www.hotelbelgica.com* ⊅*20 rooms* ⌖*In hotel: some pets allowed* ▭*MC, V* ⧀*EP.*

NIGHTLIFE & THE ARTS

NIGHTLIFE

BARS & CLUBS

Catering mostly to a gay crowd, **Backstage** (⊠*Off Rte. 123, Ponce Centro* ☎*787/448–8112*) has a huge dance floor surrounded by intimate lounges where groups of friends inevitably gather. Don't get here before midnight, or you might arrive before the staff. On the main square, **Café Palermo** (⊠*Calle Union at Calle Villa, Ponce Centro* ☎*787/448–8112*) is a hole in the wall. Still, locals can be found crowding around the bar every night of the week. **Fusion** (⊠*28 Calle Isabel, Ponce Centro* ☎*787/842–254*) has a laid-back lounge area that makes you want to order a fancy cocktail. You can also belly up to the chic bar.

THE ARTS

The **Museo de Arte de Ponce** (⊠*2325 Av. Las Américas, Sector Santa María* ☎*787/848–0505*) occasionally sponsors chamber-music concerts and recitals by members of the Puerto Rico Symphony Orchestra. Check for Spanish-language theater productions and concerts at the **Teatro La Perla** (⊠*Calle Mayor and Calle Cristina, Ponce Centro* ☎*787/843–4322*).

SPORTS & THE OUTDOORS

DIVING & SNORKELING

You can see many varieties of coral, parrotfish, angelfish, and grouper in the reefs around the island of Caja de Muertos. Snorkeling around La Guancha and the beach area of the Ponce Hilton is also fairly good.

Rafi Vega's **Island Venture** (☎*787/842–8546* ⊕*www.island venturepr.com*) offers two-tank dive excursions for $65, as well as snorkeling trips for $35. The company also takes day-trippers from La Guancha to Caja de Muertos—a 45-minutes boat ride—for a day of relaxing on the beach.

SHOPPING

On holidays and during festivals, artisans sell wares from booths in the Plaza las Delicias. Souvenir and gift shops are plentiful in the area around the plaza, and Paseo Atocha, a pedestrian mall with shops geared to residents, runs north of it.

Den Cayá (⊠72 *Calle Isabel, Ponce Centro* ☎787/649–7763), a fun and funky store, has a wide variety of crafts from around the island as well as around the world.

Mi Coquí (⊠9227 *Calle Marina, Ponce Centro* ☎787/841–0216) has shelves filled with Carnival masks, colorful hammocks, freshly ground coffee, and bottles and bottles of rum.

Utopia (⊠78 *Calle Isabel, Ponce Centro* ☎787/848–8742) sells carnival masks and crafts.

THE SOUTHERN COAST

With sandy coves and palm-lined beaches tucked in the coastline's curves, southwestern Puerto Rico fulfills everyone's fantasy of a tropical paradise. The area is popular with local vacationers on weekends and holidays, but many beaches are nearly deserted on weekdays. Villages along the coast are picturesque places where oysters and fresh fish are sold at roadside stands.

GUÁNICA

⓮ *38 km (24 mi) west of Ponce.*

Juan Ponce de León first explored this area in 1508, when he was searching for the elusive Fountain of Youth. Nearly 400 years later, U.S. troops landed first at Guánica during the Spanish-American War in 1898. The event is commemorated with an engraved marker on the city's malecón. Sugarcane dominated the landscape through much of the 1900s, and the ruins of the old Guánica Central sugar mill, closed in 1980, loom over the town's western area, known as Ensenada. Today most of the action takes place at the beaches and in the forests outside of Guánica.

★ **Fodor'sChoice** The 9,900-acre **Bosque Estatal de Guánica** *(Guánica State Forest)*, a United Nations Biosphere Reserve, is a great place for hiking expeditions. It's an outstanding example of a tropical dry coastal forest, with some 700 species of plants ranging from the prickly pear cactus to the gumbo limbo tree. It's also one of the best places on the island for bird-watching, since you can spot more than 100 species, including the pearly eyed thrasher, the lizard cockoo, and the nightjar.

One of the most popular hikes is the **Ballena Trail,** which begins at the ranger station on Route 334. This easy 2-km (1¼-mi) walk, which follows a partially paved road, takes you past a mahogany plantation to a dry plain covered with stunted cactus. A sign reading GUAYACÁN CENTENARIO leads you to an extraordinary guayacán tree with a trunk that measures 6 feet across. The moderately difficult **Fuerte Trail** takes you on a 5½-km (3½-mi) hike to an old fort built by the Spanish Armada. It was destroyed during the Spanish-American War in 1898, but you can still see the ruins of the old observatory tower.

In addition to the main entrance on Route 334, you can enter on Route 333, which skirts the forest's southwestern quadrant. You can also try the less-explored western section, off Route 325. ⊠*Rte. 334, 333, or 325* ☏*787/821–5706* ⊟*Free* ⊙*Daily 9–5.*

Off the southwest coast, near Guánica, is **Gilligan's Island,** a palm-ringed cay skirted by gorgeous beaches. You can find picnic tables and restrooms but few other signs of civilization on this tiny island, officially part of the Bosque Estatal de Guánica. Wooden boats line up at the small dock in the San Jacinto section of Guánica, off Route 333 just past the Copamarina Beach Resort. Boats depart every hour from 10 to 5 (except Monday, when rangers close the island to visitors). Round-trip passage is $6. The island is often crowded on weekends and around holidays, but during the week you can find a spot to yourself. Nearby **Isla de Ballena,** reached by the same ferry, is much less crowded. ⊠*Rte. 333 or 334* ☏*787/821–5706* ⊟*Free* ⊙*Daily 9–5.*

BEACHES
Balneario Caña Gorda. The gentle water at this beach on Route 333 washes onto a wide swath of sand fringed with palm trees. There are picnic tables, restrooms, showers, and changing facilities. ⊠*Rte. 333, west of Copamarina Beach Resort.*

Playa Jaboncillo. Rugged cliffs make a dramatic backdrop for this little cove off Route 333, but the water can be rough. ⊠*Rte. 333, west of Copamarina Beach Resort.*

Playa Santa. You can rent Jet Skis, kayaks, and pedal boats at this beach at the end of Route 325 in the Ensenada district. ⊠*Rte. 325, west of Guánica.*

WHERE TO EAT

★ Fodor'sChoice ✕**Alexandra.** Puerto Ricans drive for miles to
$$–$$$$ reach this restaurant in the Copamarina Beach Resort. You won't find such creative cuisine anywhere else west of Ponce. The kitchen takes traditional dishes and makes them something special; take the free-range chicken with cumin and thyme butter, for example, or the grilled pork chops with pineapple chutney. A standout is the risotto, which surrounds tender mussels with rice flavored with saffron, basil, and tomatoes. The elegant dining room looks out onto well-tended gardens; if you want to get closer to the flora, take a table outside on the terrace. The only disappointment may be noisy children, who tend to run in and out. ⊠*Rte. 333, Km 6.5* ☎*787/821–0505 Ext. 766* △*Reservations essential* ═*AE, MC, V.*

$–$$ ✕**San Jacinto.** Popular with day-trippers to Gilligan's Island, this modest restaurant sits right at the ferry terminal. This doesn't mean, however, that the dining room has views of the Caribbean. For those, grab one of the concrete picnic tables outside. The menu is almost entirely seafood, running the gamut from fried snapper to broiled lobster. When it's not high season the menu can be limited to two or three items. ⊠*Off Rte. 333* ☎*787/821–4941* ═*MC, V.*

WHERE TO STAY

$$–$$$ ⌧**Copamarina Beach Resort.** Without a doubt the most beau-
☺ tiful resort on the southern coast, the Copamarina is set
★ on 16 palm-shaded acres facing the Caribbean Sea. Fruit trees and other plants are meticulously groomed, especially around the pair of swimming pools (one popular with kids, the other mostly left to the adults). All the guest rooms are generously proportioned, especially in the older building. Wood shutters on the windows and other touches lend a beach vibe. A small spa with Asian-influenced design blends seamlessly with the rest of the hotel. The red snapper is a must at the elegant Alexandra restaurant. ⊠*Rte. 333, Km 6.5, Box 805, Guánica 00653* ☎*787/821–0505 or 800/468–4553* ☎*787/821–0070* ⊕*www.copamarina. com* ⌔*104 rooms, 2 villas* ♿*In-room: safe, refrigerator.*

In-hotel: restaurant, room service, bars, tennis courts, pools, gym, spa, beachfront, diving, water sports, laundry facilities =*AE, MC, V* ⌶○⌶*EP.*

★ **Fodor's**Choice ⌶ **Mary Lee's by the Sea.** This meandering cluster
$ of apartments sits in quiet grounds full of brightly colored flowers. It's home to Mary Lee Alvarez, and she'll make you feel like it's yours as well. Most units have ocean views; in the others you can catch a glimpse of the mangroves by the shore as well as of the cactus growing in the nearby Bosque Estatal de Guánica. Each of the one-, two-, and three-bedroom units is decorated in bright colors. Each is different, but most have terraces hung with hammocks and outfitted with barbecue grills. You can rent kayaks to drift along the coast or hop a boat bound for Gilligan's Island. ⌷*Rte. 333, Km 6.7* ⌷*Box 394, 00653* ⌷*787/821–3600* ⌷*787/821–0744* ⌷*www.maryleesbythesea.com* ⌷*8 apartments* ⌷*In-room: no phones, kitchens (some), no TVs. In-hotel: laundry service* =*MC, V* ⌶○⌶*EP.*

LA PARGUERA

⑮ *13 km (8 mi) west of Guánica, 24 km (15 mi) southwest of Yauco.*

La Parguera is best known for its bioluminescent bay. Although it's not nearly as spectacular as one of the islands of Vieques, it's still a beautiful sight on a moonless night. Glass-bottom boats lined up at the town dock depart several times each evening for 45-minute trips across the bay. During the day, you can explore the nearby mangrove forest.

The town bursts at the seams with vacationers from other parts of the island on long holiday weekends and all during the summer. The town's dock area feels a bit like Coney Island, and not in a good way. Vendors in makeshift stalls hawk cheap souvenirs, and ear-splitting salsa music pours out of the open-air bars. There are signs warning people not to drink alcoholic beverages in the street, but these are cheerfully ignored.

On moonless nights, large and small boats line up along the dock to take visitors out to view the **Bahía de Fosforescente** *(Phosphorescent Bay).* Microscopic dinoflagellates glow when disturbed by movement, invading the waves with thousands of starlike points of light. The bay's glow has diminished substantially from pollution—both light pollution from the nearby communities and water pollution from toxic chemicals being dumped into the bay. (And, yes, the smoke-belching boats that take tourists to the bay are doing damage, too.) If you've seen the bioluminescent bay in Vieques, give this one a pass. If not, you may find it mildly interesting. ⊠*East of La Parguera.*

The eastern section of the **Bosque Estatal de Boquerón** *(Boquerón State Forest)* is made up of miles of mangrove forests that grow at the water's edge. Boats from the dock in La Parguera can take you on cruises through this important breeding ground for seabirds. You can also organize a kayak trip. ⊠*East of La Parguera.*

BEACHES

Cayo Caracoles. You can take a boat to and from this island for $5 per person. There are mangroves to explore as well as plenty of places to swim and snorkel. ⊠*Boats leave from marina at La Parguera, off Rte. 304.*

Isla Mata de la Gata. For about $5 per person boats will transport you to and from this small island just off the coast for a day of swimming and snorkeling. ⊠*Boats leave from marina at La Parguera, off Rte. 304.*

Playita Rosada. The small beach doesn't compare to some of the longer beaches on the southwestern coast, but it's a convenient place for a quick swim. ⊠*At end of Calle 7.*

WHERE TO EAT

$$$ ✕**La Pared.** Many restaurants in La Paraguera sit beside the bay, but very few have an actual view. This elegant, second-floor dining room at the rear of Posada Porlamar overlooks a lovely stretch of coastline ringed by mangrove trees. The menu is the best in town, going well beyond the standard surf-and-turf offerings. There's rack of lamb, for example, but here you can find it topped with goat cheese. The lobster tail is as fresh as anywhere else on the strip, but is topped with a tasty guanabana sauce. ⊠*Posada Porlamar, Rte. 304, Km 3.3* ☎787/899–4015 ═MC, V.

$$ ✕**La Casita.** The so-called "Little House" isn't little at all—it's a sizeable establishment that sits smack in the middle of the town's main road. Generous portions make this family-run restaurant one of the town's favorites. Try the *asopao*, which is made with shrimp, lobster, or other types of seafood. You can take a table in the rather bland ground-floor dining room or on the second-floor terrace, which has a

view of the water. ⊠*Rte. 304, Km 3.3* ☎*787/899–1681* ⊟*MC, V* ⊗*Closed Mon.*

WHERE TO STAY

$ ⚏**Posada Porlamar.** You might not realize it at first, but this small hotel is all about the water. Most of the comfortable rooms have views of the mangrove-ringed bay, as do the restaurant, café, and bar. In the rear you can find a dock where you can rent a boat to explore the coastline, as well as a full-service dive shop where you can arrange snorkeling and diving excursions. And when you're finished exploring, you can relax by the pretty pool. The hotel is on La Paraguera's main drag, but far enough from the action that it's quiet at night. ⊠*Rte. 304, Km 3.3* ⚏*Box 3113, Lajas 00667* ☎*787/899–4343* ⚏*787/899–4015* ⊕*www.parguerapuertorico.com* ⛵*38 rooms* ⚬*In-hotel: 2 restaurants, bar, pool* ⊟*MC, V* ⊙*EP.*

$ ⚏**Villa del Mar.** What sets this family-run inn apart is the
★ warmth of the staff, which promises to take care of anything you need. The hotel, painted refreshing shades of lemon and lime, sits on a hill overlooking the boats in the bay. Not all of the squeaky-clean rooms have views, so make sure to specify when you call for reservations. You can find an open-air lounge area near the reception desk and a shimmering pool in the courtyard. You can arrange for very tasty, reasonably priced meals in the small restaurant. To find the place, take the first left as you drive into La Paraguera. ⊠*3 Av. Albizu Campos* ⚏*Box 1297, San Germán 00667* ☎*787/899–4265* ⊕*www.pinacolada.net/villadelmar* ⛵*25 rooms* ⚬*In-room: no phones. In-hotel: Restaurant, bar, pool* ⊟*AE, MC, V* ⊙*EP.*

SPORTS & THE OUTDOORS

DIVING & SNORKELING

Endangered leatherback turtles, eels, and an occasional manatee can be seen from many of the sites that attract divers and snorkelers from all parts. There are more than 50 shore-dive sites off La Parguera. **Parguera Divers** (⊠*Posada Porlamar, Rte. 304, Km 3.3* ☎*787/899–4171* ⊕*www.pargueradivers.com*) offers scuba and snorkeling expeditions and basic instruction.

San Germán

Alcaldía Antigua, **21**	
Capilla de Porta Coeli, **16**	
Casa Acosta y Forés, **19**	
Casa Kindy, **18**	
Casa de Lola Rodríguez de Tió, **24**	
Casa Morales, **17**	
Casa Perichi, **20**	
La Casona, **22**	
Iglesia de San Germán de Auxerre, **23**	
Museo de Arte y Casa de Estudio, **25**	

SAN GERMÁN

10 km (6 mi) north of La Parguera, 166 km (104 mi) southwest of San Juan.

During its early years, San Germán was a city on the move. Although debate rages about the first settlement's exact founding date and location, the town is believed to have been established in 1510 near Guánica. Plagued by mosquitoes, the settlers moved north along the west coast, where they encountered French pirates and smugglers. In the 1570s they fled inland to the current location, but they were still harassed. Determined and creative, they dug tunnels and moved beneath the city (the tunnels are now part of the water system). Today San Germán has a population of 39,000, and its intellectual and political activity is anything but underground. It's very much a college town, and students and professors from the Inter-American University often fill the bars and cafés.

Around San Germán's two main squares—Plazuela Santo Domingo and Plaza Francisco Mariano Quiñones (named for an abolitionist)—are buildings done in every conceiv-

Lives of the Santos

When they arrived on Puerto Rico, Spanish missionaries spread the word of God and fostered a spirited folk art. Since few people were literate, the missionaries often commissioned local artisans to create pictures and statues depicting Bible stories and saints or *santos*. These figures—fashioned of wood, clay, stone, or even gold—are still given a place of honor in homes throughout the island.

Early *santeros* (carvers) were influenced by the Spanish baroque style. Later figures are simple and small, averaging about 8 inches tall. The carving of santos is usually a family tradition, and most of today's santeros have no formal art training. San Germán has been associated with santos-making since the origins of the art form, and the Rivera family has been known for its carvings for more than 150 years.

Each santo has a traditional characteristic. You can spot the Virgin by her blue robes, St. Francis by the accompanying birds and animals, St. Barbara by her tower, and the Holy Spirit by its hovering dove. St. John, the island's patron saint, is an ever-popular subject, as is the Nativity, which might be just the Holy Family, or the family with an entire cast of herald angels, shepherds, and barnyard animals.

Carvings of Los Santos Reyes (The Three Kings) are also popular. Their feast day, January 6, is important on Puerto Rico. Celebrations often continue for days before or after the actual holiday, when it's difficult to find a home without these regal characters. In Puerto Rico one king is often strumming the *cuatro*, an island guitar.

–Updated by Karen English

able style of architecture found on the island including mission, Victorian, creole, and Spanish colonial. The city's tourist office offers a free guided trolley tour. Most of the buildings are private homes; two of them—the Capilla de Porta Coeli and the Museo de Arte y Casa de Estudio—are museums. The historical center is surrounded by strip malls, and the town is hemmed to the south and west by busy seaside resorts.

TIMING

San Germán's historic district is compact, so you can cover all the sights in about 1½ hours. You'll want to budget a bit more time to stroll around the nearby streets. Be sure to wear comfortable shoes, as there will be a lot of walking uphill and downhill on cobbled streets.

WHAT TO SEE

㉑ Alcaldía Antigua *(Old Municipal Building)*. At the eastern end of Plaza Francisco Mariano Quiñones, this Spanish colonial–style building served as the town's city hall from 1844 to 1950. Once used as a prison, the building is now the headquarters for the police department. ⊠*East end of Plaza Francisco Mariano Quiñones.*

⑯ Capilla de Porta Coeli *(Heaven's Gate Chapel)*. One of the
★ oldest religious buildings in the Americas, this mission-style chapel overlooks the long, rectangular Plazuela de Santo Domingo. It's not a grand building, but its position at the top of a stone stairway gives it a noble air. Queen Isabel Segunda decreed that the Dominicans should build a church and monastery in San Germán, so a rudimentary building was built in 1609, replaced in 1692 by the structure that can still be seen today. (Sadly, most of the monastery was demolished in 1866, leaving only a vestige of its facade.) The chapel now functions as a museum of religious art, displaying painted wooden statuary by Latin American and Spanish artists. ⊠*East end of Plazuela Santo Domingo* ☎787/892–5845 ⊕*www.icp.gobierno.pr* ☞*Free* ☉*Wed.–Sun. 8:30–4:20.*

⑲ Casa Acosta y Forés. A few doors down from Casa de los Kindy is this beautiful yellow-and-white wooden house dating from 1918. Although the front of the house is typical criollo architecture, the side entrance is covered with an ornate Victorian-style porch. The house isn't open to the public. ⊠*70 Calle Dr. Santiago Veve.*

⑱ Casa Kindy. East of the Plazuela de Santo Domingo, this 19th-century home is known for its eclectic architecture, which mixes neoclassical and criollo elements. Note the elegant stained-glass windows over the front windows. It's now a private residence. ⊠*64 Calle Dr. Santiago Veve.*

㉔ Casa de Lola Rodríguez de Tió On the National Registry of Historic Places, this house bears the name of poet and activist Lola Rodríguez de Tió. A plaque claims she lived in this creole-style house, though town officials believe it actually belonged to her sister. Rodríguez, whose mother was a descendent of Ponce de León, was deported several times by Spanish authorities for her revolutionary ideas. She lived in Venezuela and then in Cuba, where she died in 1924. The museum, which contains Rodríguez's desk and papers, isn't open regular hours; call ahead to schedule a tour. ✉*13 Calle Dr. Santiago Veve* ☎*787/892–3500* 🎫*Free* ⊘*By appointment only.*

⑰ Casa Morales. Facing Plazuela de Santo Domingo, this Victorian-style house was designed in 1913 by architect Pedro Vivoni for his brother, Tomás Vivoni. The gleaming white structure has numerous towers and gables. The current owners have kept it in mint condition. It's not open to the public. ✉*38 Calle Ramos.*

⑳ Casa Perichi. You can find an excellent example of Puerto Rican ornamental architecture in this elegant mansion, which sits a block south of Plazuela Santo Domingo. This gigantic white home, on the National Register of Historic Places, was built in 1920. Note the sensuous curves of the wraparound balcony and wood trim around the doors. It's not open to the public. ✉*94 Calle Luna.*

㉒ La Casona. On the north side of Plaza Francisco Mariano Quiñones, this two-story home was built in 1871 for Tomás Agrait. (If you look closely, you can still see his initials in the wrought-iron decorations.) For many years it served as a center of cultural activities in San Germán. Today it holds several shops. ✉*Calle José Julien Acosta and Calle Cruz.*

㉓ Iglesia de San Germán de Auxerre. Dating from 1739, this neoclassical church has seen many additions over the years. For example, the impressive crystal chandelier was added in 1860. Be sure to take a look at the carved-wood ceiling in the nave. This church is still in use, so the only time you can get a look inside is during services. ✉*West side of Plaza Francisco Mariano Quiñones* ☎*787/892–1027* ⊘*Mass Mon.–Sat. at 7 AM and 7:30 PM and Sun. at 7, 8:30, 10 AM, and 7:30 PM.*

㉕ Museo de Arte y Casa de Estudio. This early-20th-century home—built in the criollo style with some obvious neoclassical influences—has been turned into a museum. Displays include colonial furnishings, religious art, and artifacts of the indigenous peoples; there are also changing exhibits by local artists. ✉*7 Calle Esperanza* ☎*787/892–8870* 🎫*Free* ⊘*Wed.–Sun. 10–noon and 1–3.*

WHERE TO EAT

$–$$ ✕**Chaparritas.** On San Germán's main drag, this place certainly feels like a traditional cantina. The Mexican food here is the real deal. Although you can find some dishes that are more Tex than Mex, such as the cheesy nachos, the kitchen does best with more authentic tacos, burritos, and enchiladas. For something a bit more off the wall, try the shrimp fried in tequila. ✉*Calle Luna 171* ☎*787/892–1078* ✆*Closed Sun.–Wed.*

¢–$ ✕**Tapas Café.** One of the biggest surprises in San Germán is
★ this wonderful little restaurant facing Plaza Santo Domingo. The dining room looks like a Spanish courtyard, complete with blue stars swirling around the ceiling. Don't expect tiny portions just because it serves tapas—several of the dishes, including the medallions of beef topped with a dab of blue cheese, could pass as full entrées anywhere. You can find old favorites on the menu, including spicy sausage in red wine, but some new creations as well, such as the yam and codfish fritters. ✉*50 Calle Dr. Santiago Veve* ☎*787/264–0610* ▭*MC, V* ✆*Closed Mon. and Tues. No lunch Wed. and Thurs.*

WHERE TO STAY

$ 🏨**Villa del Rey.** On a quiet country road, Villa del Rey is set among banana and papaya trees. This family-run inn couldn't be simpler, but it's clean and comfortable. The rooms are larger than you'll find in most of the region's lodgings. The patio around the pool is a bit run-down, but the pool itself is refreshing on a hot afternoon. A restaurant and bar are planned for the future. ✉*Rte. 361, Km 0.8, off Rte. 2* ✉*Box 3033, 00667* ☎*787/264–2542 or 787/642–2627* 🖷*787/264–1579* ⊕*www.villadelrey.net* ⟿*19 rooms* ⌂*Some kitchenettes, pool, meeting room* ▭*MC, V* ⊙*EP.*

PONCE & THE SOUTHERN COAST ESSENTIALS

To research prices, get advice from other travelers, and book travel arrangements, visit www.fodors.com.

TRANSPORTATION

BY AIR

Aeropuerto Mercedita (PSE) is about 8 km (5 mi) east of Ponce's downtown. The airport is so tiny that between flights there may be nobody in the terminal besides you and a bored-looking security guard. Needless to say, there are almost no amenities. The only international flights are on Continental, which flies from Newark, and Jet Blue, which flies from New York's JFK. Cape Air flies several times a day from San Juan.

Taxis at the airport operate under a meter system, so expect to pay about $6 to get to downtown Ponce. Some hotels have shuttles from the airport, but you must make arrangements in advance.

Airlines Cape Air (☎800/525–0280 ⊕www.flycapeair.com). **Continental** (☎800/231–0856 ⊕www.continental.com). **JetBlue** (☎800/538–2583 ⊕www.jetblue.com).

Airport Aeropuerto Mercedita (PSE ⊠Rte. 506 off Rte. 52, Ponce ☎787/842–6292).

BY BUS

There's no easy network of buses linking the towns in southern Puerto Rico with the capital of San Juan or with each other. Some municipalities and private companies operate buses or *públicos* (usually large vans) that make many stops. Call ahead; although reservations aren't usually required, you'll need to check on schedules, which change frequently. The cost of a público from Ponce to San Juan is about $15 to $20; agree on a price before you start your journey.

Information Choferes Unidos de Ponce (⊠Terminal de Carros Públicos, Calle Vives and Calle Mendéz Vigo, Ponce Centro, Ponce ☎787/842–1222). **Línea Sangermeña** (⊠Terminal de Carros Públicos, Calle Luna at entrance to town, San Germán ☎787/722–3392).

BY CAR

A car is pretty much a necessity if you're exploring Puerto Rico's southern coast. Without one you'd find getting anywhere—even to the beach or to a restaurant—frustrating. You can rent cars at the Luis Muñoz Marín International Airport and other San Juan locations. There are also car-rental agencies in some of the larger cities along the south coast. Rates run about $35 to $45 a day, depending on the car. You may get a better deal if you rent a car for a week or more. Test your vehicle before heading out to be sure it runs properly.

Information Avis (⊠Mercedita Airport, Ponce ☎787/842–6154). **Budget** (⊠Mercedita Airport, Ponce ☎787/848–0907). **Dollar** (⊠Av. Los Caobos and Calle Acacia, Ponce ☎787/843–6940). **Leaseway**

of Puerto Rico (⊠*Rte. 3, Km 140.1, Guayama* ☎*787/864–8149* ⊕*www.leasewaypr.com* ⊠*Ponce* ☎*787/843–4330*).

BANKS & EXCHANGE SERVICES

You can find plenty of banks in the region, and many supermarkets, drug stores, and gas stations have ATMs. Banks are normally open weekdays from 9 to 3 or 4. Some banks—such as the Scotiabank branch in Ponce—are also open until noon on Saturday. You can exchange foreign currency in Banco Popular branches; Scotiabank exchanges Canadian currency. Western Union service is available at Pueblo Supermarkets.

Information Banco Popular (⊠*Plaza Guayama, Rte. 3, Km 134.9, Guayama* ☎*787/866–0180* ⊠*Plaza las Delicias, Ponce Centro, Ponce* ☎*787/843–8000*). **Scotiabank** (⊠*Plaza las Delicias, Ponce Centro, Ponce* ☎*787/259–8535*).

INTERNET, MAIL & SHIPPING

Internet cafés are few and far between in this part of the island. If you'll need to be wired on your trip, make sure that your hotel has an Internet connection.

There are branches of the U.S. Post Office throughout the region. You can buy stamps in Pueblo Supermarkets and in many gift shops.

TOUR OPTIONS

Alelí Tours and Encantos Ecotours Southwest in La Parguera offer ecological tours of the southwestern area, including two- or three-hour kayak trips that cost about $25.

Information Alelí Tours (⊠*Rte. 304, Km 3.2, La Parguera* ☎*787/390–6086*). **Encantos Ecotours Southwest** (⊠*El Muelle Shopping Center, Av. Pescadores, La Parguera* ☎*787/808–0005*).

VISITOR INFORMATION

In Ponce the municipal tourist office is open weekdays from 8 to 4:30, as is the small information desk in the Parque de Bombas. The Puerto Rico Tourism Company's office in the Paseo del Sur plaza is open weekdays from 8 to 5. Smaller cities generally have a tourism office in the city hall that's open weekdays from 8 to noon and 1 to 4.

Information Ponce Municipal Tourist Office (⊠*2nd fl. of Citibank, Plaza las Delicias, Ponce Centro, Ponce* ☎*787/841–8160 or 787/841–8044*). **Puerto Rico Tourism Company** (⊠*291 Av. Los Caobos, Sector Vallas Torres, Ponce* ☎*787/843–0465* ⊕*welcome.topuertorico.org*).

Rincón & the Porta del Sol

WORD OF MOUTH

"I like Rincón, a little surfing town on the west side of the island. Many restaurant options & a very nice laid-back vibe."

—SAnParis

"Boquerón is a glorious little village on the west coast of PR."

—tripster

PORTA DEL SOL TOP 5

■ Scanning the horizon from the lighthouse at Arecibo, which overlooks a glittering sea.

■ Relaxing in your private plunge pool at the Horned Dorset Primavera, perhaps the most romantic inn in the Caribbean.

■ Sampling fresh seafood at one of the oceanfront eateries along the coast.

■ Challenging the waves at Playa Tres Palmas or any other of Rincón's world-famous surfing spots.

■ Island-hopping to Desecheo Island or Mona Island.

THE "GATEWAY TO THE SUN" is how tourism officials describe the island's western coast. Although the name calls to mind well-developed, well-traveled vacations spots like Spain's Costa de Sol, the Porta del Sol is neither. Unlike the area around San Juan, the Porta del Sol is relatively undiscovered. Even around Rincón, which has the lion's share of the lodgings, the beaches are delightfully deserted. And in places like Aguadilla and Isabela, two sleepy towns on the northwestern corner of the island, it's easy to find a stretch of shoreline all to yourself.

Less than a century ago, western Puerto Rico was still overwhelmingly rural. Some large fruit plantations dotted the coast, while farther inland coffee was grown on hillside *fincas* (farms). The slow pace began to change during the mid-20th century. New roads brought development to the once-isolated towns. They also brought surfers, who were amazed to find some of the best waves in the Caribbean. There are also long beaches of golden sand. Now there are top-notch hotels, interesting natural areas to explore, and almost every kind of water sport imaginable.

EXPLORING RINCÓN & THE PORTA DEL SOL

The speedy Highway 22 and the more meandering Highway 2 head west from San Juan and swing around the northwestern part of the island, skirting the beaches of the northern coast. A short 45 minutes from the capital you

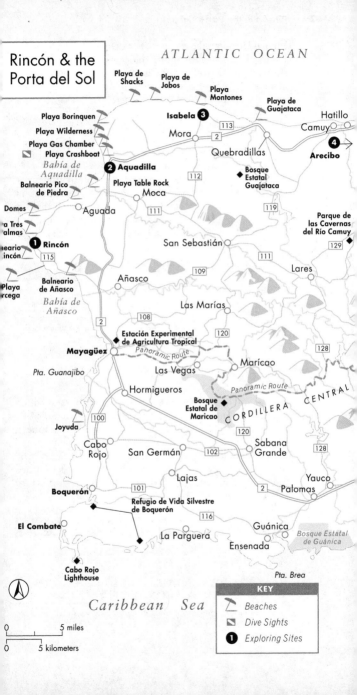

Rincón & the Porta del Sol

ATLANTIC OCEAN

Playa de Shacks
Playa de Jobos
Playa Montones
Playa de Guajataca
Hatillo
Camuy
Playa Borinquen
Isabela **3**
Playa Wilderness
Mora
113
Playa Gas Chamber
4
Playa Crashboat
Arecibo
Bahía de Aquadilla
Quebradillas
Aquadilla **2**
Bosque Estatal Guajataca
112
Balneario Pico de Piedra
Playa Table Rock
Moca
Domes
111
119
Aguada
a Tres almas
Parque de las Cavernas del Río Camuy
neario incón
Rincón **1**
San Sebastián
129
115
111
Lares
Playa rcega
Balneario de Añasco
109
Añasco
Bahía de Añasco
Las Marías
108
120
2
Estación Experimental de Agricultura Tropical
128
Mayagüez
Panoramic Route
Las Vegas
Marícao
Pta. Guanajibo
Panoramic Route
Hormigueros
CENTRAL
Bosque Estatal de Maricao
100
CORDILLERA
Joyuda
120
Cabo Rojo
San Germán
Sabana Grande
128
102
Boquerón
Lajas
Yauco
2
Palomas
101
Refugio de Vida Silvestre de Boquerón
El Combate
116
Guánica
Bosque Estatal de Guánica
La Parguera
Ensenada
Cabo Rojo Lighthouse
Pta. Brea

Caribbean Sea

KEY	
🏖	*Beaches*
🔷	*Dive Sights*
1	*Exploring Sites*

0   5 miles

0   5 kilometers

can pass through the resort town of Dorado; after Arecibo, Highway 2 continues along the coast, where the ragged shoreline holds some of the island's best surfing beaches, and a steady contingent of surfers in Aguadilla and Rincón gives the area a laid-back atmosphere.

Numbers in the text correspond to numbers in the margin and on the Northwestern Puerto Rico map.

ABOUT THE RESTAURANTS

Throughout northwestern Puerto Rico you can find wonderful *criollo* cuisine, interspersed with international restaurants ranging from French to Japanese. You can enjoy five-course meals in elegant surroundings at night, then sip coffee on an outdoor balcony the next morning. Tips, normally 15% to 20%, are usually not included in the bill, but it's always wise to double-check.

WHAT IT COSTS IN U.S. DOLLARS				
AT DINNER				
$$$$	$$$	$$	$	¢
over $30	$20–$30	$12–$20	$8–$12	under $8

Prices are per person for a main course at dinner.

ABOUT THE HOTELS

Lodging in the area runs the gamut from posh resorts offering windsurfing lessons to rustic cabins in the middle of a forest reserve. The western part of the island near Rincón has a variety of hotels, from furnished apartments geared toward families to colorful small hotels. In the central mountains a few old plantation homes have been turned into wonderful country inns that transport you back to slower and quieter times.

WHAT IT COSTS IN U.S. DOLLARS				
HOTELS FOR TWO PEOPLE				
$$$$	$$$	$$	$	¢
over $350	$250–$350	$150–$250	$80–$150	under $80

Prices are for a double room in high season, excluding 9% tax (11% for hotels with casinos, 7% for paradores) and 5%-12% service charge.

IF YOU LIKE

EATING WELL

If you like seafood, you're in the right place. If you're in Rincón, the Horned Dorset Primavera has one of the most elegant eateries in the Caribbean. But there are plenty of other more casual places, many of them overlooking the ocean, where you can enjoy the catch of the day.

ECOTOURISM

The concept of ecotourism is catching on in Puerto Rico. Not surprisingly, many outfits are based in Rincón and center around trips to Mona Island. This protected island has world-class diving as well

as a series of trails that wind their way along the edge of steep cliffs.

SURFING

The waves of northwestern Puerto Rico have long served as siren-song for traveling surfers. Rincón first drew international attention when it hosted the World Surfing Championship in 1968. Other areas on the north coast, such as Aguadilla, have impressive waves as well. The area around Isabela has some well-known breaks but this stretch of coast can reveal some hidden gems to those willing to explore a little.

TIMING

In winter the weather is at its best, but you'll have to compete with other visitors for hotel rooms; book well in advance. Winter is also the height of the surfing season on the west coast. In summer many family-oriented hotels fill up with *Sanjuaneros* escaping the city for the weekend—some hotels require a two-night stay. Larger resorts normally drop their rates in summer by at least 10%. The weather gets hot, especially in August and September, but the beaches help keep everyone cool.

RINCÓN

● *150 km (93 mi) southwest of San Juan*

Jutting out into the ocean along the rugged western coast, Rincón, meaning "corner" in Spanish, may have gotten its name because of how it's nestled in a corner of the coastline. Some, however, trace the town's name to Gonzalo Rincón, a 16th-century landowner who let poor families live on his land. Whatever the history, the name suits the town, which is like a little world unto itself.

The most famous hotel in the region is the Horned Dorset Primavera—the only Relais & Chateaux property in Puerto Rico. It's one of the most luxurious resorts on the island, not to mention the Caribbean. A couple of larger hotels have been built, but Rincón remains a laid-back place. The town is still a mecca for wave-seekers, particularly surfers from the East Coast of the United States, who can make the relatively quick flight to Aguadilla airport direct from New York–area airports instead of the long haul to the Pacific. The town continues to cater to all sorts of travelers, from budget-conscious surfers to families to honeymooners seeking romance.

For divers, **Desecheo Island,** about 20 km (13 mi) off the coast of Rincón, has abundant reef and fish life. A rocky bottom sloping to 120 feet rims the island; one formation known as Yellow Reef is distinguished by long tunnels and caverns covered with purple hydrocoral. There are other sites with plentiful fish and coral in the shallower water just off Rincón's shores.

★ About 50 mi off the coast, **Mona Island** sits brooding in the Atlantic Ocean. Known as the Galápagos of the Caribbean, the 14,000-acre island has long been a destination for adventurous travelers. It's said to have been settled by the Taíno and visited by both Christopher Columbus and Juan Ponce de León. Pirates were known to use the small island as a hideout, and legend has it that there is still buried treasure to be found here. Today, however, Mona's biggest lure is its distinctive ecosystem. It's home to a number of endangered species, such as the Mona iguana and leatherback sea turtle. Several tour operators in Rincón offer overnight camping trips to the island; they will help you with the camping permits from the Department of Natural and Environmental Resources. You need to reserve at least a few weeks ahead for an overnight stay on the island. ☏ *787/724–3724 for Department of Natural and Environmental Resources.*

Surrounding the Punta Higuera Lighthouse, **Parque Pasivo El Faro** has small kiosks at the water's edge with telescopes you can use to look for whales. (Have patience, though, even during the "season," from December through February; it could take days to spot one.) You can also glimpse the rusting dome of the defunct Bonus Thermonuclear

Energy Plant from here; it's been closed since 1974, but is being resurrected as a nuclear-energy museum. The park is a nice place to take in sunsets, and there are also benches, a shop, and a refreshment stand on the grounds. The lighthouse is closed to the public, but it's hard to walk away without taking a photo of the stately white structure. Half a block up the street are a playground and a paintball course. ⊠*End of Calle 4413, off Rte. 413* 🎟*Free* ☉*Daily 8* PM–*midnight.*

BEACHES

The best beaches north of Rincón are lined up along Route 413 and Route 4413 (the road to the lighthouse). South of town the only beach worth noting is Playa Córcega, off Route 115. The beaches below are in geographical order, north to south.

Balneario de Rincón. Swimmers can enjoy the tranquil waters at this beach. The beautiful facility has a playground, changing areas, restrooms, and a clubhouse. It's within walking distance of the center of town. Parking is $2. ⊠*Rte. 115.*

Domes. Named for the eerie green domes on a nearby power plant, this beach is extremely popular with surfers. It's also a great whale-watching spot in winter. To get here, head north on Route 4413. The beach is just north of the lighthouse. ⊠*Rte. 4413, north of lighthouse.*

Maria's. This surf spot, south of Domes, can get crowded when the waves are high. It's popular with locals, as much for its breakers as for its proximity to the Calypso Café. To get here, look for the street sign reading SURFER CROSSING. ⊠*Rte. 4413, south of lighthouse.*

Playa Córcega. The long stretch of yellow sand in front of Villa Cofresí is considered one of the best swimming beaches in Rincón. ⊠*Rte. 115. Km 12.0.*

Steps. A set of concrete steps sitting mysteriously at the water's edge gives this beach its name. The waves here can get huge. It's hard to find—look for the turnoff at a whale-shape sign indicating PLAYA ESCALERA. ⊠*Rte. 413, north of turnoff for Black Eagle Marina.*

Tres Palmas. When the surf is on here—which may be only a handful of days each year, at best—this epic wave spot is one of the world's best. At other times, it's an excellent

5

snorkeling spot. It's on the same road as Steps. ⊠*Rte. 413,
north of turnoff for Black Eagle Marina.*

WHERE TO EAT

In addition to the restaurants recommended below, the
Villa Confresí and the Lazy Parrot hotels also have good
restaurants serving fresh seafood.

$–$$ ✕ **Rincón Tropical.** Don't be scared off by the cheap plastic
tables and chairs. What you should notice is that they're
almost always full of locals enjoying the area's freshest
seafood. The kitchen keeps it simple, preparing dishes
with the lightest touch. Highlights include the mahimahi
with onions and peppers, or fried red snapper with beans
and rice. Fried plantains make a nice accompaniment to
almost anything. ⊠*Rte. 115, Km 12* ☎787/823–2017
⊟*AE, MC, V.*

$ ✕ **Tamboo.** A bar and grill that doesn't fall too much into
either category, this restaurant with an open-air kitchen
prepares any number of unusual items, from king crab
sandwiches to chicken and basil wraps. The bar, also open
to the elements, serves a mean margarita. Happy hour
sometimes starts dangerously early—at 10 AM on Saturday. The deck is a great place to watch the novice surfers
wipe out on the nearby beach. An added plus: free wireless
Internet. ⊠*Beside the Pointe, Rte. 413, Km 4.7, Rincón*
☎787/823–3210 ⊟*MC, V.*

WHERE TO STAY

★ **Fodor's**Choice ⊠ **Horned Dorset Primavera.** This is, without a
$$$$ doubt, one of the finest hotels on the island. The 22 whitewashed villas scattered around throughout the tropical gardens are designed so you have complete privacy whether
you're relaxing in your private plunge pool or admiring
the sunset from one of your balconies. The furnishings in
each of the two-story suites are impeccable, from the hand-
carved mahogany table in the downstairs dining room to
the four-poster beds in the upstairs bedroom. The marble
bathroom has a footed porcelain tub that's big enough
for two. (There's a second bath downstairs that's perfect
for showering off after a walk on the beach.) Breakfast is
served in your room, while lunch is available on a terrace
overlooking the ocean. ⊠*Rte. 429, Km 3, Box 1132, Ron-
cón 00677* ☎787/823–4030, 787/823–4050, or 800/633–

1857 ☎*787/725–6068* ⊕*www.horneddorset.com* ⇆*22 villas* ⌂*In-room: safe, kitchen, no TV. In-hotel: restaurant, bar, pools, gym, beachfront, no kids under 12* ⊟*AE, MC, V* ⦿*EP.*

$$–$$$ ▨**Rincón Beach Resort.** Part of the allure of this ocean-front hotel is that it's a bit off the beaten path. The South Seas–style decor begins in the high-ceilinged lobby, where hand-carved chaises invite you to enjoy the view through the almond trees. The rooms continue the theme with rich fabrics and dark-wood furnishings. A variety of activities are available, including whale- and turtle-watching in season. At the end of the infinity pool a boardwalk leads down to the sand. Unlike many of the beaches just a few miles north, the waters here are calm—not great for surfing, but perfect for a dip. The resort is tucked away in Añasco, about halfway between Rincón to the north and Mayagüez to the south. ⊠*Rte. 115, Km 5.8, Añasco 00610* ☎*787/589–9000* ☏*787/589–9010* ⊕*www.rinconbeach. com* ⇆*112 rooms* ⌂*In-room: safe, kitchen (some), refrigerator, dial-up. In-hotel: restaurant, room service, bars, pool, gym, beachfront, diving, water sports, public Internet, parking (no fee)* ⊟*AE, D, DC, MC, V* ⦿*EP.*

$–$$ ▨**Casa Isleña.** With its barrel-tiled roofs, wall-enclosed gardens, and open-air dining room, Casa Isleña might remind well-traveled souls of a villa on the coast of Mexico. The secret of its charm is that this little inn retains a simplicity without compromising the romantic flavor of its setting. Several of the terra-cotta-floored rooms have balconies that overlook the pool and the palm-shaded stretch of beach. Others have terraces that face the courtyard. There's also a hot tub and an indoor patio with a soothing, burbling fountain. ⊠*Rte. 413, Km 4.8, Barrio Puntas, Rincón 00677* ☎*787/823–1525 or 888/289–7750* ☏*787/823–1530* ⊕*www.casa-islena.com* ⇆*9 rooms* ⌂*In-room: refrigerator (some). In-hotel: restaurant, pool, beachfront, water sports, parking (no fee), no elevator* ⊟*AE, MC, V* ⦿*EP.*

$ ▨**Lazy Parrot.** Painted an eye-popping shade of pink, this
★ mountainside hotel doesn't take itself too seriously. Colorful murals of the eponymous bird brighten the open and airy lobby. The accommodations are a bit more subdued, though they continue the tropical theme. (The Dolphin Room has—what else?—a stuffed dolphin.) Each has a balcony where you can enjoy the view. There are two restaurants that share a similar theme—Sloppy Joe's on the lower

level serves sandwiches and other light fare, while Smilin' Joe's upstairs serves red snapper and other excellent seafood dishes. At the bar you can sample a parrot-theme concoction. ⊠*Rte. 413, Km 4.1, Rincón 00677* ☎*787823–5654 or 800/294–1752* ☎*787/823–0224* ⊕*www.lazyparrot.com* ➯*11 rooms* ⌂*In-room: refrigerator. In-hotel: 2 restaurants, bars, pool, no elevator* ⊟*AE, D, MC, V* ⭘❙*CP.*

¢ ☒**Rincón Surf & Board.** All the rooms have surfboard racks, which should give you a clue as to who is drawn to this out-of-the-way guesthouse. Two hostel-type rooms with bunk beds—remains of the original lodging concept—are available at $20 per person. One- to three-bed private rooms are ample in size and have a clean and fresh feel; some are like small apartments. All rooms have their own surf racks. Common areas are fun and friendly but not conducive to late-night partying, as the best surfing is for the early birds. ⊠*Off Rte. 413, Barrio Puntas, Rincón 00677* ☎*787/823– 0610* ☎*787/823–6440* ⊕*www.surfandboard.com* ➯*13 rooms, 2 hostel rooms* ⌂*In-room: refrigerator (some). In-hotel: restaurant, pool, beachfront, water sports, parking (no fee), no elevator* ⊟*AE, MC, V* ⭘❙*EP.*

NIGHTLIFE

Rincón attracts a younger crowd, so there are plenty of options for fun after dark. On weekends the **Calypso Café** (⊠*Rte. 4413, Maria's Beach* ☎*787/823–4151*) often has live rock-and-roll bands. The open-air establishment, more bar than grill, is also a good place to go after you've had your fill of the beach. Don't miss the second floor of the **Sandy Beach Surf Club** (⊠*Rte. 413, Km 4.3, Sandy Beach* ☎*787/823–1146*), which has a fantastic view of the town's lights.

SPORTS & THE OUTDOORS

DIVING & SNORKELING

Most of the region's dive operators also run fishing charters around Desecheo Island and whale-watching trips in season.

Along with organizing whale-watching trips, **Moondog Charters** (⊠*Black Eagle Marina, off Rte. 413* ☎*787/823– 3059* ⊕*www.moondogcharters.com*) will take a minimum of four people on a snorkeling or diving trip to Desecheo

Island. Prices are from \$45 to \$95 per person. The company also does fishing charters. **Oceans Unlimited** (✉*Rte. 115, Km 11.9* ☎787/823–2340) has snorkeling trips for \$50, including lunch. The company also offers day trips to Desecheo Island and Mona Island. **Taíno Divers** (✉*Black Eagle Marina, off Rte. 413, Rincón* ☎787/823–6429 ⊕*www.tainodivers.com*) has daily diving trips that cost \$79, including lunch. It also has daily trips to Desecheo Island, charters to Mona Island, and scuba PADI certification courses.

SURFING

Desecheo Surf & Dive Shop (✉*Rte. 413, Km 2.5* ☎787/823–0390) rents a variety of short and long surfboards (\$25 to \$30 a day). The company also organizes diving and snorkeling trips and rents Jet Skis. **Rincón Surf School** (✉*Rte. 413, Rincón* ☎787/823–0610 ⊕*www.surfandboard.com*) offers full-day lessons that include board rental and transportation. You can also arrange two-, three-, and five-day surfing seminars. Boards can be rented for \$20 without lesson.

SHOPPING

Eco-Logic-Co (✉*Parque Pasivo El Faro, end of Rte. 413* ☎787/823–1252) has fun and ecologically oriented souvenirs.

AGUADILLA

❷ *18 km (12 mi) north of Rincón*

Resembling a fishing village, downtown Aguadilla has narrow streets lined with small wooden homes. Weathered but lovely, the faded facades recall the city's long and turbulent past. Officially incorporated as a town in 1775, Aguadilla subsequently suffered a series of catastrophes, including a devastating earthquake in 1918 and strong hurricanes in 1928 and 1932. Determined to survive, the town was rebuilt after each disaster, and by World War II it became known for the sprawling Ramey Air Force Base. The base was an important link in the U.S. defense system throughout the Cold War. Ramey was decommissioned in 1973; today the former base has an airport, a golf course, and some small businesses, although many structures stand empty.

Along Route 107—an unmarked road crossing through a golf course—you can find the ruins of **La Ponderosa**, an old Spanish lighthouse, as well as its replacement Punta Borinquen at Puerto Rico's northwest point. The original was built in 1889 and destroyed by an earthquake in 1918. The U.S. Coast Guard rebuilt the structure in 1920. ⊠*Rte. 107.*

BEACHES

★ Fodor'sChoice **Playa Crashboat.** This is where you can find the colorful fishing boats that are found on postcards all over the island. Named after rescue boats used when Ramey Air Force Base was in operation, this *balneario* has picnic huts, showers, parking, and restrooms. ⊠*Off Rte. 458.*

Playa Gas Chamber. This beach with crashing waves is favored by surfers. ⊠*Rte. 107, north of Playa Crashboat.*

Playa Wilderness. This undeveloped beach north of Playa Gas Chamber is recommended only for experienced surfers, as it can have dangerous breaks. ⊠*Rte. 107, north of Playa Gas Chamber.*

WHERE TO STAY & EAT

$ ×▥**Hotel Cielomar.** Just north of the town of Aguadilla, this hotel is perched on a bluff high above the water. The good news is that nearly every room has a jaw-dropping view of the coastline; the bad news is that the beach is far, far away. The accommodations are comfortable, if a bit old-fashioned. The hotel's restaurant, El Bohío ($–$$), specializes in lobster, as well as other types of seafood. The open-air dining room is extremely pleasant, especially in the evening. There's often live music on weekends. ⊠*84 Av. Montemar, off Rte. 111, 00605* ☎*787/882–5959 or 787/882–5961* 📠*787/882–5577* @*www.cielomar.com* ⤶*72 rooms* ⚬*In-room: refrigerator. In-hotel: restaurant, bar, pool* ▤*AE, MC, V* ⦿*EP.*

SPORTS & THE OUTDOORS

DIVING & SNORKELING
Near Gate 5 of the old Ramey Air Force Base, **Aquatica Underwater Adventures** (⊠*Rte. 110, Km 10* ☎*787/890–6071*) offers scuba-diving certification courses as well as snorkeling and surfing trips. You can also rent any gear

you need. It's open Monday through Saturday from 9 to 5, Sunday from 9 to 3.

GOLF

The 18-hole **Punta Borinquen Golf Course** (⊠*Rte. 107, Km 2* ☎*787/890–2987* ⊕*www.puntaborinquengolfclub.com*), on the former Ramey Air Force Base, was a favorite of President Dwight D. Eisenhower. Now a public course, the beachfront course is known for its tough sand traps and strong crosswinds. The course is open daily. Greens fees are $20 to $22.

SABELA

❸ *20 km (13 mi) east of Aguadilla.*

Founded in 1819 and named for Spain's Queen Isabella, this small, whitewashed town on the northwesternmost part of the island skirts tall cliffs that overlook the rocky shoreline. Locals have long known of the area's natural beauty, and lately more and more offshore tourists have begun coming to this niche, which offers secluded hotels, fantastic beaches, and, just inland, hiking through one of the island's forest reserves.

Explore karst topography and subtropical vegetation at the 2,357-acre **Bosque Estatal Guajataca** *(Guajataca State Forest)* between the towns of Quebradillas and Isabela. On more than 46 walking trails you can see 186 species of trees, including the royal palm and ironwood, and 45 species of birds—watch for red-tailed hawks and Puerto Rican woodpeckers. Bring a flashlight and descend into the **Cueva del Viento** to find stalagmites, stalactites, and other strange formations. At the entrance to the forest there's a small ranger station where you can pick up a decent hiking map. (Get here early, as the rangers don't always stay until the official closing time.) A little farther down the road is a recreational area with picnic tables and an observation tower. ⊠*Rte. 446, Km 10* ☎*787/872–1045* ⊠*Free* ☉*Ranger station weekdays 8–5.*

BEACHES

Playa de Guajataca. Stretching by what is called El Tunel—part of an old tunnel used by a passenger and cargo train that ran from San Juan to Ponce from the early to mid-1900s—this beach is lined with kiosks selling local snacks

The Abominable Chupacabra

The Himalayas have their Yeti, Britain has its crop circles, New Jersey has its legendary Jersey Devil…and Puerto Rico has its Chupacabra. This "goat sucker" (as its name translates) has been credited with strange attacks on goats, sheep, rabbits, horses, and chickens since the mid-1970s. The attacks happen mostly at night, leaving the animals devoid of blood, with oddly vampirelike punctures in their necks.

Though the first references to these attacks were in the 1970s, the biggest surge of reports dates to the mid-1990s, when the mayor of Canóvanas received international attention and support from local police for his weekly search parties equipped with a caged goat as bait.

Sightings offer widely differing versions of the Chupacabra; it has gray, scraggly hair and resembles a kangaroo or wolf, or walks upright on three-toed feet. Some swear it hops from tree branch to tree branch, and even flies, leaving behind, in the tradition of old Lucifer, the acrid stench of sulfur. It peers through large, oval, sometimes red eyes, and "smells like a wet dog" as its reptilian tongue flicks the night air. It has, according to some, attacked humans, ripped through window screens, and jumped family dogs at picnics.

According to a 1995 article in the *San Juan Star*, island lore abounds with monsters predating the Chupacabra. The *comecogollo* was a version of bigfoot—but smaller and a vegetarian. In the early 1970s the Moca vampire also attacked small animals, but opinion differed on whether it was alien, animal, or really a vampire. The *garadiablo*, a swamp creature that emerged from the ooze at night to wreak havoc on the populace also struck fear in the early 1970s. This "sea demon" was described as having the face of a bat, the skin of a shark, and a humanlike body.

The Chupacabra has also been active in other spots. The list of reported sightings at ⊕ *www.elchupacabra.com* includes such unlikely locales as Maine and Missouri. And the Chupa's coverage on the Web isn't limited to sci-fi fan sites: Princeton University maintains a Web site meant to be a clearinghouse for Chupa information, and the beast's story appears on the Learning Channel's site at ⊕ *tlc.com*.

–Karl Luntta

and souvenirs. On weekends you can hear live music playing around the area. Just before El Tunel is El Merendero de Guajataca, a picnic area with cliffside trails for a spectacular view of the coastline. ⊠*Off Rte. 113.*

Playa de Jobos. This beach is famous for surfing, but it can have dangerous breaks. On the same stretch there are a couple of restaurants with oceanfront decks serving light fare and drinks. Down the road, the dunes and long stretches of golden sand are gorgeous for walks or running. Route 466 runs parallel, and there are narrow accesses to the beach scattered all along the road. ⊠*Rte. 466.*

Playa Montones. Not far from Playa de Jobos on Route 466, this is a beautiful beach for swimming and frolicking in the sand; it has a natural protected pool where children can splash safely. An outcropping of coral creates a huge wave spray on the ocean side. ⊠*Rte. 466.*

Playa de Shacks is known for its surfing and horseback riding. It also has an area called the Blue Hole, which is popular with divers. ⊠*Rte. 4446.*

WHERE TO EAT

In addition to the restaurant listed below, the restaurants at Villa Montaña and Villas del Mar Hau are known for having good food.

ECLECTIC

$-$$ ×**Happy Belly's.** In the mood for a hamburger or club sandwich? Then this laid-back restaurant is a good choice. The seating is in comfortable wooden booths that overlook Playa Jobos—but the wind that whips up the waves may also blow away your napkin. In the evening the menu changes to more substantial fare, with everything from shrimp scampi to baby back ribs. Many people just come for the socializing and the sunsets. ⊠*Rte. 4466, Km 7.5, Isabela* ☏787/872–6566 ⊟*AE, MC, V.*

WHERE TO STAY

$$-$$$ ⌷**Villa Montaña.** On a deserted stretch of beach between Isabela and Aguadilla, this secluded cluster of villas feels like its own little town. You can pull your car into your own garage, then head upstairs to your airy studio or

one-, two-, or three-bedroom suite with hand-carved mahogany furniture and canopy beds. Studios have kitchenettes, while the larger villas have full-size kitchens and laundry rooms. Eclipse ($$–$$$$), the open-air bar and restaurant, serves Caribbean-Asian fusion cuisine. Dishes include a tasty seafood risotto. Playa de Shacks, a popular beach, is nearby. ⊠*Rte. 4446, Km 1.9, Box 530, Isabela 00662* ☎*787/872–9554 or 888/780–9195* 🖷*787/872– 9553* ⊕*www.villamontana.com* ⌇*56 villas* ⌂*In-room: DVD. In-hotel: restaurant, tennis courts, pools, gym, beachfront, laundry facilities* ⊟*AE, D, MC, V* ⦿*EP.*

$–$$ ⓧ**Villas del Mar Hau.** The accommodations here aren't luxurious, but if you're looking for an unpretentious atmosphere, you'll have a hard time doing better than this small, beachfront resort. One-, two-, and three-bedroom cottages are painted in cheery pastels and trimmed with gingerbread. If you're planning on cooking, you should consider one of the studios, all of which have full kitchens. Otherwise, the open-air Olas y Arena restaurant is known for its excellent fish and shellfish; the paella is especially good. The hotel also has a stable of horses reserved for guests. ⊠*Rte. 4466, Km 8.3, Box 510, Isabela 00662* ☎*787/872–2045 or 787/872–2627* 🖷*787/872–0273* ⊕*www.paradorvillas- delmarhau.com* ⌇*40 rooms* ⌂*In-room: kitchen (some). In-hotel: restaurant, tennis court, pool, laundry facilities, no elevator* ⊟*AE, MC, V* ⦿*EP.*

SPORTS & THE OUTDOORS

DIVING & SNORKELING

Beginning and advanced divers can explore the submerged caves off Playa Shacks through **La Cueva Submarina Dive Shop** (⊠*Rte. 466, Km 6.3* ☎*787/872–1390* ⊕*www.lacuevasub marina.com*), which also offers certification courses and snorkeling trips.

HORSEBACK RIDING

Tropical Trail Rides (⊠*Rte. 4466, Km 1.9* ☎*787/872–9256* ⊕*www.tropicaltrailrides.com*) has two-hour morning and afternoon rides along the beach and through a forest of almond trees. Groups leave from Playa Shacks.

ARECIBO

④ *60 km (38 mi) west of Dorado.*

As you approach Arecibo on Highway 22, you see its white buildings glistening in the sun against an ocean backdrop. The town was founded in 1515 and is known as the "Villa of Captain Correa" because of a battle fought here by Captain Antonio Correa and a handful of Spanish soldiers to repel a British sea invasion in 1702. Today it's a busy manufacturing center, and serves as a link for visits to two of the island's most fascinating sights—the Parque de las Cavernas del Río Camuy and the Observatorio de Arecibo, both south of the city—and for deeper exploration of the central mountain region. For one of the best ocean drives on the island, get off the main road at Barceloneta and take Route 681 into Arecibo's waterfront district.

☺ A beautiful example of Spanish colonial architecture, the **Faro de Arecibo** *(Arecibo Lighthouse)* is among the loveliest on the island. Dating from 1897, it sits on a bluff high above Arecibo. Although the museum inside the lighthouse has maritime treasure that will interest everyone in your group, the rest of the park is strictly kid stuff. There are scaled-down replicas of Christopher Columbus's *Niña, Pinta,* and *Santa María* and replicas of the huts used by the island's original inhabitants, the Taíno Indians. On weekends, groups in traditional costumes play live music; there's a café with a sitting area where you can watch the revelry. Follow the signs from Highway 2. ⊠*End of Rte. 655, off Rte. 681* ☎*787/817–1936* ☎*$9* ☺*Weekdays 9–6, weekends 10–7.*

★ **Fodor's**Choice Hidden among pine-covered hills is the **Observatorio de Arecibo,** the world's largest radar–radio telescope. Operated by the National Astronomy and Ionosphere Center of Cornell University, the 20-acre dish lies in a 563-foot-deep sinkhole in the karst landscape. If the 600-ton platform hovering eerily over the dish looks familiar, it may be because it can be glimpsed in scenes from the movie *Contact.* (And yes, the dish has been used to seach for extraterrestrial life.) You can walk around the viewing platform and explore two levels of interactive exhibits on planetary systems, meteors, and weather phenomena in the visitor center. ⊠*Rte. 625, Km 3.0* ☎*787/878–2612* ⊕*www.naic. edu* ☎*$5* ☺*Wed.–Fri. noon–4, weekends 9–4.*

★ Fodor'sChoice The 268-acre **Parque de las Cavernas del Río Camuy** contains one of the world's largest cave networks. A tram takes you down a trail shaded by bamboo and banana trees to Cueva Clara, where the stalactites and stalagmites turn the entrance into a toothy grin. Hour-long guided tours in English and Spanish lead you on foot through the 180-foot-high cave, which is teeming with wildlife. You're likely to see blue-eyed river crabs and long-legged tarantulas. More elusive are the more than 100,000 bats that make their home in the cave. They don't come out until dark, but you can feel the heat they generate at the cave's entrance. The visit ends with a tram ride to Tres Pueblos sinkhole, where you can see the third-longest underground river in the world passing from one cave to another. Tours are first-come, first-served; plan to arrive early on weekends, when local families join the crowds. Tours are sometimes canceled if it's raining, as the steep walkways can get slippery. There's a picnic area, cafeteria, and gift shop. ⊠*Rte. 129, Km 18.9* ☎*787/898–3100* ⊕*www.parques nacionalespr.com* ⊑*$12* ⊗*Wed.–Sun. 8:30–3:45.*

WHERE TO EAT

$–$$ ✕**El Buen Café.** Halfway between Arecibo and Hatillo, this no-frills diner is packed with locals, especially on weekends. You can sit at the curvy counter or at one of the cozy booths. A favorite dish on the long menu is *carne mechada* (stuffed pot roast). Breakfast is served starting at 5 AM. ⊠*381 Hwy. 2, Km 84, Hatillo* ☎*787/898–3495* ⊟*AE, MC, V.*

RINCÓN & THE PORTA DEL SOL ESSENTIALS

To research prices, get advice from other travelers, and book travel arrangements, visit www.fodors.com.

TRANSPORTATION

BY AIR

Aguadilla is a convenient gateway to western Puerto Rico, thanks to several daily international flights. Continental Airlines flies from Newark to Aguadilla, and jetBlue has daily service from New York–JFK and Orlando to Aguadilla. American Eagle and Cape Air fly between San Juan and Mayagüez.

Information **American Airlines/American Eagle** (☎*800/433–7300* ⊕*www.aa.com*). **Cape Air** (☎*800/525–0280* ⊕*www.flycapeair.com*). **Continental** (☎*800/231–0856* ⊕*www.continental.com*). **JetBlue** (☎*800/538–2583* ⊕*www.jetblue.com*).

AIRPORTS & TRANSFERS

Aguadilla's Aeropuerto Internacional Rafael Hernández (BQN) is on the old Ramey Air Force Base. The renovated structure, as modern as any on the island, has a tourist information office, car-rental agencies, and a handy ATM. Tiny Aeropuerto Eugenio María de Hostos (MAZ), just north of Mayagüez on Highway 2, looks a bit like a strip mall. There's little inside besides the car-rental counters and a handy ATM. There are no airport shuttles in either Aguadilla or Mayagüez. A taxi from either airport into town is about $6 to $10, but if you're going any farther, you should rent a car.

Information **Aeropuerto Eugenio María de Hostos** (✉*Hwy. 2, Km 148.7, Mayagüez* ☎*787/833–0148 or 787/265–7065*). **Aeropuerto Internacional Rafael Hernández** (✉*Hwy. 2, Km 148.7, Aguadilla* ☎*787/891–2286*).

BY BUS & VAN

Choferes Unidos travels from San Juan to Aguadilla for about $10 per person. Linea Sultana has vans from San Juan to Mayagüez that also drop off passengers along Highway 2 in Aguada, Quebradillas, and Isabela; the price is about $12 per person.

Information **Choferes Unidos** (☎*787/751–7622*). **Linea Sultana** (☎*787/765–9377*).

BY CAR

You really need a car to see northwestern Puerto Rico, especially the mountain area. The toll road, Highway 22, makes it easy to reach Arecibo from San Juan. Highway 22 turns into Highway 2 just after Arecibo, swings by the northwestern tip of the island, then heads south to Rincón.

If you're not flying into San Juan, you can rent a car in Aguadilla or Mayagüez. Prices vary from $35 to $65 per day.

Information **Avis** (☎*787/890–3311 in Aguadilla, 787/832–0406 in Mayagüez*). **Budget** (☎*787/890–1110 in Aguadilla, 787/823–4570 in*

Mayagüez). **Hertz** (☎ 787/890–5650 *in Aguadilla, 787/879–1132 in Arecibo, 787/832–3314 in Mayagüez*). **L & M Rent a Car** (☎ 787/890–3010 *in Aguadilla*). **Leaseway of Puerto Rico** (☎ 787/833–1140 *in Mayagüez*). **Thrifty** (☎ 787/834–1590 *in Mayagüez*).

CONTACTS & RESOURCES

BANKS & EXCHANGE SERVICES

Banks are plentiful in larger cities, and smaller towns usually have at least one; banks are sometimes attached to grocery stores. All banks have ATMs (called ATHs), and many businesses accept ATM cards. If you need to change money into U.S. dollars, you can do that in banks in either Aguadilla or Rincón.

Information **Banco Popular** (✉ *Calle Mercedes Moreno, corner of Munoz Rivera, Aguadilla* ☎ 787/891–2085 ✉ *13 Av. Agustín Ramos Calero, Isabela* ☎ 787/872–3100 ✉ *1 Calle Commercio, Rincón* ☎ 787/823–2055).

INTERNET, MAIL & SHIPPING

Getting connected is a bit difficult in this part of the island. Most lodgings don't have any way for you to get online. There are only a handful of Internet cafés. The best bet is Cowabunga's, an ice-cream shop in Rincón. It's open Tuesday to Sunday noon to 9.

Larger towns like Arecibo have a main post office with smaller branches throughout the city. You can often buy stamps in grocery and drug stores. Generally, post offices are open weekdays from 7 or 8 AM until 5 or 6 PM and for a few hours Saturday morning.

Internet Cafés **Cowabunga's** (✉ *Rte. 115, Km 11.6, Rincón* ☎ 787/823–5225).

VISITOR INFORMATION

The Puerto Rico Tourism Company has an office at the Rafael Hernández Airport in Aguadilla. The town of Rincón has a tourism office on Route 115; it's open weekdays from 9 to 4.

Information **Arecibo City Hall** (☎ 787/879–2232). **Puerto Rico Tourism Company** (✉ *Rafael Hernández Airport, Aguadilla* ☎ 787/890–3315). **Rincón Tourism Office** (✉ *Rte. 115, Rincón* ☎ 787/823–5024).

Puerto Rico Essentials

PLANNING TOOLS, EXPERT INSIGHT, GREAT CONTACTS

There are planners and there are those who, excuse the pun, fly by the seat of their pants. We happily place ourselves among the planners. Our writers and editors try to anticipate all the issues you may face before and during any journey, and then they do their research. This section is the product of their efforts. Use it to get excited about your trip to Puerto Rico, to inform your travel planning, or to guide you on the road should the seat of your pants start to feel threadbare.

www.fodors.com/forums

GETTING STARTED

We're proud of our Web site: Fodors.com is a great place to begin any journey. Scan Travel Wire for suggested itineraries, travel deals, restaurant and hotel openings, and other up-to-the-minute info. Check out Booking to research prices and book plane tickets, hotel rooms, rental cars, and vacation packages. Head to Talk for on-the-ground pointers from travelers who frequent our message boards. You can also link to loads of other travel-related resources.

▌ RESOURCES

ONLINE TRAVEL TOOLS

ALL ABOUT PUERTO RICO

You can get basic information about Puerto Rico from ⊕*www. puertoricowow.com* and ⊕*www. gotopuertorico.com.* Maps are available at ⊕*www.travelmaps. com.* For information on conferences and conventions, see the Puerto Rico Convention Center Web site at ⊕*www.prconvention.com* or the Puerto Rico Convention Bureau at ⊕*www. meetpuertorico.com.*

VISITOR INFORMATION

In addition to the Puerto Rico Tourism Company's *Qué Pasa,* pick up the Puerto Rico Hotel and Tourism Association's *Bienvenidos* and *Places to Go.* Among them you can find a wealth of information about the island and its activities. All are free and available at tourism offices and hotel desks. The Puerto Rico Tourism Company has information centers at the airport, Old San Juan, Ponce, Aguadilla, and Cabo Rojo. Most island towns also have a tourism office in their city hall.

Contacts Puerto Rico Tourism Company (⊕www.gotopuertorico. com ⊡Box 902–3960, Old San Juan Station, San Juan 00902-3960 ☎787/721–2400 or 800/866–7827 ✉666 5th Ave., 15th fl., New York, NY 10103 ☎212/586–6262 or 800/223–6530 ✉3575 W. Cahuenga Blvd., Suite 560, Los Angeles, CA 90068 ☎213/874–5991 or 800/874–1330 ✉901 Ponce de León Blvd., Suite 101, Coral Gables, FL 33134 ☎305/445–9112 or 800/815–7391).

▌ THINGS TO CONSIDER

PASSPORTS & VISAS

U.S. citizens don't need passports to visit Puerto Rico; any government-issued photo ID will do. Nor is there is passport control either to or from Puerto Rico; in is respect, flying here is just like traveling on any domestic flight. Nevertheless, it's always wise to carry some form of identification that proves your citizenship, and we still recommend that you carry a valid passport when traveling to Puerto Rico; it's a necessity if you're making any other trips around the Caribbean, except to the U.S. Virgin Islands, where you will pass through customs but not passport control.

TRIP INSURANCE

What kind of coverage do you honestly need? Do you need trip insurance at all? Take a deep breath and read on.

We believe that comprehensive trip insurance is especially valuable if you're booking a very expensive or complicated trip (particularly to an isolated region) or if you're booking far in advance. Who knows what could happen six months down the road? But whether you get insurance has more to do with how comfortable you are assuming all that risk yourself.

Comprehensive travel policies typically cover trip-cancellation and interruption, letting you cancel or cut your trip short because of a personal emergency, illness, or, in some cases, acts of terrorism in your destination. Such policies also cover evacuation and medical care. Some also cover you for trip delays because of bad weather or mechanical problems as well as for lost or delayed baggage. Another type of coverage to look for is financial default—that is, when your trip is disrupted because a tour operator, airline, or cruise line goes out of business. Generally you must buy this when you book your trip or shortly thereafter, and it's only available to you if your operator isn't on a list of excluded companies.

If you're going abroad, consider buying medical-only coverage at the very least. Neither Medicare nor some private insurers cover medical expenses anywhere outside of the United States (including time aboard a cruise ship, even if it leaves from a U.S. port). Medical-only policies typically reimburse you for medical care (excluding that related to preexisting conditions) and hospitalization abroad, and provide for evacuation. You still have to pay the bills and await reimbursement from the insurer, though.

Expect comprehensive travel insurance policies to cost about 4% to 7% or 8% of the total price of your trip (it's more like 8%–12% if you're over age 70). A medical-only policy may or may not be cheaper than a comprehensive policy. Always read the fine print of your policy to make sure that you're covered for the risks that are of most concern to you. Compare several policies to make sure you're getting the best price and range of coverage available.

Trip Insurance Resources

INSURANCE COMPARISON SITES		
Insure My Trip.com	800/487–4722	www.insuremytrip.com
Square Mouth.com	800/240–0369	www.quotetravelinsurance.com
Comprehensive Travel Insurers		
Access America	866/807–3982	www.accessamerica.com
CSA Travel Protection	800/873–9855	www.csatravelprotection.com
HTH Worldwide	610/254–8700 or 888/243–2358	www.hthworldwide.com
Travelex Insurance	888/457–4602	www.travelex-insurance.com
Travel Guard International	715/345–0505 or 800/826–4919	www.travelguard.com
Travel Insured International	800/243–3174	www.travelinsured.com
MEDICAL-ONLY INSURERS		
International Medical Group	800/628–4664	www.imglobal.com
International SOS	215/942–8000 or 713/521–7611	www.internationalsos.com
Wallach & Company	800/237–6615 or 504/687–3166	www.wallach.com

BOOKING YOUR TRIP

Unless your cousin is a travel agent, you're probably among the millions of people who make most of their travel arrangements online.

But have you ever wondered just what the differences are between an online travel agent (a Web site through which you make reservations instead of going directly to the airline, hotel, or car-rental company), a discounter (a firm that does a high volume of business with a hotel chain or airline and accordingly gets good prices), a wholesaler (one that makes cheap reservations in bulk and then resells them to people like you), and an aggregator (one that compares all the offerings so you don't have to)?

▌ONLINE

You really have to shop around. A travel wholesaler such as Hotels.com or HotelClub.net can be a source of good rates, as can discounters such as Hotwire or Priceline, particularly if you can bid for your hotel room or airfare. Indeed, such sites sometimes have deals that are unavailable elsewhere. They do, however, tend to work only with hotel chains (which makes them just plain useless for getting hotel reservations outside of major cities) or big airlines (so that often leaves out upstarts like jetBlue

and some foreign carriers like Air India).

Also, with discounters and wholesalers you must generally prepay, and everything is non-refundable. And before you fork over the dough, be sure to check the terms and conditions, so you know what a given company will do for you if there's a problem and what you'll have to deal with on your own.

■TIP→ **To be absolutely sure everything was processed correctly, confirm reservations made through online travel agents, discounters, and wholesalers directly with your hotel before leaving home.**

Booking engines like Expedia, Travelocity, and Orbitz are actually travel agents, albeit high-volume, online ones. And airline travel packagers like American Airlines Vacations and Virgin Vacations—well, they're travel agents, too. But they may still not work with all the world's hotels.

An aggregator site will search many sites and pull the best prices for airfares, hotels, and rental cars from them. Most aggregators compare the major travel-booking sites such as Expedia, Travelocity, and Orbitz; some also look at airline Web sites, though rarely the sites of smaller budget airlines. Some aggregators also compare other travel products, including complex packages—a good thing, as you can sometimes get the best over-all deal by booking an air-and-hotel package.

WITH A TRAVEL AGENT

If you use an agent—brick-and-mortar or virtual—you'll usually pay a fee for the service. And know that the service you get from some online agents isn't comprehensive. For example Expedia and Travelocity don't search for prices on budget airlines like jetBlue, Southwest, or small foreign carriers. That said, some agents (online or not) *do* have access to fares that are difficult to find otherwise, and the savings can more than make up for any surcharge.

A knowledgeable brick-and-mortar travel agent can be a godsend if you're booking a package trip that's not available to you directly, an air pass, or a complicated itinerary including several overseas flights. What's more, travel agents that specialize in a destination may have exclusive access to certain deals and insider information on things such as charter flights. Agents who specialize in types of travelers (senior citizens, gays and lesbians, naturists) or types of trips (cruises, luxury travel, safaris) can also be invaluable.

■TIP➔ Remember that Expedia, Travelocity, and Orbitz are travel agents, not just booking engines. To resolve any problems with a **reservation made through these companies, contact them first.**

Complain about the surcharges all you like, but when things don't work out the way you'd hoped, it's nice to have an agent to put things right.

ACCOMMODATIONS

San Juan's high-rise hotels on the Condado and Isla Verde beach strips cater primarily to the cruise-ship and casino crowd, though several target business travelers. Outside San Juan, particularly on the east coast, you'll find self-contained luxury resorts that cover hundreds of acres. In the west, southwest, and south—as well as on the islands of Vieques and Culebra—smaller inns, villas, condominiums, and government-sponsored *paradores* are the norm.

CATEGORY	COST
$$$$	over $350
$$$	$250–$350
$$	$150–$250
$	$80–$150
¢	under $80

All prices are for a standard double room in high season, based on the European Plan (EP) and excluding 9% tax and service charges.

Most hotels and other lodgings require you to give your credit-card details before they will confirm your reservation. If you don't feel comfortable e-mailing this information, ask if you

Online Booking Resources

AGGREGATORS		
Kayak	www.kayak.com;	also looks at cruises and vacation packages.
Mobissimo	www.mobissimo.com	
Qixo	www.qixo.com	also compares cruises, vacation packages, and even travel insurance.
Sidestep	www.sidestep.com	also compares vacation packages and lists travel deals.
Travelgrove	www.travelgrove.com	also compares cruises and packages.
Booking Engines		
Cheap Tickets	www.cheaptickets.com	a discounter.
Expedia	www.expedia.com	a large online agency that charges a booking fee for airline tickets.
Hotwire	www.hotwire.com	a discounter.
lastminute.com	www.lastminute.com	specializes in last-minute travel the main site is for the U.K., but it has a link to a U.S. site.
Onetravel.com	www.onetravel.com	a discounter for hotels, car rentals, airfares, and packages.
Orbitz	www.orbitz.com	charges a booking fee for airline tickets, but gives a clear breakdown of fees and taxes before you book.
Travel.com	www.travel.com	allows you to compare its rates with those of other booking engines.
Travelocity	www.travelocity.com	charges a booking fee for airline tickets, but promises good problem resolution.
Online Accommodations		
Hotelbook.com	www.hotelbook.com	focuses on independent hotels worldwide.
Hotel Club	www.hotelclub.net	good for major cities worldwide.
Hotels.com	www.hotels.com	a big Expedia-owned wholesaler that offers rooms in hotels all over the world.

can fax it (some places even prefer faxes). However you book, get confirmation in writing and have a copy of it handy when you check in.

Be sure you understand the hotel's cancellation policy. Some places allow you to cancel without any kind of penalty—even if you prepaid to secure a discounted rate—if you cancel at least 24 hours in advance. Others require you to cancel a week in advance or penalize you the cost of one night. Small inns and B&Bs are most likely to require you to cancel far in advance. Most hotels allow children under a certain age to stay in their parents' room at no extra charge, but others charge for them as extra adults; find out the cutoff age for discounts.

■TIP→Assume that hotels operate on the European Plan (EP, no meals) unless we specify that they use the Breakfast Plan (BP, with full breakfast), Continental Plan (CP, Continental breakfast), Full American Plan (FAP, all meals), Modified American Plan (MAP, breakfast and dinner) or are all-inclusive (AI, all meals and most activities).

HOTELS

In the most expensive hotels your room will be large enough for two to move around comfortably, with two double beds (*camas matrimoniales*) or one queen- or king-size bed, air-conditioning (*aire acondicionado*), a phone (*teléfono*), a private bath (*baño particular*), an in-room safe, cable TV, a hair dryer, iron and ironing

board, room service (*servicio de habitación*), shampoo and toiletries, and possibly a view of the water (*vista al mar*). There will be a concierge and at least one hotel restaurant and lounge, a pool, a shop, and an exercise room or spa. In Puerto Rico's smaller inns rooms will have private baths with hot water (*agua caliente*), air-conditioning or fans, a double to king-size bed, possibly room service, and breakfast (Continental or full) included in the rates. In some hotels several rooms share baths—it's a good idea to ask before booking. All hotels listed in this guide have private baths unless otherwise noted.

PARADORES

Some paradores are rural inns offering no-frills apartments, and others are large hotels; all must meet certain standards, such as proximity to an attraction or beach. Most have a small restaurant that serves local cuisine. They're great bargains (from $60 to $125 for a double room). You can make reservations by contacting the Puerto Rico Tourism Company. Small Inns of Puerto Rico, a branch of the Puerto Rico Hotel & Tourism Association, is a marketing arm for some 25 small hotels island-wide. The organization occasionally has package deals including casino coupons and LeLoLai (a cultural show) tickets.

Contacts Puerto Rico Tourism Company (☎787/721–2400 or 800/866–7827 ⊕www.goto paradores.com). **Small Inns of**

Puerto Rico (☎787/725-2901
⊕www.prhtasmallhotels.com).

▌ AIRLINE TICKETS

Most domestic airline tickets are electronic; international tickets may be either electronic or paper. With an e-ticket the only thing you receive is an e-mailed receipt citing your itinerary and reservation and ticket numbers.

The greatest advantage of an e-ticket is that if you lose your receipt, you can simply print out another copy or ask the airline to do it for you at check-in. You usually pay a surcharge (up to $50) to get a paper ticket, if you can get one at all.

The sole advantage of a paper ticket is that it may be easier to endorse over to another airline if your flight is canceled and the airline with which you booked can't accommodate you on another flight.

▌TIP→ Discount air passes that let you travel economically in a country or region must often be purchased before you leave home. In some cases you can only get them through a travel agent.

▌ RENTAL CARS

When you reserve a car, ask about cancellation penalties, taxes, drop-off charges (if you're planning to pick up the car in one city and leave it in another), and surcharges (for being under or over a certain age, for additional drivers, or for driving across state or country borders or beyond a specific distance from your point of rental). All these things can add substantially to your costs. Request car seats and extras such as GPS when you book.

Rates are sometimes—but not always—better if you book in advance or reserve through a rental agency's Web site. There are other reasons to book ahead, though: for popular destinations, during busy times of the year, or to ensure that you get certain types of cars (vans, SUVs, exotic sports cars).

▌TIP→ Make sure that a confirmed reservation guarantees you a car. Agencies sometimes overbook, particularly for busy weekends and holiday periods.

Rates start as low as $35 a day (not including insurance), with unlimited mileage. Discounts are often offered for long-term rentals, for cars that are booked more than 72 hours in advance, and to automobile association members. All major U.S. car-rental agencies are represented on the island, but be sure to look into local companies. Most are reliable and some offer competitive rates.

If you're visiting during peak season or over holiday weekends, reserve your car before arriving on the island—not only because of possible discounts but also to ensure that you get a car and that it's a reliable one. Faced with high demand, the agencies may be forced to drag out the worst of their fleet; waiting until the last minute could leave you stranded without a car or stranded with one on the side of the road.

You can find offices for dozens of agencies at San Juan's Aeropuerto Internacional Luis Muñoz Marín, and a majority of them have shuttle service to and from the airport and the pickup point. Most rental cars are available with automatic or standard transmission. Four-wheel-drive vehicles aren't necessary unless you plan to go way off the beaten path or along the steep, rocky roads of Culebra or Vieques; in most cases a standard compact car will do the trick. If you're given a choice, always opt for air-conditioning. You'll be glad you did when it's high noon and you're in a San Juan traffic jam. Don't rent a car on mainland Puerto Rico and expect to take it to Culebra or Vieques.

CAR RENTAL RESOURCES

Local Agencies AAA Car Rental (☎787/726-7355 in San Juan ⊕www.aaacarrentalpr.com). **Charlie Car Rental** (☎787/728-2418 in San Juan ⊕www.charliecars.com). **Island Car Rental** (☎787/741-1666 in Vieques). **L & M Car Rental** (☎787/791-1160 in San Juan, 787/831-4740 in Mayagüez).

Major Agencies Alamo (☎800/522-9696 ⊕www.alamo. com). **Avis** (☎800/331-1084 ⊕www.avis.com). **Budget** (☎800/472-3325 ⊕www.budget. com). **Hertz** (☎800/654-3001 ⊕www.hertz.com). **National Car**

Rental (☎800/227-7368 ⊕www. nationalcar.com).

CAR-RENTAL INSURANCE

Everyone who rents a car wonders whether the insurance that the rental companies offer is worth the expense. No one—including us—has a simple answer. It all depends on how much regular insurance you have, how comfortable you are with risk, and whether money is an issue.

If you own a car and carry comprehensive car insurance for both collision and liability, your personal auto insurance will probably cover a rental, but read your policy's fine print to be sure. If you don't have auto insurance, then you should probably buy the collision- or loss-damage waiver (CDW or LDW) from the rental company. This eliminates your liability for damage to the car.

Some credit cards offer CDW coverage, but it's usually supplemental to your own insurance and rarely covers SUVs, minivans, luxury models, and the like. If your coverage is secondary, you may still be liable for loss-of-use costs from the car-rental company (again, read the fine print). But no credit-card insurance is valid unless you use that card for *all* transactions, from reserving to paying the final bill.

■TIP→Diners Club offers primary CDW coverage on all rentals reserved and paid for with the card. This means that Diners

Club's company—not your own car insurance—pays in case of an accident. It doesn't mean that your car-insurance company won't raise your rates once it discovers you had an accident.

You may also be offered supplemental liability coverage; the car-rental company is required to carry a minimal level of liability coverage insuring all renters, but it's rarely enough to cover claims in a really serious accident if you're at fault. Your own auto-insurance policy will protect you if you own a car; if you don't, you have to decide whether you are willing to take the risk.

U.S. rental companies sell CDWs and LDWs for about $15 to $25 a day; supplemental liability is usually more than $10 a day. The car-rental company may offer you all sorts of other policies, but they're rarely worth the cost. Personal accident insurance, which is basic hospitalization coverage, is an especially egregious rip-off if you already have health insurance.

■ TIP→ You can decline the insurance from the rental company and purchase it through a third-party provider such as Travel Guard (www.travelguard.com)—$9 per day for $35,000 of coverage. That's sometimes just under half the price of the CDW offered by some car-rental companies.

▮ VACATION PACKAGES

Packages *are not* guided excursions. Packages combine airfare, accommodations, and perhaps a rental car or other extras (theater tickets, guided excursions, boat trips, reserved entry to popular museums, transit passes), but they let you do your own thing. During busy periods packages may be your only option, as flights and rooms may be sold out otherwise.

Packages will definitely save you time. They can also save you money, particularly in peak seasons, but—and this is a really big "but"—you should price each part of the package separately to be sure. And be aware that prices advertised on Web sites and in newspapers rarely include service charges or taxes, which can up your costs by hundreds of dollars.

■ TIP→ Some packages and cruises are sold only through travel agents. Don't always assume that you can get the best deal by booking everything yourself.

Each year consumers are stranded or lose their money when packagers—even large ones with excellent reputations—go out of business. How can you protect yourself?

First, always pay with a credit card; if you have a problem, your credit-card company may help you resolve it. Second, buy trip insurance that covers default. Third, choose a company that belongs to the United States Tour

Operators Association, whose members must set aside funds to cover defaults. Finally, choose a company that also participates in the Tour Operator Program of the American Society of Travel Agents (ASTA), which will act as mediator in any disputes.

You can also check on the tour operator's reputation among travelers by posting an inquiry on one of the Fodors.com forums.

**Organizations American So-
ciety of Travel Agents** (ASTA
☎703/739–2782 or 800/965–2782
⊕www.astanet.com). **United States
Tour Operators Association**
(USTOA ☎212/599–6599 ⊕www.
ustoa.com).

TRANSPORTATION

TIP→ Ask the local tourist board about hotel and local transportation packages that include tickets to major museum exhibits or other special events.

BY AIR

Nonstop flights to San Juan from New York are 3¾ hours; from Miami, 2½ hours; from Atlanta, 3½ hours; from Boston, 4 hours; from Chicago, 4¾ hours; from Los Angeles, 8 hours; from the United Kingdom, 5 hours; from Germany, 9¾ hours.

There are many daily flights to Puerto Rico from the United States, and connections are particularly good from the East Coast, although there are a few nonstop flights from the Midwest as well. San Juan's international airport is a major regional hub, so many travelers headed elsewhere in the Caribbean make connections here. Because of the number of flights, fares to San Juan are among the most reasonably priced to the region.

Airlines & Airports Airline and Airport Links.com (⊕www.airlineandairportlinks.com) has links to many of the world's airlines and airports.

Airline Security Issues Transportation Security Administration (⊕www.tsa.gov) has answers for almost every question that might come up.

AIRPORTS

Aeropuerto Internacional Luis Muñoz Marín (SJU) is 20 minutes east of Old San Juan in the neighborhood of Isla Verde. San Juan's other airport is the small Fernando L. Rivas Dominici Airport (SIG) in Isla Grande, near the city's Miramar section. From either airport you can catch flights to Culebra, Vieques, and other destinations on Puerto Rico and throughout the Caribbean. (Note that although the Dominicci airport was still operating at this writing, its ultimate future was uncertain.)

Other Puerto Rican airports include Aeropuerto Internacional Rafael Hernández (BQN) in the northwestern town of Aguadilla, Aeropuerto Eugenio María de Hostos (MAZ) in the west coast community of Mayagüez, Mercedita (PSE) in the south coast town of Ponce, Aeropuerto Diego Jiménez Torres (FAJ) in the east coast city of Fajardo, Antonio Rivera Rodríguez (VQS) on Vieques, and Aeropuerto Benjamin Rivera Noriega (CPX) on Culebra.

Airport Information Aeropuerto Antonio Rivera Rodríguez (⊠Vieques ☎787/741–8358). Aeropuerto Benjamin Rivera Noriega (⊠Culebra ☎787/742–0022). Aeropuerto Diego Jiménez Torres (⊠Fajardo ☎787/860–3110). Aeropuerto Eugenio María de Hostos (⊠Mayagüez ☎787/833–0148).

Aeropuerto Fernando L. Rivas Dominici (⌧Isla Grande, San Juan ☎787/729–8711). **Aeropuerto Internacional Luis Muñoz Marín** (⌧Isla Verde, San Juan ☎787/791–3840). **Aeropuerto Mercedita** (⌧Ponce ☎787/842–6292). **Aeropuerto Rafael Hernández** (⌧Aguadilla ☎787/891–2286).

Before arriving, check with your hotel about transfers: some hotels and resorts provide transport from the airport—free or for a fee—to their guests; some larger resorts run regular shuttles. Otherwise, your best bets are *taxis turísticos* (tourist taxis). Uniformed officials at the airport can help you make arrangements. They will give you a slip with your exact fare to hand to the driver. Rates are based on your destination. A taxi turístico to Isla Verde costs $10. It's $14 to Condado and $19 to Old San Juan. There's a 50¢ charge for each bag handled by the driver.

FLIGHTS

San Juan's busy Aeropuerto Internacional Luis Muñoz Marín is the Caribbean hub of American Airlines, which flies nonstop from Baltimore, Boston, Chicago, Dallas, Fort Lauderdale, Miami, Newark, New York–JFK, Orlando, Philadelphia, Tampa, and Washington, D.C.–Dulles. Continental Airlines flies nonstop from Houston and Newark. Delta flies nonstop from Atlanta, Orlando, and New York–JFK. JetBlue flies nonstop from New York–JFK. Spirit Air flies nonstop from Fort Lauderdale and Orlando. United flies nonstop from Chicago, New York–JFK, Philadelphia, and Washington, D.C.–Dulles. US Airways flies nonstop from Baltimore, Boston, Charlotte, Chicago, Philadelphia, and Washington, D.C.–Dulles. International carriers serving San Juan include Air Canada from Toronto, Air France from Paris, Iberia from Madrid, and British Airways from London.

San Juan is no longer the only gateway to Puerto Rico. If you're headed to the western part of the island, you can fly directly into Aguadilla. Continental flies here from Newark, and jetBlue flies here from New York–JFK. If the southern coast is your goal, Continental flies to Ponce from Newark.

If you're flying on to Vieques or Culebra, you no longer have to transfer to Aeropuerto Fernando L. Rivas Dominici. Now all the carriers servicing the islands also have flights from the international airport, including Air Flamenco, Isla Nena Air Service, and Vieques Air Link; of course, these airlines do still fly daily from Isla Grande airport as well. American Eagle and Cape Air fly between the international airport and Vieques.

Puerto Rico is also a good spot from which to hop to other Caribbean islands. American Eagle serves many islands in the Caribbean; Cape Air connects San Juan to St. Thomas and St. Croix. Seaborne Airlines has seaplanes departing from San Juan

Piers 6 and 7 to St. Thomas and St. Croix.

Airline Contacts Air Canada (☎888/247–2262 ⊕www.aircanada. com). **Air France** (☎800/237–2747 ⊕www.airfrance.com). **American Airlines** (☎800/433–7300 ⊕www. aa.com). **ATA** (☎800/435–9282 or 317/282–8308 ⊕www.ata.com). **British Airways** (☎800/247–9297 ⊕www.britishairways.com). **Continental Airlines** (☎800/523–3273 for U.S. and Mexico reservations, 800/231–0856 for international reservations ⊕www.continental.com). **Delta Airlines** (☎800/221–1212 for U.S. reservations, 800/241–4141 for international reservations ⊕www.delta.com). **Iberia** (☎787/725–7000 ⊕www.iberia. com). **jetBlue** (☎800/538–2583 ⊕www.jetblue.com). **Northwest Airlines** (☎800/225–2525 ⊕www.nwa.com). **Spirit Airlines** (☎800/772–7117 or 586/791–7300 ⊕www.spiritair.com). **United Airlines** (☎800/864–8331 for U.S. reservations, 800/538–2929 for international reservations ⊕www.united.com). **USAirways** (☎800/428–4322 for U.S. and Canada reservations, 800/622–1015 for international reservations ⊕www.usairways.com).

Regional Airlines Air Flamenco (☎787/724–1105 ⊕www.airflamenco.net). **Cape Air** (☎800/352–0714 ⊕www.flycapeair.com). **Isla Nena Air Service** (☎877/812–5144 ⊕www.islanena.8m.com). **Seaborne Airlines** (☎888/359–8687 ⊕www. seaborneairlines.com). **Vieques Air Link** (☎888/901–9247 ⊕www. vieques-island.com/val).

▌ BY BOAT

The Fajardo Port Authority's 400-passenger ferries run between Fajardo and the out-islands of Vieques and Culebra; either trip takes about 90 minutes. The vessels carry cargo and passengers to Vieques three times daily ($2 one-way) and to Culebra twice-daily from Sunday through Friday, three times a day on Saturday ($2.25 one-way). Get schedules for the Culebra and Vieques ferries by calling the Port Authority in Fajardo, Vieques, or Culebra. You buy tickets at the ferry dock.

Ferry service by Ferries del Caribe runs between Mayagüez and Santo Domingo. Trips are overnight, leaving at 8 PM and arriving at 8 AM. Small cabins with sleeping accommodations for two, three, and four persons are provided. Tickets are usually available, but reserve well in advance if you're bringing your car. Ships leave from the Zona Portuaria, past the Mayagüez Holiday Inn on Highway 2.

Information Autoridad de los Puertos (☎787/788–1155 in San Juan, 787/863–4560 in Fajardo, 787/742–3161 in Culebra, 787/741–4761 in Vieques). **Ferries del Caribe** (☎787/832–4800 ⊕www. ferriesdelcaribe.com).

▌ BY BUS

The Autoridad Metropolitana de Autobuses (AMA) operates buses that thread through San Juan, running in exclusive lanes on major thoroughfares and stopping at signs marked PARADA. Destinations are indicated above the windshield. Bus B-21 runs through Condado all the way to Plaza Las Américas in Hato Rey. Bus A-5 runs from San Juan through Santurce and the beach area of Isla Verde. Service starts at around 6 AM and generally continues until 9 PM. Fares are 50¢ or 75¢, depending on the route, and are paid in exact change upon entering the bus. Most buses are air-conditioned and have wheelchair lifts and lock-downs.

There's no bus system covering the rest of the island. If you do not have a rental car, your best bet is to travel by *públicos*, which are usually shared 17-passenger vans. They have yellow license plates ending in "P" or "PD," and they scoot to towns throughout the island, stopping in each community's main plaza. They operate primarily during the day; routes and fares are fixed by the Public Service Commission, but schedules aren't set, so you have to call ahead.

Bus Information Autoridad Metropolitana de Autobuses (☎787/767–7979).

▌ BY CAR

Several well-marked multilane highways link population centers. Route 26 is the main artery through San Juan, connecting Condado and Old San Juan to Isla Verde and the airport. Route 22, which runs east–west between San Juan and Camuy, and Route 52, which runs north–south between San Juan and Ponce, are toll roads (35¢–50¢). Route 2, a smaller highway, travels along the west coast, and routes 3 and 53 traverse the east shore.

Five highways are particularly noteworthy for their scenery and vistas. The island's tourism authorities have even given them special names. Ruta Panorámica (Panoramic Route) runs east–west through the central mountains. Ruta Cotorra (Puerto Rican Parrot Route) travels along the north coast. Ruta Paso Fino (Paso Fino Horse Route, after a horse breed) takes you north–south and west along the south coast. Ruta Coquí, named for the famous Puerto Rican tree frog, runs along the east coast. Ruta Flamboyán, named after the island tree, goes from San Juan through the mountains to the east coast.

All types of fuel—unleaded regular, unleaded super-premium, diesel—are available by the liter. Most stations have both full- and self-service. Hours vary, but stations generally operate daily from early in the morning until 10 or 11 PM; in metro areas many are open 24 hours. Stations are few and far between in the Cordillera Central and other rural areas; plan accordingly. In cities you can pay with cash and bank or credit cards; in the hinterlands cash is often your only option.

uerto Rico has some of the Caribbean's best roads. That said, potholes, sharp turns, speed umps, sudden gradient changes, nd poor lighting can sometimes nake driving difficult. Be especially cautious when driving after eavy rains or hurricanes; roads nd bridges might be washed out or damaged. Many of the mountain roads are very narrow and steep, with unmarked curves and liffs. Locals are familiar with uch roads and often drive at igh speeds, which can give you quite a scare. When traveling on a narrow, curving road, it's best to honk your horn as you take ny sharp turn.

Traffic around cities—particularly San Juan, Ponce, and Mayagüez—is heavy at rush hours weekdays from 7 to 10 and 4 to 7).

n an emergency, dial 911. If your car breaks down, call the rental company for a replacement. Before renting, make sure you investigate the company's policy regarding replacement vehicles and repairs out on the island, and ask about surcharges that might be incurred if you break down in a rural area and need a new car.

U.S. driving laws apply in Puerto Rico, and you'll find no problem with signage or directionals. Street and highway signs are most often in Spanish but use international symbols; brushing up on a few key Spanish terms before your trip will help. The following words and phrases are especially useful: *calle sin salida* (dead end street), *cruce de peatones* (pedestrian crossing), *cuidado* (caution), *desvío* (detour), *estación de peaje* (toll booth), *no entre* (do not enter), *prohibido adelantar* (no passing), *salida* (exit), *tránsito* (one way), *zona escolar* (school zone).

Distances are posted in kilometers (1.6 km to 1 mi), whereas speed limits are posted in miles per hour. Speeding and drunk-driving penalties are much the same here as on the mainland. Police cars often travel with their lights flashing, so it's difficult to know when they're trying to pull you over. If the siren is on, move to the right to get out of their way. If the lights are on, it's best to pull over—just be sure that the vehicle is a *marked* police car before doing so.

ON THE GROUND

■ ADDRESSES

Addresses in Puerto Rico, especially in and around San Juan, can be confusing because Spanish terms like *avenida* and *calle* are used interchangeably with English terms like avenue and street. This means that the shopping strip in Old San Juan may be called Calle Cristo or Cristo Street. (And it might just be called Cristo, as it is on many maps.) A highway is often called a *expreso,* and an alley or pedestrian-only street is labeled a *paseo.*

Outside a metropolitan area, addresses are most often given by the kilometer mark along the road. That means that the address for Parque de las Cavernas del Río Camuy, south of Arecibo, is given as Route 129, Kilometer 18.9.

■ COMMUNICATIONS

INTERNET

Internet cafés are more common than they once were, but are still few and far between. As if that weren't bad enough, many hotels have yet to install high-speed Internet access in their rooms. Your best bet is to use your hotel business center.

Contacts Cowabunga's
(☎787/823–5225). **Cyber Net**
(☎787/724–4033 ☎787/728–4195).
Internet Active (☎787/791–1916).

Cybercafes (⊕www.cybercafes.com)
lists more than 4,000 Internet
cafés worldwide.

PHONES

The good news is that you can now make a direct-dial telephone call from virtually any point on earth. The bad news? You can't always do so cheaply. Calling from a hotel is almost always the most expensive option; hotels usually add huge surcharges to all calls, particularly international ones. In some countries you can phone from call centers or even the post office. Calling cards usually keep costs to a minimum, but only if you purchase them locally. And then there are mobile phones *(⇨below),* which are sometimes more prevalent— particularly in the developing world—than land lines; as expensive as mobile phone calls can be, they are still usually a much cheaper option than calling from your hotel.

All Puerto Rican phone numbers—like those throughout the United States—consist of a three-digit area code and a seven-digit local number. Puerto Rico's area codes are 787 and 939. Toll-free numbers (prefix 800, 888, or 877) are widely used in Puerto Rico, and many can be accessed from North America. You can also access many North American toll-free numbers from the island.

Pay phones, which are abundant in tourist areas, use coins or pre-paid phone cards; some accept credit cards. Local calls are 25¢, and on-island, long-distance calls cost about 50¢.

The country code for the United States is 1.

Access Codes AT&T Direct (☎787/725–0300). **Cellular One** (☎787/505–2273 or 787/505–4636). **MCI WorldPhone** (☎787/782–6244 or 800/939–7624). **Sprint International Access** (☎800/473–3037 or 800/298–3266).

Phone cards are widely available. The Puerto Rico Telephone Company sells its "Ring Cards" in various denominations that can be used for both local and international calls. They're available in shops, supermarkets, and drugstores as well as from the phone company.

Information Ring Cards (☎800/981–9105).

If you have a multiband phone (some countries use different frequencies than what's used in the United States) and your service provider uses the world-standard GSM network (as do T-Mobile, Cingular, and Verizon), you can probably use your phone abroad. Roaming fees can be steep, however: 99¢ a minute is considered reasonable. And overseas you normally pay the toll charges for incoming calls. It's almost always cheaper to send a text message than to make a call, since text messages

have a very low set fee (often less than 5¢).

If you just want to make local calls, consider buying a new SIM card (note that your provider may have to unlock your phone for you to use a different SIM card) and a prepaid service plan in the destination. You'll then have a local number and can make local calls at local rates. If your trip is extensive, you could also simply buy a new cell phone in your destination, as the initial cost will be offset over time.

■TIP→ **If you travel internationally frequently, save one of your old mobile phones or buy a cheap one on the Internet; ask your cell phone company to unlock it for you, and take it with you as a travel phone, buying a new SIM card with pay-as-you-go service in each destination.**

Cell phones are a viable alternative to using local service if you need to keep records of your bills. Call your cell-phone company before departing to get information about activation and roaming charges. Companies that have service on the island include Cellular One, Cingular, and Sprint. For many cell-phone users, Puerto Rico is considered part of their regular nationwide calling area; for others, it's considered international.

▐ EATING OUT

Throughout the island you can find everything from French haute cuisine to sushi bars, as well as superb local eateries serving *comidas criollas,* traditional Caribbean-creole meals. Note that the *mesón gastronómico* label is used by the government to recognize restaurants that preserve culinary traditions. *For information on food-related health issues see Health, below.* The restaurants we list are the cream of the crop in each price category. Properties indicated by a ×⊡ are lodging establishments whose restaurant warrants a special trip.

For information on food-related health issues, see Health below.

MEALS & MEALTIMES

Puerto Ricans' eating habits mirror those of their counterparts on the mainland United States: they eat breakfast, lunch, and dinner, though they don't tend to down coffee all day long. Instead, islanders like a steaming, high-test cup in the morning and another between 2 and 4 PM. They may finish a meal with coffee, but they never drink coffee *during* a meal.

People tend to eat dinner late in Puerto Rico; you may find yourself alone in the restaurant if you eat at 5 PM; at 6, business will pick up a little, and from 7 to 10, it may be quite busy.

Unless otherwise noted, the restaurants listed in this guide are open daily for lunch and dinner.

RESERVATIONS & DRESS

Regardless of where you are, it's a good idea to make a reservation if you can. We only mention them specifically when reservations are essential (there's no other way you'll ever get a table) or when they are not accepted. We mention dress only when men are required to wear a jacket or a jacket and tie.

Puerto Ricans generally dress up to go out, particularly in the evening. And always remember: beach attire is only for the beach.

WINES, BEER & SPIRITS

Puerto Rico isn't a notable producer of wine, but there are several well-crafted local beers to choose from. Legends trace the birthplace of the piña colada to any number of San Juan establishments, from the Caribe Hilton to a Calle La Fortaleza bar. Puerto Rican rum is popular mixed with cola (known as a *cuba libre*), soda, tonic, juices, or water, or served on the rocks or even straight up. Rums range from light mixers to dark, aged sipping liqueurs. Look for Bacardí, Don Q, Ron Rico, Palo Viejo, and Barrilito. The drinking age in Puerto Rico is 18.

▐ EMERGENCIES

Emergencies are handled by dialing 911. You can expect a quick response by police, fire, and medical personnel, most of whom speak at least some English. San Juan's Tourist Zone Police are particularly helpful to visitors.

Canada and the United Kingdom have consulates in San Juan.

General Emergency Contacts
Ambulance, police, and fire
(☎911). **Air Ambulance Service**
(☎800/633–3590 or 787/756–3424).

GAY & LESBIAN TRAVEL

In sophisticated San Juan, gays and lesbians will find it easy to mingle. There are many gay-friendly hotels, restaurants, and clubs throughout the city, and the beaches at Condado and Ocean Park tend to attract a gay crowd. The first Sunday in June sees a gay pride parade in Condado that's preceded by a week of events. The bohemian Old San Juan crowd is particularly friendly and—just as in Ocean Park and Condado—many businesses there are owned by gays or lesbians. Some clubs and bars also have a weekly "gay night." Other welcoming areas of the island include Ponce in the South, Boquerón in the southwest, and the town of Fajardo and the outslands of Vieques and Culebra in the east. To find out more about events and gay-friendly businesses, pick up a copy of the *Puerto Rico Breeze,* the island's gay and lesbian newspaper.

Frank Fournier of Connections Travel—which is a member of the International Gay & Lesbian Travel Association—is a reliable local travel agent for gay and lesbian travelers.

HEALTH

The most common types of illnesses are caused by contaminated food and water. Especially in developing countries, drink only bottled, boiled, or purified water and drinks; don't drink from public fountains or use ice. You should even consider using bottled water to brush your teeth. Make sure food has been thoroughly cooked and is served to you fresh and hot; avoid vegetables and fruits that you haven't washed (in bottled or purified water) or peeled yourself. If you have problems, mild cases of traveler's diarrhea may respond to Imodium (known generically as loperamide) or Pepto-Bismol. Be sure to drink plenty of fluids; if you can't keep fluids down, seek medical help immediately.

Infectious diseases can be airborne or passed via mosquitoes and ticks and through direct or indirect physical contact with animals or people. Some, including Norwalk-like viruses that affect your digestive tract, can be passed along through contaminated food. If you are traveling in an area where malaria is prevalent, use a repellant containing DEET and take malaria-prevention medication before, during, and after your trip as directed by your physician. Condoms can help prevent most sexually transmitted diseases, but they aren't absolutely reliable and their quality varies from country to country. Speak with your physician and/or check the CDC or World Health Organization Web sites for health alerts, particularly if you're pregnant, traveling with children, or have a chronic illness.

For information on travel insurance, shots and medications, and medical-assistance companies see Shots & Medications under Things to Consider in Before You Go, above.

SPECIFIC ISSUES IN PUERTO RICO

Health care in Puerto Rico is among the best in the Caribbean, but expect long waits and often a less-than-pleasant bedside manner. At all hospitals and medical centers you can find English-speaking medical staff, and many large hotels have an English-speaking doctor on call.

Tap water is generally fine on the island; just avoid drinking it after storms (when the water supply can become mixed with sewage). Thoroughly wash or peel produce you buy in markets before eating it.

Do not fly within 24 hours of scuba diving.

OVER-THE-COUNTER REMEDIES

All the U.S. brands of sunscreen and over-the-counter medicines (Tylenol, Advil, Robitussin, Nyquil, etc.) are available in pharmacies, supermarkets, and convenience stores.

▌ HOURS OF OPERATION

Bank hours are generally weekdays from 9 to 5, though a few branches are also open Saturday from 9 to noon or 1. Post offices are open weekdays from 7:30 to 4:30 and Saturday from 8 to noon. Government offices are open weekdays from 9 to 5.

Most stations are open daily from early in the morning until 10 or 11 PM. Numerous stations in urban areas are open 24 hours.

As a rule, San Juan area museums are closed on Monday, and in some cases, Sunday. Hours otherwise are 9 or 10 AM to 5 PM, often with an hour off for lunch between noon and 2. Sights managed by the National Parks Service, such as Fuerte San Felipe del Morro and San Cristóbal, are open daily from 9 to 5.

In cities, pharmacies are generally open from 9 to 6 or 7 weekdays and on Saturday. Walgreens operates numerous pharmacies around the island; some are open 24 hours.

Street shops are open Monday through Saturday from 9 to 6; mall stores tend to stay open to 9 or sometimes even later. Count on convenience stores staying open late into the night, seven days a week. Supermarkets are often closed on Sunday, although some remain open 24-hours, seven days a week.

MAIL

uerto Rico uses the U.S. post-
l system, and all addresses on
he island carry zip codes. The
ates to send letters and post-
ards from Puerto Rico are the
ame as those everywhere else
n the United States. However,
nail between Puerto Rico and
he U.S. mainland can take more
han a week.

Main Branches U.S. Post Office
(⊠153 Calle Fortaleza, Old San
uan, San Juan ⊠163 Av. Fernández
uncos, San Juan ⊠102 Calle Gar-
do Morales, Fajardo ⊠60 Calle
McKinley, Mayagüez ⊠94 Calle
tocha, Ponce).

SHIPPING PACKAGES

Many shops—particularly those
n Old San Juan and Condado—
will ship purchases for you.
Shipping services are especial-
y common at art galleries. Pay
by credit card, and save your
eceipts. Make sure the propri-
tor insures the package against
oss or damage, and ships it first-
class or by courier. Grab a business card with the proprietor's
name and phone number so you
can readily follow-up with him
or her if needed.

Post offices in major Puerto
Rican cities offer express mail
(next-day) service to the U.S.
mainland and to Puerto Rican
destinations. In addition, you
can send packages via FedEx or
UPS. Ask at the concierge desk
of your hotel; most have regu-
ar courier pickups or can call
for one. Hotels that offer business services will take care of

the entire ordeal for you. Cave-
at emptor: courier delivery and
pickup is not available on Saturday, and even "overnight" packages often take two to three days
to reach the U.S. mainland.

Express Services FedEx
(☎787/793–9300). **UPS**
(☎787/253–2877).

▍ MONEY

Puerto Rico, which is a commonwealth of the United States, uses
the U.S. dollar as its official currency. Prices for most items are
stable and comparable to those
in the States, and that includes
restaurants and hotel rates. As
in many places, city prices tend
to be higher than those in rural
areas, but you're not going to
go broke staying in the city: soft
drinks or a cup of coffee run
about $1; a local beer in a bar,
$2.75; museum admission, $2.

Prices throughout this guide are
given for adults. Substantially
reduced fees are almost always
available for children, students,
and senior citizens.

ATMS & BANKS

Your own bank will probably
charge a fee for using ATMs
abroad; the foreign bank you use
may also charge a fee. Nevertheless, you'll usually get a better
rate of exchange at an ATM than
you will at a currency-exchange
office or even when changing
money in a bank. And extracting
funds as you need them is a safer option than carrying around a
large amount of cash.

■TIP→ PIN numbers with more than four digits are not recognized at ATMs in many countries. If yours has five or more, remember to change it before you leave.

Automated Teller Machines (ATMs; known here as ATHs) are readily available and reliable in the cities; many are attached to banks, but you can also find them in gas stations, drug stores, supermarkets, and larger hotels. Just about every casino has one—the better to keep people in the game—but these can carry large surcharges, so check before you withdraw money. ATMs are found less frequently in rural areas, but there's usually at least one in even the smallest village. Look to local banks, such as Banco Popular.

CREDIT CARDS

Throughout this guide, the following abbreviations are used: **AE**, American Express; **D**, Discover; **DC**, Diners Club; **MC**, MasterCard; and **V**, Visa.

It's a good idea to inform your credit-card company before you travel, especially if you're going abroad and don't travel internationally very often. Otherwise, the credit-card company might put a hold on your card owing to unusual activity—not a good thing halfway through your trip. Record all your credit-card numbers—as well as the phone numbers to call if your cards are lost or stolen—in a safe place, so you're prepared should something go wrong. Both MasterCard and Visa have general numbers you can call (collect if you're abroad) if your card is lost, but you're better off calling the number of your issuing bank, since MasterCard and Visa usually just transfer you to your bank; your bank's number is usually printed on your card.

Reporting Lost Cards American Express (☎800/528-4800 in U.S., 336/393-1111 collect from abroad ⊕www.americanexpress.com). **Diners Club** (☎800/234-6377 in U.S., 303/799-1504 collect from abroad ⊕www.dinersclub.com). **Discover** (☎800/347-2683 in U.S., 801/902-3100 collect from abroad ⊕www.discovercard.com). **MasterCard** (☎800/627-8372 in U.S., 636/722-7111 collect from abroad ⊕www.mastercard.com). **Visa** (☎800/847-2911 in U.S., 410/581-9994 collect from abroad ⊕www.visa.com).

TRAVELER'S CHECKS & CARDS

Some consider this the currency of the caveman, and it's true that fewer establishments accept traveler's checks these days. Nevertheless, they're a cheap and secure way to carry extra money, particularly on trips to urban areas. Both Citibank (under the Visa brand) and American Express issue traveler's checks in the United States, but Amex is better known and more widely accepted; you can also avoid hefty surcharges by cashing Amex checks at Amex offices. Whatever you do, keep track of all the serial numbers in case the checks are lost or stolen.

American Express now offers a stored-value card called a Travels Cheque Card, which you can se wherever American Express edit cards are accepted, including ATMs. The card can carry a inimum of $300 and a maximum of $2,700, and it's a very fe way to carry your funds. lthough you can get replacement funds in 24 hours if your rd is lost or stolen, it doesn't eally strike us as a very good eal. In addition to a high initial ost ($14.95 to set up the card, lus $5 each time you "reload"), ou still have to pay a 2% fee or each purchase in a foreign urrency (similar to that of any redit card). Further, each time ou use the card in an ATM you ay a transaction fee of $2.50 n top of the 2% transaction fee or the conversion—add it all up nd it can be considerably more han you would pay when simly using your own ATM card. egular traveler's checks are just s secure and cost less.

ontacts **American Express**
☎888/412-6945 in U.S., 801/945-450 collect outside of the U.S. to dd value or speak to customer serice ⊕www.americanexpress.com).

SAFETY

an Juan, Mayagüez, and Ponce, ke most big cities, have their hare of crime, so guard your walet or purse in markets, on buses, nd in other crowded areas. Avoid eaches at night, when muggings ave been known to occur even n Condado and Isla Verde. Don't eave anything unattended on the each. If you must keep valuables

in your vehicle, put them in the trunk. Always lock your car. The exception is at the beaches of Vieques, where rental-car agencies advise you to leave the car unlocked so thieves don't break the windows to search for valuables. This happens extremely rarely, but it does happen.

We recommend that women carry only a handbag that closes completely and wear it bandolier style (across one shoulder and your chest). Open-style bags and those allowed to simply dangle from one shoulder are prime targets for pickpockets and purse snatchers. Avoid walking anywhere alone at night, and don't wear clothing that's skin-tight or overly revealing.

■TIP→ **Distribute your cash, credit cards, IDs, and other valuables between a deep front pocket, an inside jacket or vest pocket, and a hidden money pouch. Don't reach for the money pouch once you're in public.**

▌ TAXES

You must pay a tax on your hotel room rate: for hotels with casinos it's 11%, for other hotels it's 9%, and for government-approved paradores it's 7%. Ask your hotel before booking. The tax, in addition to each hotel's discretionary service charge (which usually ranges from 5% to 12%), can add a hefty 12% to 23% to your bill. There's no sales tax on Puerto Rico. Airport departure taxes are usually included in the cost of your plane ticket rather than being collected at the airport.

TIME

Puerto Rico operates on Atlantic Standard Time, which is one hour later than the U.S. Eastern Standard Time in winter. The island does not keep U.S. daylight savings time. This means that when it's noon on a winter day in New York, it's 1 PM in Puerto Rico. In summer Puerto Rico and the East Coast of the United States are on the same time, and three hours ahead of the West Coast. Sydney is 14 hours ahead of Puerto Rico, Auckland is 16 hours ahead, and London is 4 hours ahead.

TIPPING

Some hotels automatically add a 5% to 12% service charge to your bill. Check ahead to confirm whether this charge is built into the room rate or will be tacked on at check-out. Tips are expected, and appreciated, by restaurant waitstaff (15% to 20% if a service charge isn't included), hotel porters ($1 per bag), maids ($1 to $2 a day), and taxi drivers (10% to 15%).

INDEX

NOTES

NOTES

NOTES

ABOUT OUR WRITER

It was a trip to Bahía Mosquito that convinced Mark Sullivan that Puerto Rico was not just another spot in the Caribbean. Diving into the bioluminiscent bay—and watching the trail of blue-green sparks he left in his wake—made him realize that this is truly an *isla encantada*. Since that time he's explored every nook and cranny, from the bat-filled caverns of the the Parque de las Cavernas del Río Camuy to the cactus-lined trails of the Bosque Estatal de Guánica. A few of his favorite pastimes? Trying the *lechón* (suckling pig roasted on a spit) at roadside stands near Cayay was an experience, as was eating the *mofongo* (mashed plantains stuffed with lobster and other delicacies) in several of the seafood shacks at Joyuda. He has written or edited dozens of travel guides, including *Fodor's Central America, Fodor's South America,* and *Fodor's Pocket Aruba.* His cultural reporting has also appeared in many magazines, including *Billboard, InStyle,* and *Interview.* When not on the road, he splits his time between a shoebox apartment in New York City and a rambling Victorian in the Catskills.

Acknowledgments

Few travel guides, even ones like this that have a single author, are the work of one person. Many people made this book possible. I'd like to thanks Glorimar Alvarez and Nelly Cruz at the offices of the Puerto Rico Tourism Company. They provided me with a stack—quite literally—of information about the island. Several people along the way were especially helpful, introducing me to places I might otherwise have missed, including Estaban Haigler and Emeo Cheung at the Andalucia Guest House, Evy Garcia at the Westin Río Mar Beach Golf Resort & Spa, and Sigrid Velez at the recently closed (and much missed) Hyatt Dorado Beach Resort & Country Club. A big help on Vieques was Hacienda Tamarindo's Burr Vail, who pointed the way to secluded beaches and off-the-beaten-path eateries. Everyone on Culebra seemed to want to lend a hand, but I'm especially grateful to Ginny Tawalski at Posada La Hamaca and Jim Petersen of the *Culebra Calendar.* (His "office," on the sunny patio of his wife's restaurant, is one of the friendliest spots in Puerto Rico.) The biggest thanks goes to my editor, Doug Stallings, whose ability to juggle many projects but still give each writer his full attention is amazing.